DANGEROUS FAMILIARS

DANGEROUS FAMILIARS

Representations of Domestic Crime

in England, 1550–1700

FRANCES E. DOLAN

CORNELL UNIVERSITY PRESS

ITHACA AND LONDON

First published 1994 by Cornell University Press.

Library of Congress Cataloging-in-Publication Data

Dolan, Frances E. (Frances Elizabeth), 1960–
    Dangerous familiars : representations of domestic crime in
England, 1550–1700 / Frances E. Dolan.
        p.   cm.
    Includes bibliographical references and index.
    ISBN 0-8014-2901-3 (alk. paper)
    1. Crime—England—History—16th century.   2. Crime—England—
History—17th century.   3. England—Social conditions —16th
century.   4. England—Social conditions—17th century.   I. Title.
    HV6949.E5D65   1994
364.942—dc20   93-40060

Printed in the United States of America

⊗ The paper in this book meets the minimum requirements
of the American National Standard for Information Sciences—
Permanence of Paper for Printed Library Materials, ANSI Z39.48-1984.

For Robyn and Mary Jean,
heroines of the everyday

and in memory of my brother, Tom,
who walked me to school

CONTENTS

LIST OF ILLUSTRATIONS

ACKNOWLEDGMENTS

I could not have imagined and written this book without the support of two communities: the Miami University Department of English and the Newberry Library. Miami funded research and writing with a Summer Research Appointment and an Assigned Research Appointment; a Monticello College Foundation Fellowship at the Newberry also provided vital time and resources. As votes of confidence in the project at an early stage, these awards meant far more than the hours and dollars they put at my disposal. I have also benefited from the company and conversation of colleagues in both communities. Barry Chabot, Eric Goodman, Britton J. Harwood, Frank Jordan, Susan Morgan, Kerry Powell, John Romano, and James Sosnoski encouraged my development as a teacher and scholar. At the Newberry Library, which excels at fostering rigorous, congenial exchange, Dympna Callaghan, Rosemary Kegl, Peggy McCracken, Julie Solomon, and Jane Tylus all offered advice and friendship.

I was first won over to sixteenth- and seventeenth-century literature by Suzanne Gossett's eager, responsive, strict instruction. She helped me to explore an expanded range of possibilities. I have received many gifts from Mary Beth Rose, in many contexts. She helped me become a professional by treating me as one from the beginning; my work has been inspired by our conversations and by the model of her scholarship. I was also fortunate in my teachers at the University of Chicago, David Bevington, Janel Mueller, and Richard Strier. These mentors have never encouraged me to imitate them and have always engaged in the demanding task of helping me to find my own voice.

Writing this book has been a particularly interactive process—in person, through the mail, and over the phone. I am most grateful to those who read and critiqued the whole manuscript: Susan Amussen, Mary Jean Corbett, Jean Howard, and Janel Mueller; each of them helped me to define and realize the project. Margot Finn, Cynthia Herrup, Constance Jordan, Carole Levin, Phyllis Mack, Lynn Voskuil, and Joy Wiltenburg also offered comments on various chapters. Scott C. Shershow not only read drafts but talked me through the revision process with seemingly endless patience, interest, and good cheer. I am also grateful to Sharon Achinstein, Susan Amussen, Mark Thornton Burnett, Dympna Callaghan, Mitchell Greenberg, Cynthia Herrup, Jane Kamensky, Gail Paster, Julie A. Sikkink, Julie R. Solomon, Deborah Symonds, Betty Travitsky, Frank Whigham, and Deborah Willis for sharing unpublished work with me. The staffs of the British, Folger, and Newberry libraries graciously assisted me. Closer to home, William Wortman and Teresa Lyle made me think that anything was possible. I am grateful to my editor, Bernhard Kendler, for supporting the project and to Lesley Beneke for her careful copy editing.

I thank the *Yale Journal of Law and the Humanities* for permission to reprint a revised version of " 'Home-rebels and House-traitors': Murderous Wives in Early Modern England," 4.1 (1992): 1–31, and *Shakespeare Quarterly* for permission to reprint a revised version of "The Subordinate('s) Plot: Petty Treason and the Forms of Domestic Rebellion," 43.3 (1992):317–40. Following standard practice, I have retained original orthography in quoting from primary texts or facsimile editions, except for silently modernizing i, j, u, and v.

My mother, father, and sisters, relieved that there are no chapters on the murder of parents or siblings, have supported what my father calls the "killer women project," as they have supported all my endeavors. My brother, who encouraged the early interests that led me to the book and inquired into every detail of my research, did not live to see the project finished. I dedicate it to him in meager recompense for all he did to help me out into the world. I also dedicate the book to the two women whose friendship I depend on daily. With Robyn Muncy, I have redefined what home means: Robyn on the other end of the phone. Gifted at ignoring my limitations, Robyn always makes me feel inexhaustible and hopeful. Although Mary Jean Corbett does not suffer praise gladly, she'll just have to accept that she is the ne plus ultra of colleagues and neighbors. Finally, I thank the people who have made homes for me as I have written this book, despite my alarming habit of talking about domestic crime over dinner. Laurie Maguire, Lynn Voskuil, Doug Patton, and John Johnson have all reminded me that domesticity has pleasures as well as perils; Scott Shershow shared with me the wonders of the domestic resurrection circus.

FRANCES E. DOLAN

Cincinnati, Ohio

DANGEROUS FAMILIARS

INTRODUCTION

In early modern England, as now, the home could function as a locus of conflict, an arena in which the most fundamental ideas about social order, identity, and intimacy were contested. Although the contests took many forms, they emerged into public scrutiny and intervention most dramatically when they erupted into violence. I focus here on the most extreme, violent instances of domestic conflict. Early modern English culture recognized nonmurderous domestic violence, for example, wife- and child-beating, sexual abuse, and verbal abuse, as a problem that local communities might address in ecclesiastical courts or through informal interventions, including shaming rituals. Common law, however, did not define these kinds of violence as criminal, and popular culture rarely represented actual instances of domestic violence that had no clear legal status, that is, those that did not lead to death.[1] I look

1. Although there are many conventional, comic representations of wife-beating and shrew-taming, these ally themselves more to the tradition of folktales than to representations of recent, local instances of domestic violence. They also tend to censure the unruly wife more than her brutal "tamer." On this literature see, among many others, Lynda E. Boose, "Scolding Brides and Bridling Scolds: Taming the Woman's Unruly

at those forms of domestic violence that occurred least often, but attracted most attention, and that the culture defined as felonies: acts of murder (petty treason, wife murder, infanticide) and of witchcraft.

Although there were other possible kinds of domestic murder, such as the killing of a parent or sibling, the law did not mark these out for special attention. In contrast, legal statutes explicitly define the killing of a husband, master, or newborn, or the causing of harm through witchcraft as capital offenses. Statutes may locate sources of disorder differently than do other legal documents, such as court records; they also do not necessarily correspond to how local judges and juries actually defined and prosecuted crimes. Yet statutes, by codifying the ruling elite's dominant ideology and by regulating the conduct of all the realm's subjects, demonstrate how legal fictions pervade a culture, shaping as well as articulating its conceptions of order and disorder.

The domestic crimes that attracted the most legal attention also generated the most extensive representations in a range of popular texts that began to proliferate in the late sixteenth century and became increasingly varied and numerous in the course of the seventeenth century. Constantly changing, coalescing, and diverging in form, these included pamphlets (ranging, roughly, from two to twenty-five pages), ballads, and plays based on actual crimes as well as published trial transcripts, scaffold speeches, and confessions. Some historians who have compared such texts to assize indictments and other legal records have found them accurate; they have also depended on these sources for evidence about the legal process that would not otherwise be available.[2] Some literary critics specializing in the eighteenth century have argued that these texts

Member," *Shakespeare Quarterly* 42.2 (1991): 179–213; and Linda Woodbridge, *Women and the English Renaissance: Literature and the Nature of Womankind, 1540–1620* (Urbana: University of Illinois Press, 1984), pp. 201–7.

2. On the value of popular literature as "evidence" about domestic crime and its punishment, see J. S. Cockburn, "Introduction," *Calendar of Assize Records,* ed. Cockburn (London: Her Majesty's Stationers Office, 1985), 1: 14, 97–98; Peter Lake, "Puritanism, Arminianism and a Shropshire Axe-Murder," *Midland History* 15 (1990): 37–64; J. H. Langbein, *Prosecuting Crime in the Renaissance: England, Germany, France* (Cambridge: Harvard University Press, 1974), pp. 45–54; Alan Macfarlane, *Witchcraft in Tudor and Stuart England: A Regional and Comparative Study* (London: Routledge, 1970), chap. 5; and J. A. Sharpe, *Crime in Early Modern England, 1550–1700* (London: Longman, 1984), chap. 5, "Domestic Homicide in Early Modern England," *The Historical Journal* 24.1 (1981): 29–48, esp. pp. 40–41, and " 'Last Dying Speeches': Religion, Ideology and Public Execution in Seventeenth-Century England," *Past and Present* 107 (May 1985): 144–67.

contribute to the development of the novel.[3] Generally, however, even those scholars who attend to ephemeral popular materials relegate them to the margins, where they add color to the "real" evidence (legal records) or lay the groundwork for the "real" literature (the novel).

Operating on the assumption that accounts of domestic crime should be read as both evidence and artifacts, I value them not as records of particular crimes but as evidence of the processes of cultural formation and transformation in which they participated. I interrogate the disparities among kinds of evidence—court records, legal theory, popular materials—and I concentrate on those published materials in widest circulation; I emphasize that all these sources are *representations* that often conform to conventions and may or may not correspond to the range of actual experiences of domestic violence in the early modern period. Yet I insist that representations had material consequences, shaping as well as being shaped by early modern cultural practices.

In broadening the range of texts available for sustained critical attention, I follow in the steps of cultural materialist and new historicist critics. I shift the focus, however, from the court to the household, from elite texts to popular culture, from major authors to cultural contests that incorporate many differently located, adversarial voices and texts that span social and literary hierarchies. I also investigate what interests were served when literary and social histories subsequently authorized some of these voices and texts as representative or aesthetically pleasing, while silencing others. Wary of flattening discourses into homogeneity, I attend throughout to the distinctions among audiences, genres, and texts.[4] This emphasis enables me to reclaim form as a category of feminist materialist analysis without privileging any one text as a centerpiece that reduces the other materials to "background" or "context." My assumption that culture is a site of struggle, my decision

3. I cite this scholarship in the Epilogue, but see, especially, Lennard J. Davis, *Factual Fictions: The Origins of the English Novel* (New York: Columbia University Press, 1983); and J. Paul Hunter, *Before Novels: The Cultural Contexts of Eighteenth-Century English Fiction* (New York: W. W. Norton, 1990).

4. On the importance of attending to differences within and among discourses, see Walter Cohen, "Political Criticism of Shakespeare," in *Shakespeare Reproduced: The Text in History and Ideology*, ed. Jean E. Howard and Marion F. O'Connor (New York: Methuen, 1987), pp. 18–46; and Vincent P. Pecora, "The Limits of Local Knowledge," in *The New Historicism*, ed. H. Aram Veeser (New York: Routledge, 1989), pp. 243–76.

to focus on collectivities (of persons and texts) rather than individuals, and my engagement in a cross-genre, transdisciplinary interrogation of the cultural contestations over canonical inclusion and exclusion all link my practice to recent work in cultural studies.[5] All of these methods have provided invaluable resources for my pursuit of the feminist questions and commitments that remain crucial for me. I take gender as my central category of analysis, always observing how constructions of gender intersect with, interrupt, or evade those of class, race, and sexuality.[6]

I argue that, in representations of domestic crime, the threat usually lies in the familiar rather than the strange, in the intimate rather than the invader. These representations most often depict an insider who threatens order as a woman or a servant, although legal records suggest that women and servants were more often the victims than the perpetrators of domestic violence. Pressing this disparity between popular representation and the reported occurrence of domestic violence, I emphasize that the former depicts such figures as "familiar"—that is, as members of the family or household, associated with the domestic, intimate, habitual, ordinary, and daily—and as "dangerous"—meaning not only threatening but also fraught with the particular early modern

5. See Lawrence Grossberg, Cary Nelson, and Paula Treichler, "Introduction," in *Cultural Studies,* ed. Grossberg, Nelson, and Treichler (New York: Routledge, 1992), pp. 1–22, esp. p. 12; and the many essays in the volume, most of which ruminate on what cultural studies is and should be. Also helpful are Stuart Hall, "Cultural Studies and the Centre: Some Problematics and Problems," *Culture, Media, Language: Working Papers in Cultural Studies, 1971–79* (London: Hutchinson, 1980), pp. 15–47; and Richard Johnson, "What Is Cultural Studies Anyway?" *Social Text* 17 (1987): 38–80.

6. On the importance of combining materialist and feminist analyses, see Gayle Greene and Coppelia Kahn, "Feminist Scholarship and the Social Construction of Woman," in *Making a Difference: Feminist Literary Criticism,* ed. Greene and Kahn (London: Routledge, 1985), pp. 1–36; Jean E. Howard, "Towards a Postmodern, Politically Committed, Historical Practice," in *Uses of History: Marxism, Postmodernism, and the Renaissance,* ed. Francis Barker, Peter Hulme, and Margaret Iversen (Manchester and New York: Manchester University Press/St. Martin's Press, 1991), pp. 101–22; Carol Thomas Neely, "Constructing the Subject: Feminist Practice and the New Renaissance Discourses," *English Literary Renaissance* 18.1 (1988): 5–18; Judith Lowder Newton, "History as Usual? Feminism and the 'New Historicism'," in *The New Historicism,* ed. Veeser, pp. 152–67; Carolyn Porter, "History and Literature: 'After the New Historicism'," *New Literary History* 21.2 (1990): 253–72; Mary Beth Rose, "Where Are the Mothers in Shakespeare?: Options for Gender Representation in the English Renaissance," *Shakespeare Quarterly* 42.3 (1991): 291–314; and Joan W. Scott, "Gender: A Useful Category of Historical Analysis," in her *Gender and the Politics of History* (New York: Columbia University Press, 1988), pp. 28–50.

associations of "difficult to deal with," "hard to please," and "reluctant to comply."[7] In the witch's familiar, a demonic domestic pet who serves as companion and agent of mischief, I find a useful model for this pervasive conflation of dangerous and familiar.

Representations of crime, however diverse, construct the subjectivities of these dangerous familiars in predominantly negative terms. When they represent these perpetrators sympathetically, it is at the cost of ascribing them any agency. When they represent such persons as subjects and agents, they show them as violent transgressors whose interiorities and voices are disruptive and destructive, prior to and apart from the actions to which they are shown to lead. In reconstructing the processes by which the subjectivities of the socially marginalized, particularly women, were produced as resistant, criminal, and violent, we must depend on what Carlo Ginzburg describes as the often "hostile testimonies, originating from or filtered by" the legal process that criminalized and executed them. In such testimonies, "the voices of the accused reach us strangled, altered, distorted; in many cases, they haven't reached us at all."[8] These are still some of our richest resources for recovering those voices and for reflecting on the conditions under which the socially marginalized (for example, poor, unmarried women) could be constructed as subjects and their voices recorded.

By focusing on representations of women as the perpetrators of domestic crime, I participate in recent efforts to uncover the possibilities, however contingent and circumscribed, for human agency in historical process. Turning to accounts of domestic violence as one set of scripts in which women could be cast as agents, albeit in problematic terms, I focus on how such extreme cases force the contradictions within and between the available constructions of subjectivity into visibility. These contradictions themselves can facilitate resistance. As Joan Scott argues: "Subjects are constituted discursively, but there are conflicts among discursive systems, contradictions within any one of them, multiple meanings possible for the concepts they deploy. And subjects do have agency. They are not unified, autonomous individuals exercising free will, but rather subjects whose agency is created through situations and statuses

7. For these obsolete meanings, see the *Oxford English Dictionary*.
8. Carlo Ginzburg, *Ecstasies: Deciphering the Witches' Sabbath,* trans. Raymond Rosenthal (New York: Pantheon, 1991), p. 10.

conferred on them."[9] In the process of subject-formation, the contradictions within and among various constructions of subjectivity create
possibilities for agency. Early modern culture did not associate subjectivity only with resistance, nor did it limit resistance to violent crime.
Other cultural scripts delineate a range of less visible, less violent re-
sistances and self-assertions—mental reservation, passive disobedience,
patient suffering. Nor do the representations that survive neatly overlap
with or exhaust the possibilities that actual women must have explored,
the subtle ways in which they outwitted ideological constraints. They
do show, however, the complex processes by which legal and popular
representations conspired to associate the self-assertion of the socially
marginalized, particularly women, with disobedience, crime, and
violence.

Most pamphlets and ballads about actual crimes were printed soon
after the condemned's execution; some even appeared just after a suspect's apprehension but before sentencing and execution. Plays that
dramatized actual crimes also tended to emerge shortly after the crime
had come to public attention. Production and consumption of these
representations centered on London: Pamphlets and ballads were published and sold in London even when the crimes they depicted had
taken place far from the city; the theaters, too, were located in London.[10]

I join with other scholars in assuming that, in London, a wide, varied
group of spectators and readers had access to ephemeral entertainments.[11] In theater audiences, privileged and unprivileged (except for

9. Joan W. Scott, "The Evidence of Experience," *Critical Inquiry* 17 (Summer 1991):
773–97, esp. p. 793. My understanding of subjectivity has been informed by Louis
Althusser, "Ideology and Ideological State Apparatuses (Notes towards an Investiga-
tion)," in *Lenin and Philosophy and Other Essays,* trans. Ben Brewster (New York: Monthly
Review Press, 1971), pp. 127–86; Teresa de Lauretis, "Eccentric Subjects: Feminist
Theory and Historical Consciousness," *Feminist Studies* 16.1 (1990): 115–50; Louis A.
Montrose, "Renaissance Literary Studies and the Subject of History," *English Literary
Renaissance* 16.1 (1986): 5–12; and Paul Smith, *Discerning the Subject* (Minneapolis:
University of Minnesota Press, 1988).

10. See the introduction, "The Significance of the Metropolis," and other essays in
London, 1500–1700: The Making of the Metropolis, ed. A. L. Beier and Roger Finlay
(London: Longman, 1986), pp. 1–33; Steven Mullaney, *The Place of the Stage: License,
Play, and Power in Renaissance England* (Chicago: University of Chicago Press, 1988);
and Sandra Clark, *The Elizabethan Pamphleteers: Popular Moralistic Pamphlets, 1580–1640*
(Rutherford, N.J.: Fairleigh Dickinson University Press, 1983), pp. 22, 33.

11. On popular culture, see Peter Burke, *Popular Culture in Early Modern Europe*

the very poorest) men and women commingled; the public, outdoor theaters, in which most dramatizations of domestic crime were staged, attracted the most diverse audiences, drawing tradespeople and servants as well as lords and ladies, pickpockets and whores.[12] Of all the representations of domestic crime, ballads were the most accessible. Sung in the streets by those who hawked them, they mediated between oral and written culture. They were printed on one side of a single sheet of paper making them cheap and portable. Ballads were widely circulated in printed form and by memory; they were consumed by those with neither spending money nor reading skills.[13] Pamphlets recounting the "news" of recent crimes, which make up the bulk of my evidence, probably reached a somewhat more limited audience. Published in quarto by mainstream publishers who approached news as a sideline, these pamphlets were brief, unbound, and thus relatively cheap.[14] Retailing at about twopence, they cost about as much as "two quarts of strong beer at the alehouse," by Tessa Watt's calculation.[15] We know

(New York: Harper, 1978); Steven L. Kaplan, ed., *Understanding Popular Culture: Europe from the Middle Ages to the Nineteenth Century* (Berlin: Mouton, 1984); Barry Reay, ed., *Popular Culture in Seventeenth-Century England* (London: Croom Helm, 1985); Peter Stallybrass and Allon White, *The Politics and Poetics of Transgression* (Ithaca: Cornell University Press, 1986); and James B. Twitchell, "The Imaging of Violence in Early Modern Popular Culture," in his *Preposterous Violence: Fables of Aggression in Modern Culture* (Oxford: Oxford University Press, 1989), pp. 48–89.

12. Martin Butler, Appendix 2, "Shakespeare's Unprivileged Playgoers, 1576–1642," in his *Theatre and Crisis, 1632–1642* (Cambridge: Cambridge University Press, 1984); and Andrew Gurr, *Playgoing in Shakespeare's London* (Cambridge: Cambridge University Press, 1987). See also R. A. Foakes, "Playhouses and Players," in *The Cambridge Companion to English Renaissance Drama*, ed. A. R. Braunmuller and Michael Hattaway (Cambridge: Cambridge University Press, 1990), pp. 1–52, esp. pp. 32–39. Although the repertoires and clienteles of the indoor and outdoor theaters were distinct, they also overlapped.

13. On ballads, see Natascha Wurzbach, *The Rise of the English Street Ballad, 1550–1650*, trans. Gayna Walls (Cambridge: Cambridge University Press, 1990); and Joy Wiltenburg, *Disorderly Women and Female Power in the Street Literature of Early Modern England and Germany* (Charlottesville: University of Virginia Press, 1992).

14. Tessa Watt, *Cheap Print and Popular Piety, 1550–1640* (Cambridge: Cambridge University Press, 1991), p. 265.

15. Ibid., p. 262, see also pp. 260–64. On the cost of pamphlets and ballads, see also Wiltenburg, *Disorderly Women*, p. 30, and chap. 3, passim; Lincoln B. Faller, *Turned to Account: The Forms and Functions of Criminal Biography in Late Seventeenth- and Early Eighteenth-Century England* (Cambridge: Cambridge University Press, 1987), Appendix I; Margaret Spufford, *Small Books and Pleasant Histories: Popular Fiction and Its Readership in Seventeenth-Century England* (Cambridge: Cambridge University Press, 1981), esp. p. 48.

less about the distribution of news pamphlets than we do about ballads and chapbooks, which were published by specialist printers who distributed them through their own networks of peddlers.[16] These peddlers traveled the countryside as well as working the streets of London; they may well have included some news pamphlets among their wares. Bookstalls in larger towns as well as in London would also have sold such pamphlets.

The purchasers of printed texts were most probably the middling or industrious sort, the London craftsmen, tradesmen, and merchants, and their households, who had attained moderate levels of both literacy and disposable income, as well as some members of the upper classes.[17] Heads of household were not the only people with the money to buy texts or the ability to read them. I assume that if women of the middling sort had the money to purchase poison, as accounts of domestic crime suggest they did, then they might also have been able to purchase cheap texts. The texts themselves suggest that tradesmen's and gentlemen's wives and servants, and even witches, could sometimes read, undercutting any simple division between literate elite and illiterate popular cultures. Reading ability, a much more common skill than writing, was spread unevenly throughout all but the most impoverished classes.[18] Black-letter type, in which most of the texts under discussion here were printed, was more widely legible than other kinds of type or, certainly, script.

Literacy did not wholly determine access to the stories. Those who could not read might still attend assize sessions (trials), executions, and plays; they might hear ballads sung on the street by their sellers and learn them by heart; they might have a pamphlet read to them or hear

16. Spufford, *Small Books,* and Watt, *Cheap Print,* both focus on chapbooks, which were small-format "merry" and "godly" books. Both scholars base their categories on those Samuel Pepys used and virtually exclude accounts of actual crimes.

17. Wiltenburg, *Disorderly Women,* p. 39.

18. On literacy, see David Cressy, *Literacy and the Social Order: Reading and Writing in Tudor and Stuart England* (Cambridge: Cambridge University Press, 1980); Thomas Laqueur, "The Cultural Origins of Popular Literacy in England, 1500–1850," *Oxford Review of Education* 2.3 (1976): 255–75; Margaret Spufford, "First Steps in Literacy: The Reading and Writing Experiences of the Humblest Seventeenth-Century Spiritual Autobiographers," *Social History* 4.3 (1979): 407–34; and Keith Thomas, "The Meaning of Literacy in Early Modern England," in *The Written Word: Literacy in Transition,* ed. Gerd Baumann (New York: Oxford University Press, 1986), pp. 97–131.

it recited (roughly) from memory.[19] Inns and alehouses would have been important arenas for the reading or the memorial reconstruction of popular texts. During the process of transmission, those who disseminated songs and stories must also have changed them.[20] Although little evidence survives of consumers' strategic appropriations and adaptations, we should assume that the texts that survive offer only one of the versions in circulation and that textual reception was a dynamic, interactive process.

The elite were not necessarily remote from and uninterested in scandalous domestic crimes among the nonelite and their popular depictions. They, too, may have formed part of the audience for printed texts, as they did for plays. Indeed, some pamphlets reveal attempts to cater to the learned with scraps of Latin and classical allusions.[21] In my discussion of witchcraft, I emphasize that popular and elite, oral and print cultures were not sharply segregated in the early modern period, but were intertwined and overlapping.

Published legal texts vividly demonstrate how popular and elite cultures intersect, sometimes antagonistically, sometimes collaboratively, in the process of defining, detecting, punishing, and representing crime.[22] Written by the relatively elite—learned, male legal personnel (justices of the peace or legal clerks)—texts such as manuals for justices

19. Roger Chartier, "Leisure and Sociability: Reading Aloud in Early Modern Europe," in *Urban Life in the Renaissance,* ed. Susan Zimmerman and Ronald F. E. Weissman (Newark: University of Delaware Press, 1989), pp. 103–20, and "Texts, Printing, Readings," in *The New Cultural History,* ed. Lynn Hunt (Berkeley: University of California Press, 1989), pp. 154–75, esp. pp. 158–59.

20. As Roger Chartier argues: "Cultural consumption, whether popular or not, is at the same time a form of production, which creates ways of using that cannot be limited to the intentions of those who produce" ("Culture as Appropriation: Popular Cultural Uses in Early Modern France," in *Understanding Popular Culture,* ed. Kaplan, pp. 229–53, esp. p. 234). See also Chartier, "Texts," pp. 164–65, 169–70; Ann Rosalind Jones, *The Currency of Eros: Women's Love Lyric in Europe, 1540–1620* (Bloomington: Indiana University Press, 1990), esp. pp. 2–4; and Wiltenburg, *Disorderly Women,* pp. 28–29. On inns and alehouses as centers "where ballads and chapbooks and corantos were handed round, or read aloud," see Spufford, *Small Books,* pp. 66–67; and Bernard Capp, "Popular Literature," in *Popular Culture in Seventeenth-Century England,* ed. Reay, pp. 198–243, esp. pp. 203–4.

21. Watt, *Cheap Print,* p. 265.

22. On how "literary" convention shapes even legal documents about crime, see Natalie Z. Davis, *Fiction in the Archives: Pardon Tales and Their Tellers in Sixteenth-Century France* (Stanford: Stanford University Press, 1987).

of the peace, a legal encyclopedia for women, or lengthy, published trial transcripts address a fairly privileged audience that is assumed to be more interested in upholding the law than in breaking it. These texts publish the legal assumptions and controversies that inform judgments on all subjects, from the most to the least privileged; they also induct new initiates into legal mysteries. Given the widespread interest and participation in administering justice at the local level (quarter sessions and assize courts), we should not assume that knowledge of the law was the exclusive province of the elite. Even men or women without property may have participated not just as defendants but as victims, who initiated the process by bringing charges and assembling evidence, or as witnesses; additionally, they may have sat in on the proceedings. Men of the middling sort—yeomen, husbandmen, and established tradesmen who owned some property—played a central role in the administration of justice as members of juries and justices of the peace. In the choices they made, these community members created and exploited what Cynthia Herrup calls "the gap between law as written and law as lived," making law enforcement flexible and collaborative.[23] Popular accounts of crime may also have spread knowledge of the legal process even to those excluded from participation.[24]

We know most about the relatively learned writers of these diverse legal discourses. The authors of the most cheaply produced and widely disseminated representations of domestic crime never identify themselves, so I can say little about their social status, education, or gender. Some seem to have made a living through the popular press, particularly as writers of ballads; others supported themselves through paid labor— John Taylor, "the water poet," was a waterman on the Thames—while writing occasional ballads or pamphlets as a sideline.[25] Most frequently, familiarity with a particular case moved a participant observer (neighbor, legal clerk, or witness) to write and publish an account. Such writers may have published only one text. No evidence suggests that the accused

---

23. Cynthia Herrup, *The Common Peace: Participation and the Criminal Law in Seventeenth-Century England* (Cambridge: Cambridge University Press, 1987), esp. p. 193; James Sharpe, "The People and the Law," in *Popular Culture in Seventeenth-Century England,* ed. Reay, pp. 244–70.

24. See Sharpe, "People and the Law," p. 256.

25. On Taylor's unique career, see Victor E. Neuburg, *Popular Literature: A History and Guide* (Harmondsworth: Penguin, 1977), pp. 96–101.

ever wrote their own accounts, although many pamphlets reproduce their examinations and confessions, their remarks on the scaffold, or letters written from prison.[26] In presenting the convicts' remarks, such texts can be seen as a kind of collaboration between author and subject. In addition, plays, pamphlets, and ballads were often collaboratively written; widespread practices of revising, borrowing, compiling, and copying also made many texts "collaborations."[27]

Henry Goodcole may be representative of these mysterious writers; he wrote a pamphlet on each of the three female domestic offenses central to the book, yet he did not support himself by writing. As minister to the condemned in Newgate prison, he wrote from intimate knowledge of particular criminals, their crimes, and their spiritual preparations for death. Goodcole records his active engagement in extracting and shaping confessions; the contradictions within his own narrative frames, as well as between those frames and the statements he attributes to his condemned "patients," expose the hard work of producing moral lessons out of the social and ethical complexities of criminals' stories.

His texts also expand from the focus on a single criminal (*The Wonderfull Discoverie of Elizabeth Sawyer a Witch* [1621]) to more general discussions of the phenomenon of domestic crime, especially as perpetrated by women (*The Adultresses Funerall Day* [1635]). The more Goodcole expands his format and ruminates on the implications of the crimes, the less control he seems to have over his material, resulting in texts far more ambiguous than their harshly judgmental titles. As a minister of relatively modest birth and education, Goodcole stands between the law and the condemned, not quite belonging with either. Urging, directing, and recording confessions, he participates in the process of convicting and punishing offenders; counseling the condemned, he professes care for their spiritual welfare and attends to the details of their stories.[28]

26. On the extent to which we can consider the condemned as the "authors" of the speeches and documents attributed to them, see my " 'Gentlemen, I have one thing more to say': Women on Scaffolds in England, 1563–1680," *Modern Philology*, forthcoming.

27. On the collaborative nature of dramatic composition, see Gerald E. Bentley, *The Profession of Dramatist in Shakespeare's Time, 1590–1642* (Princeton: Princeton University Press, 1971), chap. 8, and passim. On the extent to which pamphleteers drew on one another's work, see Clark, *Elizabethan Pamphleteers*, pp. 33, 96–97.

28. Goodcole wrote two texts, also on criminals, which I do not discuss: *Heavens Speedie Hue and Cry Sent after Lust and Murther* (London, 1635) and *A True Declaration*

The extant evidence on "cheap print" suggests that although not everyone had absolutely equal access to "popular" texts, even wage laborers might have thought of them as an occasionally affordable luxury.[29] Since London's population grew from 120,000 in 1550 to 490,000 in 1700, accounts of domestic crime probably circulated among ever-increasing numbers of readers, spectators, and listeners.[30] The fact that so many of these pamphlets survive is evidence in itself that they were mass-produced and widely distributed. Quickly and cheaply published to capitalize on the interest in sensational crimes, these ephemeral texts would have been passed hand-to-hand, affixed to walls, or "recycled" as a source of much-needed paper, becoming, in John Dryden's wonderful phrase, "martyrs of pies, and relics of the bum."[31] Since they were accorded little value as objects, it is amazing that so many of them have survived.

In Chapters 1, 2, and 3, I explore the fluid boundaries between the domestic and political spheres as revealed through commonplace analogies between the household and the Commonwealth. I am particularly interested in how the meanings and functions of these analogies change in the course of the seventeenth century and its dramatic political upheavals. Although many scholars have focused on the political consequences of analogical thinking, I focus on its *domestic* implications and the pressure it places on the household and its members.[32] Challenging

of the Happy Conversion, Contrition, and Christian Preparation of Francis Robinson, Gentleman (London, 1618). On Goodcole, and on pamphleteers in general, see Clark, *Elizabethan Pamphleteers*, pp. 26–29, 87–88; see also her introduction and chap. 2, passim.

29. According to Wiltenburg, such texts were even more affordable at the end of our period because rising wages outpaced their cost (*Disorderly Women*, p. 30).

30. Beier and Finlay, *London*, p. 2.

31. John Dryden, "Mac Flecknoe" (circa 1679), in *The Norton Anthology of English Literature*, gen. ed. M. H. Abrams, 2 vols., 6th ed. (New York: W. W. Norton, 1993), 1: 1818, line 101; see also Spufford, *Small Books*, pp. 48–49.

32. On the analogy between the household and Commonwealth, see Susan Dwyer Amussen, *An Ordered Society: Gender and Class in Early Modern England* (Oxford: Basil Blackwell, 1988); Dympna Callaghan, *Woman and Gender in Renaissance Tragedy: A Study of "King Lear," "Othello," "The Duchess of Malfi" and "The White Devil"* (Atlantic Highlands, N.J.: Humanities Press International, 1989), pp. 14–27; Natalie Z. Davis, "Women on Top," in her *Society and Culture in Early Modern France* (Stanford: Stanford University Press, 1975), esp. pp. 127–28; Christopher Hill, *Society and Puritanism in Pre-Revolutionary England*, 2d ed. (New York: Schocken, 1967), chap. 13; Karen Newman, *Fashioning Femininity and English Renaissance Drama* (Chicago: University of Chicago Press, 1991), chap. 2; Mary Beth Rose, *The Expense of Spirit: Love and Sexuality in*

Jonathan Goldberg's argument that "Renaissance families need to be read from the outside in: from the state to the family," I argue that early modern culture needs to be read from the inside out: from the family to the state.[33]

In Chapter 1, I examine legal and popular representations of husband-murder, which was defined as petty treason, that is, as a crime against civil authority. This crime captured the popular imagination and generated extensive representations, especially before 1650, despite the fact that it was never very common. Exploring the connections between legal and literary fictions, I argue that the fictions circulating in the courtroom, on the stage, and on the street attempt to restore the order threatened by wifely insubordination. Yet these fictions reveal the irreconcilable contradictions within and among early modern constructions of married women's status, as well as the anxieties surrounding intimacy in this period.

Chapter 2 continues the focus on petty treason, extending it to the relations between masters and servants. I investigate likeness between the two kinds of dependents, wives and servants, and the two kinds of petty treason, husband-killing and master-killing, examining how legal and literary narratives of petty treason work to subordinate the story of the rebellious dependent within social and literary structures. The interplay between the master('s) plot and the subordinate('s) plot(s) reveals the interdependency of superiors and subordinates and the precariousness of the master's authority. I focus on this interplay in three cases: Shakespeare's fictional *Tempest;* the anonymous, quasi-fictional *Arden of Faversham* (based on an actual case); and, finally, narratives of the actual trial of the earl of Castlehaven.

Around mid century, pamphlets and ballads shift their focus from insubordinate dependents to the murderous husband, depicting his abuse of his authority as petty tyranny. In Chapter 3, I trace how this relocation of domestic threat corresponds to the suspicion and circumscription of authority that builds from the Civil War, through the Restoration, to the 1688 Revolution. Demonizing the murderous hus-

---

English Renaissance Drama (Ithaca: Cornell University Press, 1988), chap. 3; and Debora Kuller Shuger, *Habits of Thought in the English Renaissance: Religion, Politics, and the Dominant Culture* (Berkeley: University of California Press, 1990), chap. 6.

33. Jonathan Goldberg, *James I and the Politics of Literature* (Baltimore: Johns Hopkins University Press, 1983), p. 89.

band as a lunatic exception, pamphlets and ballads deny his relationship to other husbands, refusing to reflect on the potential for abuse built into marriage or the imbalances of power within the household. To chart the shift from one dominant narrative of domestic conflict to the next, I examine texts (such as *Othello*) that work as palimpsests, simultaneously telling the stories of the domestic tyrant and of the petty traitor.

While the first three chapters focus on the relationships of authority and subordination that structure the early modern household and how these change over time, in Chapters 4 and 5 I expand my focus to include figures who exist largely outside the patriarchal household, especially unmarried women.[34] Obviously, not all women who lived outside marriage and the traditional family were criminalized, but legal and popular representations of infanticide and witchcraft explicitly target those women who live outside direct male supervision, revealing the anxieties such women provoked. Accounts of infanticide and witchcraft demonize women's self-assertions as attacks directly on the family they stand outside (and, the logic goes, therefore against): Such women slaughter infants, undermine domestic production, and hold secret rites.

Although accounts of petty treason usually focus on a wife-servant conspiracy—which reproduces the heterosexual couple even as it overturns domestic hierarchy—and almost never depict women plotting together, accounts of infanticide and witchcraft teem with women acting either alone or with other women.[35] Such female separatism suggests the frightening possibility of an alternative social space dominated by women. Representations of this threatening space outside the patriarchal household are especially infrequent in the drama, which rarely

34. As Patricia Crawford argues: "Clearly men thought that [the family] was central to order in society, but women did not always live their lives in the bounds imposed by the family, and it may be useful to reconsider the idea of the family as the basic social unit" (review of Susan Amussen's *An Ordered Society, Renaissance Quarterly* 45.1 [1992]: 178–79, esp. p. 179).

35. The one exception I know of is *Murther, Murther. Or, A Bloody Relation How Anne Hamton . . . by Poyson Murthered Her Deare Husband . . . Being Assisted and Counselled thereunto by Margeret Harwood* (London, 1641). In her work with assize and quarter sessions records in Hertfordshire, Carol Z. Wiener sees a similar pattern by which those women who engage in violent crime have at least one male accessory ("Sex Roles and Crime in Late Elizabethan Hertfordshire," *Journal of Social History* 8.4 [1975]: 38–60, esp. p. 45).

focuses on women who are neither married nor to be married.[36] There are remarkable exceptions, like Moll Cutpurse, the roaring girl, who is the central protagonist of her play despite her resolute refusal to marry. But plays about the crimes generally attributed to unmarried women skillfully avoid placing such women at the center. Plays about child abuse or abandonment focus on fathers as perpetrators, despite the fact that most other representations of these crimes, including legal statutes, focus on mothers. Plays about witchcraft either relegate witches to the subplot or present them as married, contained, comic.

Most women who lived on the margins of households and communities were neither independent nor powerful; they lived in terrible poverty, poverty that drove them to make demands of those more securely positioned, who then feared them. By attributing power to such women, popular culture collaborated with the law in criminalizing poverty. Like fictions of petty treason, representations of infanticide and witchcraft locate the threat to domestic and social order in the least powerful and privileged, in those most likely to be the victims rather than the perpetrators of violence, vilification, and exploitation.

In the last two chapters, I pay particular attention to how the processes of canon-formation transformed Shakespeare's plays into high culture, simultaneously excluding many of the other texts and issues from the cultural contests in which the plays engaged. Reconnecting plays such as *The Winter's Tale* and *Macbeth* to heterogeneous cultural materials debating domestic crime, I consider why these plays are now so much more familiar than the other materials. Of what contests did they emerge the victors? Depending on what Dominick LaCapra has called the "noncanonical reading of canonical texts," I demonstrate that these plays are more conventional than is readily visible when we view them in isolation, as well as more actively engaged in contestation.[37]

Chapter 4, then, focuses on how dramatizations of infanticide and infant abandonment participated in a complex cultural process that displaced blame for abuse and neglect of children onto poor, unmarried

36. In *The Lawes Resolutions of Womens Rights: Or, The Lawes Provision for Woemen* (London, 1632), compiled by I.L. and revised by T.E., T.E. explains that all women are "understood either married or to bee married" (sig. B3v).

37. Dominick LaCapra, *History and Criticism* (Ithaca: Cornell University Press, 1985), chap. 3, esp. pp. 93, 79.

women. Throughout the chapter, I emphasize that representations of child murder associate it with self-destructive acts: suicide, in the case of mothers, and prodigality, in the case of fathers. By reconstructing Leontes's relationship to poor spinsters who threw their newborns in the privy, I demonstrate *The Winter's Tale*'s engagement both in a cultural debate about the vexed, violent relationship between parent and child and in the process of canon-formation, itself violent. Just as Perdita was not "lost" but abandoned, the legal and popular representations of child abuse on which *The Winter's Tale* depends were not lost but were absorbed and repressed in the very process of transforming them into a self-consciously literary artifact and mainstay of the Renaissance drama canon.

In Chapter 5, I approach witchcraft as another kind of domestic crime, showing how the tensions within families, especially stepfamilies, could be displaced and negotiated through accusations of witchcraft. Witches were themselves well known to, even intimate with, their victims. Their "imps" or "familiars," popularly perceived as both small household pets and fiendishly busy embodiments of the devil, further exemplify how accounts of domestic crime conflate the familiar and the dangerous, the self and the other. English witch belief at popular and elite levels understood the subject as diffusing itself into the material world of bodily effluvia, clothing, and items of personal property, animating these objects as extensions of the subject that the witch could maliciously appropriate and manipulate. Through subject-extensions, even the most socially empowered people could become vulnerable to the relatively disenfranchised and marginalized. Witchcraft was believed to destabilize the distributions of power within the culture and the foundations of social order.

The threat witches posed, like that murderous wives and servants posed, lay in their capacity for agency, again construed as wholly negative. At the height of witchcraft prosecutions, popular and elite belief conjoined in attributing power and agency to women in order to justify persecuting them. In contrast, the learned skepticism that spread among the elite and eventually spared witches from legal prosecution worked by depriving them of agency. The central section of Chapter 5 locates the many dramatic representations of witchcraft, including *Macbeth,* at an intersection of popular and elite beliefs and charts the drama's participation in the controversy over witches' agency.

Throughout, I use the term "early modern" to avoid the standard literary periodizations of "Renaissance" and "Restoration" that divide up the seventeenth century and elide the middle. Since these terms are associated with change at the top of social and literary hierarchies, they are not relevant to the ephemeral materials and socially marginalized figures on whom I focus.[38] Furthermore, the crimes central to the book are seventeenth-century, rather than Renaissance or Restoration, phenomena. In most cases, the statutes that define them as crimes were enacted in the late Tudor period and repealed or disregarded by the early eighteenth century; in a parallel development, popular representations emerged in the late sixteenth century and dwindled, like prosecutions, in the late seventeenth century. By ignoring literary periodizations, I can chart changes across the whole of the seventeenth century. The shift in popular interest from the murderous wife to the murderous husband that occurs around mid century is one example of a pattern one can see only when considering the seventeenth century as a whole.

Many social historians agree that early modern England witnessed a crisis of order, focusing on gender relations, that began around 1550, peaked in 1650, and passed by 1700. According to Susan Amussen, after 1660 concerns about disorder ceased to be displaced directly onto women. Political theorists such as John Locke and Thomas Hobbes discarded the analogy between the household and Commonwealth to argue that the father's authority over his family was neither "natural" nor a model for the relationship between a king and his subjects. As a result, Amussen says, "women's role in family government lost its public significance."[39] At the local level, fewer efforts were made to interfere in and regulate households or to control disorderly women. Pointing to the declining frequency in prosecutions of both witches and scolds after the Restoration, David Underdown argues that "the witch and the scold had risen together as alienated outsiders, casualties of a chang-

38. On how attention to gender challenges us to reconsider traditional periodizations, see Joan Kelly, "Did Women Have a Renaissance?" in her *Women, History, and Theory* (Chicago: University of Chicago Press, 1984), pp. 19–50; and Margaret W. Ferguson, with Maureen Quilligan and Nancy J. Vickers, "Introduction," in *Rewriting the Renaissance: The Discourses of Sexual Difference in Early Modern Europe*, ed. Ferguson, Quilligan, and Vickers (Chicago: University of Chicago Press, 1986), pp. xv–xxxi.

39. Amussen, *Ordered Society*, pp. 187, 132. See also pp. 33, 109, 130, 177–78 on the shift from formal to informal methods of control.

ing social order; when a different kind of order was consolidated its defenders found less need to discipline them."[40] In their work on witches and prophets, respectively, Christina Larner and Phyllis Mack agree that women ceased to be regarded as either spiritual authorities or as threats by 1700.[41] By 1700, representations of domestic conflict and of disorderly, violent women receded from the center of popular culture. Women were spared persecution and execution, yet they were taken less seriously. Less feared, they were also perceived as less powerful and dangerous.

By emphasizing the mixed results of these changes for women—the disparities among kinds of evidence, the gap between the surviving evidence and how women may actually have experienced change, the different consequences for differently positioned women—I avoid arguing that "women's status" either improved or declined in the period.[42] Certainly eighteenth-century English culture continued to attribute power to women; popular representations of criminal women contributed to the novel with its bold, criminal heroines such as Roxana and Moll Flanders. But the conjunction of law and popular culture in criminalizing female agency breaks down. While female thieves, whores, and deceivers abound, women as agents of domestic violence recede from the spotlight of legal regulation and popular attention. In a brief Epilogue, I examine the representations of domestic conflict and constructions of women's subjectivities in the eighteenth century, particularly in the novel. Selectively examining Daniel Defoe's *Moll Flanders* and *Roxana,* Elizabeth Inchbald's *Nature and Art,* and George Lillo's *The London Merchant,* I argue that these texts depend on domestic conflict but displace its violence onto characters other than the protagonists or

40. David Underdown, *Revel, Riot, and Rebellion: Popular Politics and Culture in England, 1603–1660* (Oxford: Oxford University Press, 1985), pp. 286–87.

41. Christina Larner, *Witchcraft and Religion: The Politics of Popular Belief,* ed. Alan Macfarlane (Oxford: Basil Blackwell, 1984), p. 87; Phyllis Mack, "Women as Prophets during the English Civil War," *Feminist Studies* 8.1 (1982): 19–45, esp. p. 34. See also Sharpe, *Crime in Early Modern England,* pp. 17–18, 184–85; and Wiltenburg, *Disorderly Women,* pp. 256–57.

42. One way to chart the changes in women's status as public figures, idealized as well as demonized, is to consider the difference between Elizabeth I, with her wily refusals to marry, and Princess Mary of Orange, who "declared her intention to renounce the crown to William, should she inherit it, on grounds that a wife must obey her husband" (Lois G. Schwoerer, "Images of Queen Mary II, 1689–95," *Renaissance Quarterly* 42.4 [1989]: 717–48, esp. p. 729).

into dreams and visions; they also explore nonviolent means of separating from spouses and children.

Although I wish to demonstrate my work's relevance to scholarship on "the origins of the novel," I also challenge the assumption that popular materials such as pamphlets are sub- or at best preliterary, base metals awaiting their alchemical transformation into the novel: My contention is not that they "would be gold if they had time."[43] Like Shakespearean drama, the novel, subsequently valorized as the consummate genre of its era, absorbed and digested ephemeral, widely disseminated materials. If this is a story of origins, it is a violent one in which the children eat their parents and bury the bones. Exhuming the remains of those repudiated progenitors, I narrate the process of their defeat, writing literary history as itself a violent story of conflict among intimates.

43. Ben Jonson, *The Alchemist,* in *Drama of the English Renaissance II: The Stuart Period,* ed. Russell A. Fraser and Norman Rabkin (New York: Macmillan, 1976), 2.3.137.

I. "HOME-REBELS AND HOUSE-TRAITORS": PETTY TREASON AND THE MURDEROUS WIFE

In Thomas Heywood's *An Apology for Actors* (1612), which contributes to the lively debate over the theater in Renaissance England, two murderous wives make cameo appearances. Against claims that the theater displays and corrupts women, Heywood argues for the theater as an arena in which criminal women can be found out and controlled. For Heywood, to imagine women as theatergoers and spectators is to imagine them as adulterous and murderous wives, waiting to be discovered. Arguing that plays are not only morally instructive but have been "the discoverers of many notorious murders," Heywood offers two "domestike and home-borne" examples of the "education" of murderous wives. In one, for instance, a woman who sees an unusual murder enacted on stage—a nail driven through the victim's skull—confesses to killing her husband in a similar way. Heywood remarks approvingly: "This being publicly confest, she was arraigned, condemned, adjudged, and burned."[1] In defending the theater as a means rather than an

---

1. Thomas Heywood, *An Apology for Actors* (Nendeln, Liechtenstein: Kraus Reprint, 1966), pp. 57, 60. Catherine Belsey also connects Heywood's *Apology* to representations

obstacle to social control, Heywood employs the figure of the murderous wife as a representative of the social disorder that the theater
can correct by exposing. In his narrative, women are spectators and
spectacles, agents of violent action and objects of control, murderers
and wives. In this chapter, I am interested in the cultural conditions
particular to early modern England that enabled a writer like Heywood
to use the figure of the murderous wife as the embodiment of such
irreconcilable contradictions.

Defining Petty Treason: Legal and Popular Fictions

In *The Crowne Conjugall* (1632), John Wing reminds readers that "an
undutifull wife is a *home-rebell*, a *house-traitor*."[2] As Wing's hyphenated
terms reveal, the analogical relation between the household and the
commonwealth could elide distinctions between the two. The resulting
conflation of the domestic and the political informed legal as well as
literary representation; the possibility that a wife might actually kill her
husband was so disturbing that the crime had a special legal status. In
legal statutes after 1352 (25 Edward 3), killing one's husband, defined
as petty treason, was carefully distinguished from other forms of murder
and pronounced analogous to high treason—any threat to or assault
on the monarch and his or her government. While a man who killed
his wife or servant was accused of murder, the statutes provided that
"if any servant kill his Master, any woman kill her husband, or any
secular or religious person kill his Prelate to whom he owes Obedience,
this is treason."[3] One justice of the peace succinctly explained that a
wife or servant who "maliciously killeth" a husband or master was
accused of treason while a husband or master who "maliciously killeth"

---

of petty treason; see her *The Subject of Tragedy: Identity and Difference in Renaissance
Drama* (London: Methuen, 1985), esp. p. 137.

2. John Wing, *The Crowne Conjugall* (London, 1632), p. 297. Similarly, William
Whately advises that a husband should promote cooperation with his wife because "it is
harmfull to nourish as it were a domestick faction in this little common-weale" (*A Bride-
Bush. Or, A Direction for Married Persons* [London, 1623], pp. 96–97).

3. For 25 Edward 3, St. 5, cap. 2 (the Statute of Treasons), see William Rastall, *A
Collection in English of the Statutes Now in Force* (London, 1603), p. 460.b. According to
J. H. Baker, "Petty treason was abolished, and the offence converted to murder, in 1858"
(*An Introduction to English Legal History* [London: Butterworths, 1971], p. 284).

a wife or servant was accused of murder "for that the one is in subjection and oweth obedience, and not the other."[4]

In the statute that first defined killing a husband or master as a form of treason, killing a king and killing a husband or master were not explicitly distinguished as high and low, grand and petty, treasons but were instead described simply as versions of the same act, that is, kinds of treason. According to many legal historians, the definition of petty or domestic treason did not grow out of the definition of high treason, nor was the definition of the latter applied to the household analogously; instead, the understanding of treason against the sovereign, and even more abstractly, against the state, may well have evolved out of the more local, particular concept of betrayal of one's feudal lord.[5] In marking any distinction between the two kinds of treason, the 1352 statute might be seen as defining high as well as petty treason, marking a difference between king and lord and placing greater value on loyalty to the king. Although it is unclear exactly when the term "petty" or "petit" was first used to describe acts of domestic treason, the term "petty treason" was widely used in popular and legal discussions of the crime by the early seventeenth century.

Until 1790, the punishments for petty treason were different than those for murder and drew attention to the crime as a particularly egregious assault on social and political order. Men convicted of petty treason were drawn to the place of execution on a hurdle and then were hanged. This punishment emphasized the shameful display of the disciplined body, but was not as heinous as the notorious executions for high treason, which involved mutilation, disembowelment, and decapitation. Women convicted of petty treason, however, were sentenced to the same punishment as those convicted of high treason: They were burned at the stake (see Fig. 1).[6] In legal theory, then, if not always in

4. Michael Dalton, *The Countrey Justice* (London, 1618), p. 205.

5. Frederick Pollock and Frederic W. Maitland, *The History of English Law*, 2 vols. (Boston: Cambridge University Press, 1895), 2:502, see also 2:501–7; W. S. Holdsworth, *A History of English Law*, 7 vols., 3d ed. (London: Methuen, 1923), 2:450, see also 2:449–50. I am grateful to Julie A. Sikkink for these references and for her help in understanding the complexities of petty treason in legal theory and practice in early modern England.

6. These punishments were standard for men by the thirteenth century and for women by the fourteenth. On punishments, see Francis Bacon, *Cases of Treason* (London, 1641), chaps. 2 and 6; Dalton, *The Countrey Justice*, p. 206; and J. H. Baker, "Criminal Courts and Procedure in Common Law, 1550–1800," in *Crime in England, 1550–1800*, ed.

The Adultreſſes Funerall Day:

In flaming, ſcorching, and conſuming fire:

OR

The burning downe to aſhes of *Alice Clarke* late of *Vx-bridge* in the County of *Miadleſex,* in *Weſt-ſmith-field,* on *Wenſday* the 20. of *May,* 1635. for the unnaturall poiſoning of *Fortune Clarke* her Husband.

A breviary of whoſe Confeſſion taken from her owne mouth, is here unto annexed : As alſo what ſhe ſayd at the place of her Execution.

By her daily Viſiter H. G. *in life and death. And now publiſhed by Authority and Commaund.*

LONDON

Printed by *N.* and *I. Okes,* dwelling in *Well-yard* in lit-tle St. *Bartholmews,* neare unto the *Lame Hoſpitall* gate, 1635.

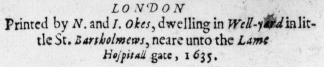

Figure 1. A petty traitor burns at the stake. Title page from *The Adultresses Funerall Day* (1635). By permission of the Houghton Library, Harvard University.

practice, the punishment of female petty traitors collapsed the distinction between the two kinds of treason. For women, these capital offenses were not only analogous but virtually the same.

Although the legal definition of petty treason constructs the subordination of wives and servants to the master of the household as the foundation of domestic and civil order, as natural and inevitable, it also acknowledges that wives and servants did not always cooperate; their subordination was *not* a given. The very need to define such a crime and the fairly regular opportunities to see or read about the offenders who committed it suggest the pervasive fear that wives and servants could and would rebel; they might not acquiesce to their subordination, which was achieved only by a complex network of constraints and coercions. The statute thus tells two stories that contradict one another: "These are the incontrovertible, non-negotiable principles according to which our world works"; and, simultaneously, "Our world does not always work according to these principles, so perhaps they are controvertible and negotiable."

The transgressions of curates against their ministers and male servants against their masters inscribed in the legal definition of petty treason offer a useful reminder that domestic hierarchy and gender hierarchy are not the same thing and that gender and class categories do not neatly overlap. Some discussions of petty treason, although not the legal statute itself, suggest that a female servant who kills her mistress or a child who kills his or her mother could be considered guilty of petty treason. Such texts grant women positions of authority analogous to those of the king or queen—or husband or master—and present crimes against them, in their roles as mothers and mistresses, as crimes against familial and domestic authority. Although it was possible for female gender to coincide with domestic authority, as the relatively frequent murders of women by their rebellious servants and children confirm, the popular texts that survive seldom tell these stories, nor does the statute of treasons explicitly address this possibility.[7] Petty

---

J. S. Cockburn (Princeton: Princeton University Press, 1977), p. 42. On the 1790 revocation of burning as the punishment for women adjudged of petty or high treason, see Ruth Campbell, "Sentence of Death by Burning for Women," *Journal of Legal History* 5 (1984): 44–54.

7. For discussions of whether killing a mistress was petty treason, see Dalton, *The Countrey Justice*, pp. 204–6; T.E., *The Lawes Resolutions of Womens Rights: or, The Lawes*

treason narratives inevitably present the story of the murderous wife (and, often, of her servant-lover); when they grant a woman an important role in a story of domestic violence, she is usually the perpetrator rather than the victim of that violence. The many popular versions of the story of the betrayed male authority figure and the female home-rebel and house-traitor exclude the complexities with which the justices of the peace wrestled.

The murderous wife invited representation and debate in a huge array of seventeenth-century printed texts, including legal treatises, pamphlets, scaffold speeches, political polemic, ballads, and plays. Depicting actual domestic crimes, these texts serve a variety of functions—spreading news, correcting false reports with "true relations," offering moral lessons and "warnings," debating legal issues, and fulfilling the taste of a burgeoning audience for titillation and retribution.

The proliferation of texts about petty treason does not demonstrate that wives and servants suddenly began killing their husbands and masters in record numbers. Nor does the relative paucity of texts on husbands killing their wives (especially before 1650) mean that they rarely did so or, more important, that they did so less frequently than wives killed their husbands. Indeed, statistics on domestic homicide in this period suggest that husbands murdered their wives at least twice as often as wives murdered their husbands. Using assize indictments from Essex, Hertfordshire, and Sussex from 1559 to 1625, J. S. Cockburn calculates that women were the victims of almost three-fourths of the instances of "marital killing." In Essex assizes from 1560 to 1709, J. A. Sharpe finds that women outnumber men as the victims of spousal murders two to one. Servants, too, were more often the victims than the perpetrators of violence.[8] Although women and servants committed

---

Provision for Woemen, compiled by I.L., and revised by T.E. (London, 1632), sigs. O8v–P; and Ferdinando Pulton, *De Pace Regis et Regni* (London, 1623), sigs. T6v–U. For accounts of female servants who kill or attempt to kill their mistresses, see the story of Joane Burs in Henry Goodcole, *Natures Cruell Step-Dames* (London, 1637); and Thomas Brewer, *The Bloudy Mother* (London, 1609).

8. J. S. Cockburn, "The Nature and Incidence of Crime in England, 1559–1625: A Preliminary Survey," in *Crime in England,* ed. Cockburn, p. 57; J. A. Sharpe, "Domestic Homicide in Early Modern England," *The Historical Journal* 24.1 (1981): 29–48, esp. pp. 36–38. I am also grateful to Susan Dwyer Amussen for sharing her unpublished essay, " 'Being Stirred to Much Unquietness': Violence and Domestic Violence in Early Modern England" forthcoming in *Journal of Women's History;* hereafter cited as "Violence and Domestic Violence." On patterns of interpersonal violence in England, see J. S.

proportionately fewer acts of violence, the story of the murderous wife or the murderous servant is far more frequently narrated and published than the story of the murderous husband or master. The process of textual representation amplifies rather than suppresses women's violent assertions of self, revealing and contributing to an anxiety about murderous wives in inverse proportion to the actual threat they posed.

Although popular texts offer varying accounts of the extent and nature of the contradictions inherent in the story of the murderous wife, all of them constitute a wife's subjectivity as violent in its interiority and speech as well as in its action.[9] These texts represent married women's consciousness of their conflict with and separateness from their husbands, their articulation of themselves as speaking subjects, and their plotting and execution of murder as interrelated and as equally violent. They also portray the subjectivities of their protagonists as produced through the hierarchies ordering gender, class, and domestic relations (they are wives) and their resistance to those hierarchies (they are *murderous* wives).

By asserting her entitlement to grievance and self-will and endeavoring to reshape her circumstances by means of violence, the murderous wife calls into question the legal conception of a wife as subsumed by her husband and largely incapable of legal or moral agency. She also violates the vigorous and persistent, if not necessarily descriptive, cultural constructions of women as incapable of initiative or autonomous action. While evidence suggests that actual early modern women found many ways of challenging, outwitting, or ignoring such sexual ideologies, the representations of the murderous wife explore the most extreme, visible, threatening scenarios of resistance. The heterogeneous narratives of the murderous wife construct the conditions of wifely

---

Cockburn, "Patterns of Violence in English Society: Homicide in Kent, 1560–1985," *Past and Present* 130 (February 1991): 70–106; J. A. Sharpe, "The History of Violence in England: Some Observations," *Past and Present* 108 (August 1985): 206–15; and Lawrence Stone, "Interpersonal Violence in English Society, 1300–1980," *Past and Present* 101 (November 1983): 22–33.

9. As Teresa de Lauretis explains: "The constitution of the social subject depends on the nexus language/subjectivity/consciousness" ("Eccentric Subjects: Feminist Theory and Historical Consciousness," *Feminist Studies* 16.1 [1990]: 115–50, esp. p. 115). For a discussion of other work that has influenced my understanding of subjectivity, see the Introduction.

subjectivity as criminal, because, in violent action, the contradictions of wives' social and legal status prove uncontainable.

Legal and literary discussions of the murderous wife and her crime, petty treason, interrogated the contradictory, disturbing nature of wifely subjectivity in its most extreme and uncontainable form. But it is in those moments of violent criminality that prescription constituted married women as subjects. As numerous scholars have noted, in early modern England, husband and wife became one legal agent—the husband—by means of the husband's "subsumption" of his wife into himself.[10] In this process, the wife became a *feme covert,* meaning that she was "vailed, as it were, clouded and over-shadowed." The wife emerged from this coverture into legal responsibility when her husband ("her sterne, her *primus motor,* without whom she cannot doe much at home, and lesse abroad") died or deserted her, or when she committed a serious crime on her own: "In matters criminall and capitall causes, a Feme covert shall answere without her husband."[11] As Catherine Belsey explains, "Women became capable while and only while they had no husbands, but were always accountable," especially when it would cost them most.[12]

Contemporary discussions of married women's legal status reveal that criminality was the most extreme instance of one strategy by which women accommodated themselves to the demands of coverture. In *The Lawes Resolutions of Womens Rights* (1632), an encyclopedia written to inform women, T.E. explains that the husband's incorporation of his wife into himself is the reason "that Women have no voyse in Parliament, They make no Lawes, they consent to none, they abrogate none. All of them are understood either married or to bee married and their desires [are] subject to their husband, I know no remedy though some women can shift it well enough."[13] T.E. simultaneously constitutes wives as subjects of desire and, in that very desire, as subject to their

10. See Peter Laslett, *The World We Have Lost: England before the Industrial Age—Further Explored,* 3d ed. (New York: Scribners, 1984), p. 20.

11. T.E., *Lawes Resolutions,* sigs. I7, O6v, and O7v.

12. Belsey, *Subject of Tragedy,* p. 153; see also Joy Wiltenburg, *Disorderly Women and Female Power in the Street Literature of Early Modern England and Germany* (Charlottesville: University of Virginia Press, 1992), pp. 15–16.

13. T.E., *Lawes Resolutions,* sig. B3v.

husbands. In pursuing their desire, married women are represented as "shifting it," as managing a demanding, repressive situation, by bending, if not breaking, the rules.[14] Married women are "covert" both in that they are subsumed by their husbands and in that they are stealthy, sly maneuverers within that subsumption. In T.E.'s text, it is only in infractions (presented as "shifting or managing within" rather than "transgressing against") that subjectivity is conferred on married women, even when they are not criminal or violent.

By this formulation, T.E. constitutes married women as subjects, but never challenges the sexual ideologies within which they must operate. If, by presenting wives as "shifting it," T.E. constructs them as subjects without fracturing marriage or reshaping their legal status, she or he also describes a strategy that works only if it does not draw attention to itself. Women who abandoned the covert tactic of "shifting it" in favor of violence and thereby challenged the subordinate place allotted them in the institution of marriage and in legal discourse employed tactics that were conceptually allied with the more widespread strategy of "shifting it." Yet, because they were less covert in either meaning of that word, these wives gained more attention—and more censure.

Scholars have demonstrated the contradictions and tensions *within* prescriptive discourses about love, sexuality, and marriage that construct wives as authorities and dependents, partners and subordinates, sometimes allied with their husbands and sometimes with the children and servants.[15] Just as contradictions inhered in the cultural construction

14. On how Tudor women "shifted it" in regard to property, see Thomas Smith, *De Republica Anglorum* (London, 1583), sig. O3v; and Pearl Hogrefe, "Legal Rights of Tudor Women and the Circumvention by Men and Women," *Sixteenth Century Journal* 3.1 (1972): 97–105.

15. See Amussen, *An Ordered Society: Gender and Class in Early Modern England* (Oxford: Basil Blackwell, 1988), esp. pp. 41–47, 72–85; Belsey, *Subject of Tragedy*, chap. 6; Lynda E. Boose, "Scolding Brides and Bridling Scolds: Taming the Woman's Unruly Member," *Shakespeare Quarterly* 42.2 (1991): 179–213, esp. p. 194; Margaret J. M. Ezell, *The Patriarch's Wife: Literary Evidence and the History of the Family* (Chapel Hill: University of North Carolina Press, 1987), chap. 2; Rosemary Kegl, " 'Those Terrible Approches': Sexuality, Social Mobility, and Resisting the Courtliness of Puttenham's *The Arte of English Poesie*," *English Literary Renaissance* 20.2 (1990): 179–208, esp. pp. 191–92; Mary Beth Rose, *The Expense of Spirit: Love and Sexuality in English Renaissance Drama* (Ithaca: Cornell University Press, 1988), esp. pp. 126–29; and Lawrence Stone, *The Family, Sex, and Marriage in England, 1500–1800* (New York: Harper and Row, 1977), pp. 195–202.

of the role of wife, the lived experience of many married women may have contradicted the prescriptions for and representations of their conduct.[16] But the legal process could also counter women's attempts to outfox constraints through fictions that maximize their accountability. For instance, in her assessment of assize indictments that paradoxically describe defendants as married spinsters, Carol Wiener argues that the married spinster was "a useful legal fiction" invented by judges to permit the prosecution of married women for crimes.[17]

Wiener's discovery of the married spinster demonstrates the centrality of fictions to the maintenance of social order and the ways these fictions can simultaneously make contradictions visible and work to occlude them. Although such fictions did have consequences and did inform practice, my focus throughout is on *representations* in popular literature and in legal theory. While the legal definition of petty treason was not new to the early modern period and the crime did not actually increase in this period, the representation of petty treason was a phenomenon particular to the late Tudor and Stuart periods.

These representations express fears that the home was unsafe and could not be protected against those who would rise against it from within. If surviving court records suggest that murderous men generally killed men who were not members of their households, and did so in public places, they also suggest that murderous women most often killed their family members at home.[18] Texts about petty treason dwell on the violation of domesticity and marital intimacy entailed by this crime, which generally occurred in the central locations of marital life—the dining table and the bed. The formulation of legal separation as a divorce *a mensa et thoro*, "from table and bed," reinforces the significance of these furnishings as sites of intimacy and estrangement.[19] Most accounts

16. See Amussen, *Ordered Society*, pp. 92–93; Ralph A. Houlbrooke, *The English Family, 1450–1700* (London: Longman, 1984), pp. 112–13; Phyllis Rackin, *Stages of History: Shakespeare's English Chronicles* (Ithaca: Cornell University Press, 1990), pp. 192–93; and Keith Wrightson, *English Society, 1580–1680* (New Brunswick, N.J.: Rutgers University Press, 1982), p. 92.

17. Carol Z. Wiener, "Is a Spinster an Unmarried Woman?" *American Journal of Legal History* 20.1 (1976): 27–31, esp. p. 30. Wiltenburg argues that: "Women are given a larger place in the popular literature of crime than their proportion among criminals would have warranted" (*Disorderly Women*, p. 212).

18. Sharpe, "Domestic Homicide," pp. 36–37.

19. Either husband or wife could seek such a divorce, which did not free either spouse to remarry, by petitioning to the ecclesiastical courts, claiming adultery or physical cruelty.

of petty treason present the transgressors as acting on these sites. Mistress Page of Plymouth and her lover, George Strangwidge, after strangling her husband with his own kerchief and breaking his neck against the bedside, "stretched him and laid him in his bed again . . . as though no such act had been attempted."[20] Lowe, a curate, smothers Leonard James, the minister under whom he serves and whose wife he has seduced, in his own bed; despite admonitory thunder and lightning, "like a bestyall savage . . . hee layd vyolent and bloudy hands upon the body of his sleeping Master."[21]

In administering poison—the early modern housewife's method of choice, perhaps because it is a stealthy, tidy, nonconfrontational method that relies more on cunning than on physical strength—wives manipulate their husbands' dependence on them for physical sustenance.[22] Anne Hamton so heavily laces her husband's food with poison, "enough to have destroyed ten men," that he swells and bursts; Anne Welles fixes her husband "a measse of suger soppes" laced with "a strong deadly poyson"; Elizabeth Caldwell gives her husband poisoned "oaten cakes . . . for that she knewe [he] much affected them."[23] In these violations of domesticity, vividly figured through disrupted sleep and contaminated food, the dependent who should share the bed and table, and solace and nurture her husband's body, abuses intimacy to invade and destroy that body.

See Amussen, "Violence and Domestic Violence"; and Martin Ingram, *Church Courts, Sex, and Marriage in England, 1570–1640* (Cambridge: Cambridge University Press, 1987), esp. chap. 5.

20. "The Murder of Page of Plymouth," from *Sundry Strange and Inhumaine Murthers, Lately Committed* (1591), reprinted in *Blood and Knavery: A Collection of English Renaissance Pamphlets and Ballads of Crime and Sin*, ed. Joseph H. Marshburn and Alan R. Velie (Rutherford, N.J.: Fairleigh Dickinson University Press, 1973), p. 62.

21. *A True Relation of the Most Inhumane and Bloody Murther, of Master James . . . Committed by One Lowe His Curate, and Consented unto by His Wife* (London, 1609), sigs. A4v–B.

22. In his work with assize court records, Cockburn also finds that murderous wives are associated with stealth and poison ("Nature and Incidence," p. 57).

23. *Murther, Murther. Or, A Bloody Relation How Anne Hamton . . . by Poyson Murthered Her Deare Husband* (London, 1641), reprinted in *Miscellanea Antiqua Anglicana: The Old Book Collectors Miscellany*, ed. Charles Hindley (London: Reeves and Turner, 1872), 2.4–5; *The Trueth of the Most Wicked and Secret Murthering of John Brewen . . . Committed by His Owne Wife* (London, 1592), reprinted in *Illustrations of Early English Popular Literature*, ed. J. Payne Collier (New York: Benjamin Blom, 1966), 1.9; Gilbert Dugdale, *A True Discourse of the Practises of Elizabeth Caldwell . . . on the Person of Ma: Thomas Caldwell . . . to Have Murdered and Poysoned Him* (London, 1604), sig. B.

Such representations of the violated home both reinforce the household as the sphere in which women act and suggest that women were not only confined to the household but were empowered within it. There they may suffer frustrations and annoyances so great that they turn to violence, but at home they also dare to transform their household tasks into the occasions of retribution and their household tools into the weapons they need. By depicting the home as an arena of female power as well as subordination and by representing the *feme covert* as both subsumed by her husband and stealthily insubordinate, accounts of petty treason show how the analogy between the household and commonwealth could work to grant the household significance as a locus of conflict. As Mary Beth Rose argues, many Puritan writers insist that marriage "constitutes the arena in which the individual can struggle and meet death or defeat, triumph or salvation."[24] The discourses of petty treason similarly construct both marriage and the household as arenas of contest and striving, but refuse the concept of shared heroism that Protestant discourses of marriage attempt to idealize and disseminate, suggesting instead that there will be only one winner—indeed, only one survivor.

The Battered Wife and the Economy of Marital Subjectivity

Texts about petty treason clearly depict where and how women murder their husbands, but they have more trouble explaining *why* women do so. Just as the murderous wife challenged the conceptions of women's legal and moral stature on which marriage and social order depended, she also posed a problem for the many writers—hacks, ministers, legal personnel (judges, justices of the peace, clerks, and theorists), chroniclers, playwrights, and balladeers—who rushed to tell and sell her story. These authors attempt to tell a story in which a wife becomes the protagonist without conferring too much authority, prestige, or sympathy on a criminal, married woman. For only through transgression could such women, usually wives of yeomen, shopkeepers, tradesmen, and small landowners, demand attention outside of the household and

24. Rose, *Expense of Spirit*, p. 121.

neighborhood;[25] only thus could they become the topic of debate in legal treatises and on streetcorners, the focus of attention in courtrooms and on scaffolds; only through transgression could they command a place at the center of a popular narrative as the protagonist of the story.[26]

If killing her husband made it possible for a wife to be at the center of a story, it remained a difficult story to tell. Certainly pamphlets describe who did what to whom with ease. Yet the texts that struggle to tell the story of a wife's transgression attempt to redress it through a didacticism that restricts the narration of her motives and desires. Once the writers begin to explore motives, they lose control of the moral of the story, for the more the reader engages with the wife the less simple the lesson becomes. To imagine, let alone sympathize or identify with, the frustrations of a wife is to question the legal and moral assumption that in the household there is only one citizen, one legal agent, one property owner, one decision maker: the husband.

Some sixteenth- and seventeenth-century texts employ an explanation for the behavior of murderous wives that we often see in today's news and in popular culture; they represent the murderer as a battered wife who resorts to violence in despair and self-defense. Contrary to reductive analyses of the early modern family and the position of women in it, these period texts suggest a popular perception that husbands sometimes beat their wives to an extent that exceeded lawful correction and prudence and that beatings put wives in "a fit humour for the devill to worke on." Alice Clarke, for instance, is described as having visible bruises at the time that she is apprehended and examined for killing her husband. Even Henry Goodcole, the minister who counsels her and writes the gruesomely titled *The Adultresses Funerall Day* (1635) about her case, sees a connection between those bruises and her actions. The beatings described in such texts include not only drunken and

25. Among the cases that I have examined, husbands' occupations include: locksmith, goldsmith, farmer, innkeeper, hatter, and turner; I have also encountered murderous wives with their own occupations outside of the home: midwifery and nursing.

26. On the prospects for women as protagonists and authority figures in early modern England, see Elaine V. Beilin, *Redeeming Eve: Women Writers of the English Renaissance* (Princeton: Princeton University Press, 1987), chap. 6; Frances E. Dolan, " 'Gentlemen, I have one thing more to say': Women on Scaffolds in England, 1563–1680," *Modern Philology*, forthcoming; Margaret Doody, " 'Those Eyes Are Made So Killing': Eighteenth-Century Murderesses and the Law," *Princeton University Library Chronicle* 46.1 (1984): 49–80; Rackin, *Stages of History*, pp. 147–48 and 161–62; and Rose, *Expense of Spirit*, chap. 3.

impulsive assaults "with the next cudgell that came accidentally unto his hand" but also sadistic, eroticized rituals, such as "tying her to his bed-post to strip her and whippe her, &c."[27] Although pamphlets exploit the titillation of such stories, despite the coy propriety of that "etc.," they also suggest that husbands could be uncontrolled, savage, and "unnatural," and that wives, especially those isolated from friends and neighbors by shame, distance, and religious or ethnic difference, might have felt that violence was their only recourse.[28]

Under common law, husbands had a legal right to beat their wives; however, the limits on this right were debated in conduct literature and explored in ecclesiastical courts when members of the community feared that excessive beatings threatened the wife's life and the peace of the neighborhood. The law did not spell out the limits on discipline except to assume that husbands did not have the right to kill their wives. As Martin Ingram explains, "Domestic relations were thus on the borders of public and private morality in this period—matters to be influenced by exhortation but not ordinarily by the exercise of formal discipline."[29] To say that domestic relations remained outside "formal" discipline is not to say that they were unobserved or unregulated; neighbors and the local community exerted informal control over marriage and domesticity in many ways, including confrontation, shaming rituals, and bringing the offending couple before the justice of the peace for "unquietness." A husband's authority over his wife remained legally and morally ambiguous, even if the community's scrutiny constrained him.

Since a husband's treatment of his wife remained largely beyond legal regulation, conduct literature appealed to the husband's judgment, urging him to regulate himself. In one of the many discussions of wife-beating in conduct literature, William Gouge suggests that beating one's

---

27. Henry Goodcole, *The Adultresses Funerall Day: In Flaming, Scorching, and Consuming Fire; Or the Burning Downe to Ashes of Alice Clarke . . . for the Unnaturall Poisoning of Fortune Clarke Her Husband* (London, 1635), sigs. B2v and Bv.

28. Amussen, *Ordered Society,* pp. 128–29 and 167–68, and "Violence and Domestic Violence."

29. Ingram, *Church Courts,* p. 142, see also pp. 143, 183; Constance Jordan, *Renaissance Feminism: Literary Texts and Political Models* (Ithaca: Cornell University Press, 1990), p. 249, pp. 286–97; and Sharpe, "Domestic Homicide," p. 31. Wiltenburg argues that, in the course of the seventeenth century, English popular literature increasingly depicted wife-beating as a lower-class, vulgar activity (*Disorderly Women,* p. 128).

wife undermines household governance because it opens up a space between the husband and wife, revealing that they are not one flesh, not one legal agent, but two: "Now a wife having no ground to be perswaded that her husband hath authority to beat her, what hope is there that she will patiently beare it, and be bettered by it? Or rather is it not likely that she will if she can, rise against him, over-master him (as many do) and never doe any duty aright?"[30] The husband's violence threatens to incite a contest for mastery; once the context of violence enables the wife to enter the fray as a combatant, the outcome is uncertain.

One account of a wife's reaction to a marital rape, which we might not expect to find recognized as an offense in this period, clearly shows how a wife's subjectivity is constructed as violent, as a choice of her own life over her husband's life. In her examination recorded in *A Hellish Murder* (1688), Mary Aubrey (or Hobry), a French midwife, describes a history of dissension with her husband because she would not cooperate with him "in Villanies contrary to Nature." On the night of the murder, after beating her savagely, "he attempted the Forcing of this Examinate to the most Unnatural of Villanies, and acted such a Violence upon her Body in despite of all the Opposition that she could make, as forc'd from her a great deal of Blood, this Examinate crying out to her Landlady, who was (as she believes) out of distance of hearing her."[31] When she insists that she cried out, Aubrey employs the strategy of the rape victim, who had to demonstrate that she had made a "hue and cry" and thus had not consented.[32]

In presenting Aubrey's compelling testimony about this assault, *A Hellish Murder* not only suggests limits on a husband's rights to and power over his wife's body but also constructs a subjectivity for Mary Aubrey out of her despair, her sense of grievance, and her determination to escape. Aubrey finally demands of her husband, "Am I to lead this Life for ever?" only to receive more threats in response. In asking that

30. William Gouge, *Of Domesticall Duties* (London, 1622), pp. 396–97. I am grateful to Susan Amussen for bringing this passage to my attention.

31. *A Hellish Murder Committed by a French Midwife, on the Body of Her Husband* (London, 1688), sigs. E3v, F. Amussen briefly discusses another account of this case, "A Warning Piece to All Married Men and Women" (London, 1688), which openly condemns Mary Aubrey (see "Violence and Domestic Violence"). As Amussen mentions, there are at least two more accounts.

32. Dalton, *The Countrey Justice* (1635 ed.), p. 281.

question, Mary Aubrey is portrayed as raising a voice and imagining herself as having a life separate from and in conflict with her husband's. By depicting her reaction to abuse and her contemplation of retaliatory violence, this text constitutes Aubrey as a self-conscious, speaking subject. Later, beside her sleeping husband, she thinks "with her self," "What will become of me? What am I to do! Here am I Threatned to be Murder'd, and I have no way in the World to Deliver my self, but by Beginning with him."[33] Aubrey's subjectivity is seen not only as the midwife's deliverance of herself but as a birth that depends on a death. "Immediately upon these thoughts," she stoutly undertakes the murder of her husband, strangling and dismembering him, and lugging parts of his body around in her petticoat to dispose of them.

Popular accounts of petty treason usually shy away from such risky representation of a wife's conscious articulation of rights that are allied to violence by their very conception. The resulting attempts both to account for the complexities of domestic friction and to achieve some sympathy for the abused wife, while keeping authority vested in the husband, however tyrannous, can verge on the absurd. Goodcole describes one "young and tender" wife, who, repenting after administering poison to her "old, peevish," and abusive husband, fruitlessly pleads with him to take an antidote to preserve his life. "Nay thou Strumpet and murderesse," Goodcole reports him as saying, "I will receive no helpe at all but I am resolvd to dye and leave the world, be it for no other cause, but to have thee burnt at a stake for my death."[34] Although the wife is executed at Smithfield, Goodcole regards the husband, in his spiteful insistence on dying, as the agent. Sarah Elston, in her scaffold confession as recorded in *A Warning for Bad Wives* (1678), "protested again most seriously, that she never in her life had the least designe or thoughts of killing [her husband], onely it was an unfortunate Accident; and whether it came by a blow from her, or his violent running upon the point of the Sizzars as she held them out to defend her self, she could not to this minute certainly tell."[35] These comic moments reveal how pamphleteers who wish to portray murderous wives as penitent and pitiful must awkwardly scramble to shield them from the imputation

33. *A Hellish Murder,* sig. Fv.
34. Goodcole, *The Adultresses Funerall Day,* sigs. Bv–B2.
35. *A Warning for Bad Wives: Or, The Manner of the Burning of Sarah Elston* (London 1678), pp. 6–7.

of intending to kill, just as they are presented as shielding themselves from blows.

To characterize such women as assessing their hopeless situations and deciding to take violent action to escape them, that is, to present them as subjects, is also to remove them from sympathy and to open up disturbing implications about the marital relation of authority and submission. Writers in effect displace responsibility onto the husbands, positioning them as still in charge, even if drunken, violent, and absurdly self-destructive.

In representations of domestic conflict in early modern popular culture—ballads, pamphlets, and plays, shaming rituals and jokes—the wife diminishes or usurps her husband's claims to authority as she asserts herself by committing adultery, beating or bossing her husband, or plotting to kill him.[36] For instance, *Arden of Faversham* (1592), a play about an actual case of petty treason, can be seen as an extended cuckold joke. Like such jokes, and like popular shaming rituals such as the charivari, the play holds the cuckolded husband responsible for his wife's adultery and insubordination. If the husband and wife become a joint subject at marriage, then, these popular representations seem to suggest, the wife's enlargement into volition, speech, and action necessarily implicates, diminishes, and even eliminates the husband. These popular representations push the logic of coverture to suggest an economy of marital subjectivity that leaves room for only one subject. They constitute the wife as a subject only to the extent that they qualify her husband's claims to subject status by silencing and immobilizing him and casting doubt on his authority and potency.

The fact that popular accounts of such crimes acknowledge the role of abuse in inciting women to murder challenges assumptions we still have about women's rights within marriage and the monolithic power

36. On how the participants in charivari held husbands responsible for tolerating wives who defied their authority, see Boose, "Scolding Brides," pp. 189–91; Natalie Z. Davis, "Women on Top," in her *Society and Culture in Early Modern France* (Stanford: Stanford University Press, 1975), pp. 124–51, esp. p. 140; Martin Ingram, "Ridings, Rough Music, and the 'Reform of Popular Culture' in Early Modern England," *Past and Present* 105 (November 1984): 79–113; David Underdown, "The Taming of the Scold: The Enforcement of Patriarchal Authority in Early Modern England," in *Order and Disorder in Early Modern England,* ed. Anthony Fletcher and John Stevenson (Cambridge: Cambridge University Press, 1985), pp. 116–36; Wiltenburg, *Disorderly Women,* esp. chap. 8; and Linda Woodbridge, *Women and the English Renaissance: Literature and the Nature of Womankind, 1540–1620* (Urbana: University of Illinois Press, 1984), chap. 8.

of the patriarchy during this period. It also complicates the notion of petty treason by introducing the possibility of tyrannous household government and by suggesting, albeit hesitantly, that there are some justifications for rebellion. Certainly, contemporary debates about the limits on conscientious submission to civil and domestic authorities have a bearing on relations within the household and the understanding of petty treason. Writers of sermons and conduct books about marriage explicitly include the situation of the godly wife in their considerations of the limits on obedience to earthly authority; they advocate a demanding balance between submission and resistance, silence and good counsel.[37] In those cases of petty treason that resulted in convictions and made it into print, however, the circumstances in the household did not mitigate the wife's guilt. These women were executed as petty traitors despite their husbands' inadequacies as household governors. Although juries may actually have taken extenuating circumstances into consideration when they deliberated over cases of petty treason,[38] these texts hold the husband responsible as well as depict the execution of the guilty wife; they recognize limits to a husband's power over his wife, yet present a wife's violent resistance as ultimately unjustifiable and destructive of the political order.

Popular representations make these contradictions between husbandly authority and wifely submission visible, but they do not resolve them. The writers of these texts acknowledge the conflict between telling the story from the wife's perspective and creating a subjectivity for her, on the one hand, and presenting an edifying tale of sin and retribution, on the other. The writer of *A Hellish Murder,* for instance, explains that "in the womans [Mary Aubrey's] Story, I have done all the Right that Honestly I could to the Compassionable Condition of an Unhappy Wretch, but without Extenuating the *Horror* of the *Wickedness.*" Good-

37. See, for instance, Thomas Gataker, *Marriage Duties Briefely Couched Togither* (London, 1620), sigs. C4–D. On the spiritual justifications for civil (and domestic) disobedience, see Constance Jordan, "Woman's Rule in Sixteenth-Century British Political Thought," *Renaissance Quarterly* 40.3 (1987): 421–51, esp. p. 435; and Richard Strier, "Faithful Servants: Shakespeare's Praise of Disobedience," in *The Historical Renaissance: New Essays on Tudor and Stuart Literature and Culture,* ed. Strier and Heather Dubrow (Chicago: University of Chicago Press, 1988), pp. 104–33.

38. In her master's thesis, Julie A. Sikkink (Department of History, Duke University) explores the discrepancy between the legal definition of petty treason and its application in the early modern English courtroom. I am grateful to Ms. Sikkink for sharing her work with me.

cole, discussing the unnamed battered wife, concedes that "her injuries, and harsh and unmanly usage spurred on by the instigations of the divell, *almost* compeld her to what she did."[39] By making the murderous wife the protagonist and by representing the husband's inadequacy and subsequent death as the conditions under which she can be constructed as a subject, these texts disturbingly reveal the contradictions and violence underlying early modern marriage. They abruptly foreclose further exploration of these issues by asserting the moral, recording the woman's punishment, and restoring moral order and domestic hierarchy.[40]

Attacking Marriage: Adultery and/as Murder

Other popular pamphlets present murderous wives not as acting against abusive husbands but as acting (often in collusion with a lover) against the institution of marriage, which requires their subordination, restricts them to sexual partners whom they have not chosen freely or of whom they have grown tired, and prevents them from having their own way. One might expect such women to be portrayed as villainesses, against whose stories grave, chaste matrons should stop their ears, as one writer advises. But this group of texts, like those that narrate the stories of battered wives, discovers contradictions *within* the constructions of the wife's role and the ideology of marriage. Just as petty treason itself simultaneously constructs wives as subordinate and as capable of violent insubordination, this group of texts defines the married woman's subjectivity in relation to her role as wife but locates it explicitly in resistance to that role.

This resistance takes various forms, but it is always described as violent. Many representations of estranged, rebellious wives locate their subjectivity in adulterous sexual desire and willfulness, linking both to murder. In *The Adultresses Funerall Day* (1635), Goodcole wrestles with the dilemma of presenting the murderous wife both as an agent—to

39. *A Hellish Murder,* sig. F4; Goodcole, *The Adultresses Funerall Day,* sig. Bv, emphasis added.

40. Joy Wiltenburg also argues that the representations of marital violence in "street literature" depict marriage as "a relationship governed ultimately by force. One partner has to dominate.... Violence is the fundamental arbiter" (*Disorderly Women,* p. 137).

justify the way that she is held accountable for her actions, which are vividly recorded in the title and the gruesome woodcut of Alice in flames on the title page—and as a sympathetic victim (see fig. 1). In Alice's two "confessions," redacted in the third person by Goodcole, the descriptions of her various sexual alliances conflate unregulated sexuality with murderousness. All the men with whom she has sex contribute to her plan to murder her husband. Although this description depicts her as a voracious and insatiable subject of desire who will not stop even at murder, it also presents her as acted upon by the various men with whom she allies, however briefly. In Goodcole's narrative, Alice first confesses Henry White's role in giving her money for the poison and urging her to kill her husband; second, she confesses that, before she was married, her master got her pregnant and arranged the marriage to Clarke "whom shee could not love, nor no way effect"; third, she confesses that a man of Hillenden "inticed her, to run away from her Husband, with him beyond the Seas" and also urged her to poison her husband; finally, she confesses that her husband seized the poison from her and took it of his own volition.[41] In Goodcole's text, Alice admits "freely and voluntarily" not her own transgressions but those of all the men who advised her; as Goodcole tells it, through her violent rebellion against her abusive husband she does not act independently but rather submits herself to other men.[42]

By displacing blame onto these four men, Alice Clarke, in Goodcole's narrative, displays her own sexual rapacity even as she attempts to exonerate herself. Goodcole presents her transgression as the "selfe-will" to which she was "so addicted."[43] Thus, Goodcole solves his dilemma by shifting the grounds of her transgressive agency from independent, violent action to self-will, presented largely in sexual terms. Simultaneously revealing and suppressing a wife's subjectivity, he downplays the implication that women are capable of conceiving and executing violence, yet he still holds Alice responsible for her husband's death. For him, her culpability resides in her character and consciousness more than in what she actually does.

Other pamphlets about petty treason similarly conflate adultery and

41. Goodcole, *The Adultresses Funerall Day,* sigs. Cv and Cv–C2.
42. See Carol Z. Wiener, "Sex-Roles and Crime in Late Elizabethan Hertfordshire," *Journal of Social History* 8.4 (1975): 38–60.
43. Goodcole, *The Adultresses Funerall Day,* sig. B2.

murder. In *A Briefe Discourse of Two Most Cruell and Bloudie Murthers, Committed Bothe in Worcestershire* (1583), Mrs. Beast seduces her servant, and enjoys being "carnally acquaint[ed]" with him, "till lust had gotten so much power of the Woman: as she began altogether to loathe and dislike her Husband, and preferre the fleshly dealings of her new companion so much, as she must needs seeke and practise the death of her Husband." In this passage, the rapid shift from Mrs. Beast's desire for another man to her loathing for her husband and then to her plan to kill him succinctly exemplifies how these texts associate female sexual desire that quests beyond marriage with violence. As Alice Clarke was addicted "unto selfe-will," Mrs. Beast "must needs have her will." The same "devilish desire" that leads her to pursue her servant sexually leads her to incite him to kill her husband and his master, so that the lovers may "live merrily together."[44]

A similar slide from one transgression to another occurs in *A True Relation of the Most Inhumane and Bloody Murther, of Master James, Minister and Preacher* (1609), in which James's curate Lowe plots "how and which way he might raise his estate, to the very height and toppe of his desires, viz. If hee could but inauger or graft himselfe into the love of his Mistresse." The text presents this adultery as a means to Lowe's ambitious end. Although the wife's involvement in the plot begins in desire *for* the curate rather than resentment *against* her husband, once again, adulterous desire leads inevitably to murder. Correspondingly, in this text, the devil advises Lowe that "the breach of all the commandements is but death, and one is no lesse. Adultery is a sinne, and murther is no more, withal, how much more better it was to live like a Master then a slave, to command then to be commanded."[45] In tandem, the wife's sexual desire and the curate's ambition become a single desire to live like a master rather than a slave. Both *A Briefe Discourse* and *A True Relation* construct the husbands and masters only as victims, shadowy figures who fade into the background as their wives and servants move violently to the fore.

---

44. *A Briefe Discourse of Two Most Cruell and Bloudie Murthers* (London, 1583), sigs. B2–B2v, B3. On the slide from one offense to another, see Cynthia Herrup, "Law and Morality in Seventeenth-Century England," *Past and Present* 106 (February 1985): 102–23; and Peter Stallybrass, "Patriarchal Territories: The Body Enclosed," in *Rewriting the Renaissance: The Discourses of Sexual Difference in Early Modern Europe*, ed. Margaret W. Ferguson, Maureen Quilligan, and Nancy J. Vickers (Chicago: University of Chicago Press, 1986), pp. 123–42.

45. *A True Relation of the . . . Murther, of Master James,* sigs. A3r-v, A4.

Although Mrs. James takes no active role in the murder and claims not even to have known about it, *A True Relation,* and the penal process it depicts, construe the alliance with Lowe that furthers his plot against her husband as a felony punishable by death. Presenting Mrs. James as manipulated by Lowe and uninvolved in the murder plot, the text still indicts her for desires that her marriage could not fill, especially the desire to command rather than to be commanded. Condemned for petty treason, she burned at the stake.

Texts that focus on the ambitious, frustrated servant, like texts focused on the murderous wife, link dependents' insubordinations, showing a man's wife and servant as conspiring against him and representing their subjectivities in similar terms; they locate the servant's subjectivity in anger and violence, even to the point of shifting from narrated to direct speech. For instance, in "The Cruell Murther of Maister Browne in Suffolke" (1605), as Peter Golding reflects on his master's recent promise of extraordinary preferment—marriage to his daughter and a portion of land—and its abrupt reversal, the narrative all at once lurches from *"he* remembered" to *"I* will be most subtile, and *my* revenge most sodaine." Made to articulate the threat that all these texts explore, that of the dependent who nurses grievances and plots "subtile" and "sodaine" revenge, this servant is also ascribed with a sense of injury—of his violated *rights*—and as feeling and speaking his frustration. As in the accounts of wives killing their husbands, the subordinate finds a voice and is constructed as a subject at the moment that he articulates a grievance and vows to redress that wrong: "I have wrong, and you are guiltie of it."[46] The servant's threat lies in his resistance to his master's arbitrary power.[47] In this text, as in *A True Relation,* the wife is adjudged a petty traitor, a principal rather than an accessory, and burned at the stake. Mrs. Browne's involvement in the plot against her husband is even more tenuous than Mrs. James's; in fact, she is barely implicated.

46. This text is included in *Two Most Unnaturall and Bloodie Murthers* (London, 1605), reprinted in *Illustrations of Early English Popular Literature,* ed. J. Payne Collier (New York: Benjamin Blom, 1966), 1.30–31, emphases added, 1.30.

47. On violence *against* servants, see Cockburn, "Patterns," pp. 97–98; Houlbrooke, *English Family,* pp. 175–76; Michael MacDonald, *Mystical Bedlam: Madness, Anxiety, and Healing in Seventeenth-Century England* (Cambridge: Cambridge University Press, 1981), pp. 85–88; Sarah C. Maza, *Servants and Masters in Eighteenth-Century France: The Uses of Loyalty* (Princeton: Princeton University Press, 1983), pp. 190, 172–74; and Steven R. Smith, "The London Apprentices as Seventeenth-Century Adolescents," *Past and Present* 61 (November 1973): 152–53.

That she is convicted nonetheless suggests that in the structure shaping such texts the wife and servant are assumed to be in alliance, and are both defeated, regardless of their roles in the crime.

The texts that formed the substance of the investigation of Mary Stuart's complicity in her husband Darnley's murder in 1567 reveal how early one can detect the conventions shaping representations of the adulterous, murderous wife and how rapidly these conventions pervaded elite as well as popular culture, informing even the quasi-legal proceedings against a compromised queen.[48] By becoming implicated in her husband's murder and then hastily marrying a suspected coconspirator, the earl of Bothwell, Mary plunged herself into a scandal that effectively ended her rule; her half-brother, the earl of Moray, was made regent. Certainly the murder and the marriage determined much of what followed, but the texts that documented and interpreted these events, communicating them to a wider public, drew on the popular fascination with the adulterous, murderous wife to exacerbate the scandal and discredit Mary.

Although Mary was never formally tried, an investigation focused on compiling and circulating plausible narratives rather than on interviewing witnesses or examining the evidence.[49] "The casket letters," a cache of letters from Mary to Bothwell, were presented as the primary evidence against her; if these were not forged, they may well have been "manipulated," edited, or expanded. The Moray party also produced *The Book of Articles,* a "collection of presumption and circumstances," heavily indebted to George Buchanan, a professional advisor to the earl of Moray during the proceedings.[50] Since historians claim that *The Book*

48. Darnley was killed in an explosion in the early morning on February 10, 1567. Although historians have not determined exactly what role Mary played in this assassination, most agree that she was implicated in various plots against her husband, even if she was not actively engaged in the final, successful scheme.

49. Gordon Donaldson, *The First Trial of Mary, Queen of Scots* (New York: Stein and Day, 1969), p. 139.

50. On the casket letters, see ibid., p. 68, pp. 72–73; and Jenny Wormald, *Mary Queen of Scots: A Study in Failure* (London: George Philip, 1988), pp. 175–78. Since the originals of the casket letters disappeared in 1584, little progress can now be made toward determining their authenticity. Wormald argues that circumstances surrounding the discovery and use of the letters make outright forgery unlikely. George Buchanan reprints the casket letters in *Ane Detection of the Duinges of Marie Quene of Scottes, Touchand the Murder of Hir Husband, and Hir Conspiracie, Adulterie, and Pretensed Mariage with*

of Articles was largely unsubstantiated, it is particularly important to see how this complex legal narrative about an unfaithful wife participates in the conventions that shape other such narratives.

Although Mary's detractors portrayed her involvement in Darnley's murder as high treason, complicity on her part, however objectionable, indeed criminal, would not have been treasonous. Darnley was legally subject to Mary despite her own efforts to grant him royal authority.[51] As her chief advocate, John Leslie, insists: "Albe yt he was her hedd in wedlocke, yet was he otherwise but a membre of the Scottishe comon wealthe, subjecte to her, as to his principall and supreme governesse, and to her lawes."[52] As Leslie demonstrates, Mary's power and authority as a married regnant queen were exceptional not only among married women but among queens.[53] Queens consort, "as wome[n] most commonlie do take theire honour a[n]d chief dignitie of theyre husbands. Her husband encrease of adva[n]cemente came by hys matchinge with her."[54] In defending Mary, Leslie attempts to conjoin two incompatible lines of argument: He protests Mary's innocence while simultaneously challenging claims that her complicity was treasonous. Reinforcing the popular association of wives' authority and self-determination with violence and adultery, and unwittingly associating female sovereignty with the threat of the murderous wife, Leslie's arguments were destined to fail.[55]

George Buchanan successfully manipulated the widespread fears that

the Erle Bothwell (London, 1571), sigs. Q4–X2v; Donaldson reprints *The Book of Articles* in *First Trial of Mary*, pp. 142–90.

51. Revealing her ambivalence about her own authority, Mary had complicated Darnley's position by pronouncing him king, with the right to sign royal documents, the day before their wedding (Wormald, *Mary Queen of Scots*, p. 150; see also p. 156).

52. John Leslie, *A Defence of the Honour of the Right Highe, Mightye and Noble Princesse, Marie Quene of Scotlande, with a Declaration as well of Her Right, Title & Intereste to the Succession of the Crowne of Englande, as that the Regimente of Women Ys Conformable to the Law of God and Nature* (London, 1569), sigs. A4v–A5.

53. On the married regnant queen's position, see Constance Jordan, "Woman's Rule in Sixteenth-Century British Political Thought," pp. 428, 440, 450; and Lois G. Schwoerer, "Images of Queen Mary II, 1689–95," *Renaissance Quarterly* 42.4 (1989): 717–48, esp. pp. 720–21.

54. Leslie, *Defence*, sigs. B7–B7v.

55. Later, an English ambassador reported that Leslie, then Mary's ambassador, referred to her as the murderer of all three of her husbands (Donaldson, *First Trial of Mary*, p. 95). I am more interested here in the strategies Leslie used to defend Mary than in whether he believed in her innocence.

John Leslie inadvertently evoked. Buchanan's influential fictions sought to substitute familiar political and domestic stories (a virtuous and beleaguered king; a scheming wife) for the highly anomalous story of a queen regnant, her lover, and her murdered husband. Cleverly combining narratives of high and petty treason, Buchanan and the legal fictions so indebted to him construct Mary as a traitor on both domestic and political levels in order to construct Darnley as husband and king, as domestic and political authority, although he was neither.

I do not mean to elide the vital distinctions between Scottish and English culture, or between queens and housewives of the middling sort, or between court politics and popular culture. Nevertheless, many of the texts concerning Mary's role in Darnley's murder were produced with an eye to an English audience, particularly Elizabeth herself. Elizabeth monitored the publication of these texts in England and first allowed Buchanan's *Ane Detection of the Duinges of Marie Quene of Scottes* and the casket letters to be published in 1571. In his text, Buchanan represents Mary as an adulterous, violent wife rather than as a queen; he employs terms that are remarkably familiar from the narratives of petty treason we have seen.[56]

Even though she was a queen, Mary's detractors present her as perceiving her relation to her husband in "him or me" terms: "She plainly and expresly protested, that unlesse she mought by some meane or other be dispatched of the king, she should never haife ane gude day. And if by no other way she cauld atteine it, rather than she wald abide to live in sic sorow, she wald slay hir selfe."[57] Buchanan and *The Book of Articles* view this statement as an attempt by Mary to prompt various nobles to assassinate Darnley. In contrast, Leslie points out that Mary had a broader range of options than most dissatisfied wives: "For yf she had bene so desirouse to have bene ridd of him, as they falselie, and maliciouselie imagine, and reporte her to have bene, she had good and lawfull meanes to serve her turne."[58] Leslie enumerates various

56. In addition, Buchanan presents Mary as the bad mother of the heir, James, endangering both him and the succession. In contrast, Leslie presents Mary as mother not only to James but to Darnley, to whom "she was...not onlie a loyall Prince, a lovinge a[n]d deare wyfe, but a most carefull and tendre mother with all" (Leslie, *Defence,* A6v–A7).

57. Buchanan, *Ane Detection,* sigs. C1–C1v; see also *The Book of Articles* in Donaldson, *First Trial of Mary,* p. 161.

58. Leslie, *Defence,* sig. A4v.

charges Mary could have brought against Darnley to eliminate him legally. Despite Leslie's insistence on Mary's prerogatives as queen, Buchanan's more influential narratives ally her with murderous wives. Citing Cato's claim "that there is na adulteresse, but the saim is alswa a poysoner" as sufficient evidence that Mary attempted to poison her husband prior to the assassination, Buchanan also assumes that adultery would lead Mary inevitably into plots to kill her husband.[59] "Of the which disdain and extreme hatred conceived against her husband, and inordinate affection borne to Bothwell, with whom she abused her body in her said husband's lifetime in manner above expressed, *necessarily follows* the compassing and deliberation taken of his death and destruction and consequently the execution of his murder."[60] Like the accounts of Mrs. Beast's or Mrs. James's crimes, such condemnations of Mary depict her "inordinate affection" for her lover and "extreme hatred" for her husband as implying and requiring one another.

The popular story of the adulterous, murderous wife provided a resource for denigrating and discrediting Mary. Although Jenny Wormald argues that there is "an absence of any tradition, cultural or propagandist" for the image of woman that the casket letters between Mary and Bothwell portray, and therefore the letters must be authentic rather than forged, other representations of adulterous, murderous wives reveal just such a model, although one must look beyond elite culture to find it.[61] We cannot now know whether the letters were forged; I simply wish to show how well they suit the narrative of adultery and murder that Buchanan weaves and how very conventional that narrative is. Its success, first in persuading Elizabeth to imprison Mary and declare the earl of Moray regent and second in persuading the public in England and Scotland to accept Mary's deposition, depended on its skillful manipulation of convention.

Similarly conjoining adultery and murder, yet other representations of husband-killing depict murderous wives as deconstructing the institution of marriage by their violent attempts to remake it to suit them-

59. Buchanan, *Ane Detection*, sig. H2v. See *The Book of Articles* on the assumption that Mary attempted to poison Darnley (Donaldson, *First Trial of Mary*, p. 162).
60. Donaldson, *Book of Articles*, in *First Trial of Mary*, p. 160, emphasis added. Compare with Buchanan, *Ane Detection*, sig. I4.
61. Wormald, *Mary Queen of Scots*, p. 178.

selves. The conception that the husband subsumes his wife is based on the assumption that marriage permanently transforms both husband and wife, enlarging one and diminishing the other, regardless of the circumstances leading up to the marriage. A text such as *The Trueth of the Most Wicked and Secret Murthering of John Brewen, Goldsmith* (1592) explores how an enforced marriage might prepare a wife to resist the transformations that are supposed to accompany marriage.

In this text, Anne Welles must choose between two goldsmiths who are best friends and rivals for her hand. She prefers John Parker, who the narrator warns us is the less deserving. When she "despises" John Brewen's suit but refuses to return his gifts, he has her arrested and only dismisses the charges when she agrees to marry him. The narrator conveys Anne's shame and frustration: "The stout damsel, that had never before been in the like daunger, [is] so astonished and dismayed" that she submits, trading one form of imprisonment for another. As soon as Anne is released from jail, Parker, the rejected suitor, begins to work on her sense of entrapment, "and with bitter speeches so taunted and checked her, that she repented the promise she made to Brewen, although she could not any way amend it." Thus, when she enters the marriage, she is determined to escape Brewen by killing him and marrying Parker. As a result, she refuses to be a wife to Brewen from the beginning of the marriage.

> Now, she had not been maried to Brewen above three dayes, when she put in practise to poyson him. And although the honest young man loved her tenderly, yet had she conceived such deadly hatred against him, that she lay not with him after the first night of her mariage; neither would she abide to be called after his name, but still to be termed Anne Welles, as she was before: and to excuse her from his bed, she sayd she had vowed never to lie by him more till he had gotten her a better house.[62]

Refusing the shared name and shared bed of marriage, Welles also lives apart from her husband, near her lover. If marriage makes husband and wife one flesh, blurring the boundaries between them, she uses her different name and address to announce her resistance to wifely coverture and to defend her right to make demands in her own interest.

62. *The Trueth,* pp. 7, 8, 8–9.

Since, in accounts of petty treason, to stand apart from one's husband is to stand against him, Anne Welles's self-interest and separateness quickly manifest themselves in violence. Just as Brewen strategized to get Welles to marry him, she as cleverly and ruthlessly manipulates his expectations of wifely nurturance and intimacy. Entering his house only to kill him, her first wifely gesture toward him is to offer him the poisoned "measse of sugar soppes." She plays the role of the good wife only long enough to get him to eat the poisoned food. "Wife (quoth he) ... I take it very kindly that you will doe so much for me: alas! husband (quoth she), if I could not find in my heart to doe so small a matter for you (especially being so lately married) you might justly judge me unkinde: and therwithall [she] went to make ready his last meat." [63] Having played the part long enough to administer the poison, Welles abandons it, refusing to visit or nurse the dying man. Although Anne Welles is presented as daringly retaining her own name, refusing cohabitation, and, in an action presented as the inevitable outcome of such self-assertions, poisoning her husband, she is also depicted as acting in alliance with another man, and as substituting debasement for subordination.

Her violent rebellion entraps her further, making her the "slave" of a brutal man rather than the wife of an "honest young man [who] loved her tenderly." John Parker, her lover and collaborator in the murder, makes constant and unreasonable demands, which she is afraid to deny.

> To [such] slaverie and subjection did he bring her, that she must runne or goe wheresoever he pleased to appoint her, held he up but his finger at any time: if she denied him either money, or whatsoever else he listed to request, he would haule and pull her as was pittie to behold; yea, and threaten to stabbe and thrust her through with his dagger, did she not as he would have her in all things.[64]

After much mutual recrimination, Parker accuses Welles of being too dangerous to marry; her murderousness makes it impossible for him to imagine her as his wife. "Out, arrant queane! (quoth he): thou wouldst marry me to the end thou mightest poyson me, as thou didst thy husband; but for that cause I meane to keepe me as long out of

63. *The Trueth,* pp. 9–10.
64. *The Trueth,* p. 13.

thy fingers as I can, and accurst be I, if I trust thee, or hazard my life in thy hands."[65] Parker's horror at Anne Welles's crime and his fear of making himself vulnerable to her have not prevented him from bullying and impregnating her, but he cannot *marry* her. While the text presents Welles as pursuing Parker as a husband despite his role in the murder of his best friend and his bad treatment of her, it shows Parker recoiling at the conjunction of murderess and wife, irreconcilable by definition.

Parker seems to fear Welles's violence only if they are married; Welles seems to assume that marriage will prevent or ameliorate his abuses. Although Welles paradoxically seeks a second marriage through denying her first, her adultery, rebellion against wifeliness, and capacity for violence conjoin to disqualify her for the conventional role of wife and to redefine that role as one of power, cunning, and threat. By contrasting Welles's and her lover's responses to one another after the murder, the text demonstrates that the violence by which wives assert themselves marks them as threatening, unwomanly, and unmarriageable. In attempting to stretch the definition of wife to accommodate her self-determination, a woman like Anne Welles creates a contradiction in terms, the murderous wife. By enacting these irreconcilable contradictions, Welles's case parodies and undermines the available conceptions of marriage.

Performance Scripts and the Competing Voices of Petty Treason

In exploring how contradictions can conjoin in a single person—the murderous wife, the rebellious subordinate, the subsumed subject—pamphlet narratives hesitantly shape motives and voices for the female transgressors whose stories they tell. Representing wives' transgressive subjectivity creates a dilemma for the writers of pamphlets, who attempt to present a unified, unambiguous perspective on petty treason, which reassures readers that it is unjustifiable and that it will always be found out and punished. The explorations of motive and eruptions into voice that enliven these texts also disrupt them, and the writers hastily close off the avenues they open up by asserting the moral and recording the woman's punishment. Although the basic plot of petty treason—wife

65. *The Trueth*, p. 14.

and/or servant kills the master of the house—requires pamphlet writers to create multiple subject positions and voices, the attempt to restore the order disturbed by the crime limits the exploration of multiple and competing subjectivities within the household.

While the writers of pamphlet narratives struggle with their contradictory agendas, writers of performance scripts—ballads and plays—face an even greater challenge. They must invent utterances for criminal women that will be voiced by singers and players, not merely read. Ballads about murderous wives rely on a particularly ingenious way to grant female offenders a voice without seeming to sympathize with or endorse their actions. They allow condemned women to speak only from the dead *after* their executions. These ballads even attempt to convey the experience of being burned to death.

> And there in Smithfield at a stake,
> My latest breath I there did take.
>
> . . .
>
> And being chayned to the Stake,
>   both Reedes and Faggots then
> Close to my Body there was set,
>   with Pitch, Tarre, and Rozen.[66]

Ballads such as "A Warning for All Desperate Women" preserve the unified perspective essential to didacticism by making the wife articulate the moral condemnation of her own actions.

> Then hasty hairebraind wives take heed,
>   of me a warning take,
> Least like to me in coole of blood,
>   you burn't be at a stake.[67]

Singing in the petty traitor's voice, to the extent that it invites any imaginative identification, involves the singer in the process of dying,

66. "The Unnatural Wife: Or, The Lamentable Murther, of One Goodman Davis . . . by His Wife" (1628), reprinted in *A Pepysian Garland: Black-letter Broadside Ballads of the Years 1595–1639,* ed. Hyder E. Rollins (Cambridge: Cambridge University Press, 1922), p. 287.
67. "A Warning for All Desperate Women" (1628), reprinted in ibid., p. 289. On these ballads, see also Kathleen McLuskie, *Renaissance Dramatists* (Atlantic Highlands,

not of choosing to kill. Yet the woman's voice in the ballads is so unambivalently condemnatory that the first-person perspective remains estranged even from the woman's suffering. Singers and listeners are positioned as spectators of her death, as well as fellow sufferers. Despite their titles, such ballads offer more than a warning; like the public executions they represent, they also offer the ghoulish thrill of *someone else's* suffering.

As Anne Schotter argues, songs written in the voices of aggrieved women resemble those written in the voices of other creatures for whom subjectivity is an unimaginable and ludicrous possibility, such as a roast swan. Such works achieve an almost comic distancing "by pretending for a moment to take seriously the sufferings of a creature alien to the audience."[68] Margaret Doody sees a similar dynamic in Civil War ballads, which present "the self-exposition by the absurd enemy of his absurd point of view" and depend on what she calls "ventriloquism" or the singer's assumption of the persona of an opposite or other. In such cases, she suggests, "singing the ballad is not only highly aggressive, but also oddly suicidal."[69] Such ballads, then, engage the singer or auditor in both identification with and alienation from the woman's voice; they invite her to share the woman's guilt as well as to observe her punishment from a distance. Ballads in the voices of petty traitors, focusing on executions rather than crimes, never engage her in the imaginative enactment of choosing to kill one's husband.

Heywood's *An Apology for Actors,* mentioned earlier, addresses the troublesome possibility of women's identification with petty traitors by sternly resolving the ambiguity. In his account, female spectators identify with remorse, not with the desire to kill. When we examine the performance scripts based on actual crimes to which Heywood refers, we find that such plays, even more than the narratives we have already explored, might elicit responses more unpredictable and disruptive than

---

N.J.: Humanities Press International, 1989), pp. 46–48; and Lennard J. Davis, *Factual Fictions: The Origins of the English Novel* (New York: Columbia University Press, 1983), chap. 3, esp. pp. 56–61.

68. Anne Howland Schotter, "Woman's Song in Medieval Latin," in *Vox Feminae: Studies in Medieval Woman's Song,* ed. John F. Plummer (Kalamazoo: Western Michigan University Press, 1981), p. 29.

69. Margaret Doody, *The Daring Muse: Augustan Poetry Reconsidered* (Cambridge: Cambridge University Press, 1985), pp. 45, 33. See also Wiltenburg, *Disorderly Women,* pp. 49, 211.

confession. Because the drama as a form is committed to the exploration of conflict and must by its very nature present multiple subjectivities and voices, it can represent petty treason without subverting its own purposes and conventions.[70] It does not need, therefore, to present its murderous wives as safely dead or to retreat from the contradiction that they embody.

Although the drama has resources for exploring the reasons for and implications of petty treason unavailable in other popular genres, the murderous wife remains a less prominent figure on the stage than Heywood's *Apology* might lead one to believe. In *Hamlet,* Gertrude is implicated in King Hamlet's death; in *The Changeling,* Beatrice-Joanna hires De Flores to murder her betrothed so that she can choose another. However, the decision to kill one's husband and the process of doing so rarely claim center stage. Only two dramatizations of actual husband murders, committed by nonnoble women and set in England, survive. These are *Arden of Faversham* (1592) and *A Warning for Fair Women* (1599).[71] *Arden* dramatizes a case still notorious in 1592, forty-one years after it happened. It was maintained in public consciousness by Holinshed's account of it in both the 1577 and 1587 editions of his *Chronicles.*[72] The case involved a wife's conspiracy with her lover (a steward and her social inferior) and her husband's inferiors and dependents to murder him.

In their attempts to emphasize the fairness and efficacy of the judicial process and its ability to know and reform the transgressor, the pamphlets discussed so far claim that the criminal can be coerced or per-

---

70. Joel B. Altman, *The Tudor Play of Mind: Rhetorical Inquiry and the Development of Elizabethan Drama* (Berkeley: University of California Press, 1978); and Rose, *Expense of Spirit,* esp. p. 131.

71. See Frances E. Dolan, "Gender, Moral Agency, and Dramatic Form in *A Warning For Fair Women,*" *Studies in English Literature* 29 (1989): 201–18; and Betty S. Travitsky, "Husband-Murder and Petty Treason in English Renaissance Tragedy," *Renaissance Drama,* n.s. 21 (1990): 171–98.

72. M. L. Wine argues that the 1587 edition of Holinshed is the more likely influence on the play; he points to marginal glosses that may have shaped the playwright's interpretation and appear only in the later edition. Holinshed's account appears in the second edition of his *Chronicles* (2:1062–66), and, according to Wine, the probable source for his narrative of the murder is a manuscript account, "The history of a most horrible murder comytyd at ffeversham in Kent" (Harley Mss. 542, fols. 34–37B). See Wine's introduction to his edition of the play, *The Tragedy of Master Arden of Faversham,* ed. M. L. Wine (London: Methuen, 1973), pp. xxxv–xliii. Wine reprints Holinshed's account in an appendix.

suaded into "sincerity." The drama, in contrast, casts doubt on this conception of a unified, knowable self that can be enacted and articulated. *Arden of Faversham* presents Alice Arden, the murderous wife, not only as a character in a story of petty treason but also as a skillful performer who manipulates possible versions of the murderous wife narrative. While some pamphlet narratives evoke sympathy for a murderous wife by displacing responsibility onto her abusive husband, *Arden of Faversham* presents Alice as self-consciously employing the same strategy. Offering no evidence that Arden mistreats Alice, the play in effect portrays her as enacting the abused wife in order to secure sympathy and avoid blame for her adultery, her open defiance of her husband, and, eventually, her act of murder. Alice first performs this part to enlist the sympathy and assistance of Master Greene.

> Ah, Master Greene, be it spoken in secret here,
> I never live good day with him alone.
> When he is at home, then have I froward looks,
> Hard words, and blows to mend the match withal.
> And, though I might content as good a man,
> Yet doth he keep in every corner trulls;
> And, weary with his trugs at home,
> Then rides he straight to London. There, forsooth,
> He revels it among such filthy ones
> As counsels him to make away his wife.
> Thus live I daily in continual fear,
> In sorrow, so despairing of redress
> As every day I wish with hearty prayer
> That he or I were taken forth the world.[73]

By offering so vivid a description of husbandly "ill usage," Alice enables Greene to turn his own anger at Arden's landgrabbing into the chivalrous rescue of a damsel in distress: "I shall be the man / Shall set you free from all this discontent" (1.511–12).

Alice's proposed solution to her dilemma closely resembles Mary Aubrey's formulation in response to her husband's assault: "I have no

---

73. *Arden of Faversham*, 1.492–505; subsequent citations are located in the text. My reading of the play is informed by Belsey, *Subject of Tragedy,* chap. 5; Lena Cowen Orlin, "Man's House as His Castle in *Arden of Feversham*," *Medieval and Renaissance Drama in England* 2 (1985): 57–89; and Wine's excellent edition.

way in the World to Deliver my self, but by Beginning with him."[74]
While *A Hellish Murder* struggles to come to terms with Aubrey's violent
response to abuse presented as *actual*, *Arden of Faversham* shows Alice
Arden similarly proposing that the solution to marital discord is that
"he or I" must die, although the abuse and fear she describes as motivating this desperate response are *invented*.

The play also depicts Alice as playing the abused wife to manipulate
Arden and to place him at fault. After another of Alice's schemes has
backfired, she boldly accuses Arden of being a bad husband, and therefore responsible for their difficulties.

> Ah me accursed,
> To link in liking with a frantic man!
> Henceforth I'll be thy slave, no more thy wife;
> For with that name I never shall content thee.
> If I be merry, thou straightways thinks me light;
> If sad, thou sayest the sullens trouble me;
> If well attired, thou thinks I will be gadding;
> If homely, I seem sluttish in thine eye.
> Thus am I still, and shall be while I die,
> Poor wench abused by thy misgovernment.
> (13.104–13)

It is unusual to find a wife's experience of misinterpretation and mistreatment so vividly and sympathetically portrayed; it is even more
unusual to see her making a good case against a bad husband for her
own purposes. The play presents Alice as a woman whose complaints
about abuse are "cunningly performed"; she even draws attention to
her own performances (1.417–19). In addition to characterizing Alice
as a skillful manipulator of effect, the play explores the subjectivity from
which she chooses those roles and the desires that motivate her
performances.

When Alice is alone, and, apparently, speaking "sincerely," the play
presents her as a wife who acts *against* marriage, and who imagines
murder as the only way to move from one embrace to another: "I shall
no more be closed in Arden's arms, / . . . Mosby's [her lover's] arms /
Shall compass me" (14.143; 145–6). Like Anne Welles in *The Murth-*

74. *A Hellish Murder*, sig. Fv.

ering of John Brewen and other murderous wives, Alice violates domesticity and marriage. She poisons her husband's broth; welcomes a steward into their bed; and, in her husband's absence, makes her lover both master of her heart and of the house (1.639–40). She licenses Mosby to play the "husband's part" sexually and domestically (1.638).

Also like Anne Welles, Alice is portrayed as attempting to reshape marriage to fill her own needs; she wants to kill Arden principally to replace him with another husband, equally possessive and authoritative. She imagines her substitution of one man for another as a transfer of the "title" to herself.

> Sweet Mosby is the man that hath my heart;
> And he usurps it, having nought but this,
> That I am tied to him by marriage.
> Love is a god, and marriage is but words;
> And therefore Mosby's title is the best.
> Tush! Whether it be or no, he shall be mine
> In spite of him, of Hymen, and of rites.
> (1.98–104)

In this passage, Alice's vague pronouns obscure the difference between Arden and Mosby, one husband/owner and another. Here, Alice also abandons an argument in terms of men's rights and titles, finally asserting her own desire to possess ("*he* shall be *mine*") and to get what *she* wants. At certain points in the play, Alice even voices rebellion against Arden's authority over her and declares her desire for self-government.

> Why should he thrust his sickle in our corn,
> Or what hath he to do with thee, my love,
> Or govern me that am to rule myself?
> (10.83–85)

Such moments are transitory. Alice is not generally presented as seeking *self*-government; she seeks, rather, the liberty to *elect* her governor.

In *Arden of Faversham,* as in other accounts of petty treason, adultery and murder collapse into one another. Alice explains that she is driven to murder Arden because violence is the only way that she can enjoy Mosby freely and openly.

> Yet nothing could enforce me to the deed
> But Mosby's love. Might I without control
> Enjoy thee still, then Arden should not die;
> But seeing I cannot, therefore let him die.
> (1.273–76)

Mosby responds to Alice's resigned acceptance of Arden's death as a profession of devotion: "Enough, sweet Alice; thy kind words makes me melt" (1.277). Earlier, Alice asks Mosby to recall the moment of intimacy in which they pledged their troth, that is, to murder Arden.

> Remember, when I locked thee in my closet,
> What were thy words and mine? Did we not both
> Decree to murder Arden in the night?
> (1.191–93)

The play so closely associates desire, affection, and violence that the murder plot becomes the consummation of Alice's and Mosby's affair.

Like Anne Welles, whose lover is afraid to marry a woman who would murder her husband, Alice becomes unmarriageable when she undertakes to choose who her master will be. Shortly after Mosby imagines that marriage will "make us two but one," he reveals his inability to imagine that he could absorb Alice into himself, subsume her enough to sleep easily in the usurped bed.

> But what for that I may not trust you, Alice?
> You have supplanted Arden for my sake,
> And will extirpen me to plant another.
> 'Tis fearful sleeping in a serpent's bed,
> And I will cleanly rid my hands of her.
> (8.39–43)

As Alice uses violence to reassert her subjectivity and to reshape the role of wife, Mosby plans to use violence to reassert husbandly authority over Alice. Again, it looks as if husband and wife, man and woman, cannot *both* be subjects in the same bed. Alice has made it clear that the institution of marriage and the role it constructs for the wife cannot deprive her of consciousness, language, and agency. Since Mosby cannot imagine a marriage in which he and Alice could both be subjects, he must secure his own "place" at her expense, as she has secured hers at Arden's. While the play, like other accounts of the conspiracy of wife and servant, associates adultery with ambition, and presents both as leading to violence, it depicts wife and servant as rivals as much as coconspirators. In Mosby's plan to kill Alice, the spats between the lovers woven throughout the plot, and the couple's final recriminations, the play vividly dramatizes the competition between Mosby and Alice for the same place.

The conflation of social aspiration, violence, and sexual desire that fuels the lovers' competition pervades the play. For instance, the apprentice Michael plans to kill his brother and seize his land as a means of winning over Mosby's sister Susan: "Who would not venture upon house and land / When he may have it for a right-down blow?" (1.174–75). All the conspirators rely on violence to gain money or land and to resculpt their social positions. Black Will and Shakebag, the hired killers, kill Arden for ten pounds; Alice kills him to get Mosby; Mosby kills him for Alice and for Arden's house and lands; Greene conspires to regain his land; and Michael and the painter cooperate in an attempt to win Susan in marriage. In this play, to desire a lover is to be willing to kill to get him or her; to want another man's land is similarly to be willing to kill to get it.

In the climactic murder of Arden, the confluence of sexual and social insurgencies and violence finds its most vivid representation. As Mosby stabs Arden, he reminds him of an earlier confrontation in which Arden had seized Mosby's sword and sarcastically urged him to arm himself with a pressing iron instead, thereby attempting to reverse his rival's rise from tailor to steward. Settling the score, Mosby announces the murder as an act of social rebellion: "There's for the pressing iron you told me of" (14.235). In the prose accounts of the crime, Mosby actually bludgeons Arden with a pressing iron. It may not be a gentleman's weapon, but it can secure a gentleman's place. Alice, to the horror of her servant, demands the knife to strike her own blow: "What, groans thou?—Nay, then give me the weapon! / Take this for hind'ring Mosby's love and mine" (14.237–38). The play thus presents the murder as the ultimate, violent refusal of subsumption.

Since wives cannot choose new husbands, nor servants choose to become masters, such marginal figures' longings for change must be construed as potentially violent. To desire a man other than one's husband or to aspire to one's master's authority and wealth is to challenge the whole social order that regulates sexuality and reproduction, the distribution of property, and the hierarchies of authority and submission. In using the resources of the drama to act out the competing voices that characterize petty treason plots, *Arden of Faversham* registers both the violence and the vitality of scheming subordinates in their attempts to seize the master's pivotal subject-position. While the play imposes closure by listing the fates of all the conspirators, it also reveals what has been lost, silenced, and repressed in the process of restoring order. What is left is a starkly bare stage: Arden is dead and *eight* conspirators are marched off to execution, Alice as a petty traitor and the rest as murderers and accessories to murder. Arden's house is no longer a locus of conflict simply because it is empty.

While representations of murderous wives emphasize the apprehension, condemnation, and execution of the offenders, they also present violent resistance as one means by which women could be constituted and recognized as subjects in the early modern period. The process that convicts and publicly punishes petty traitors—reducing them to ashes—also holds them accountable for their actions in a way that exposes the contradictions of women's, especially wives', legal status in this period. Since men's and women's representations of women in early modern England suggest a range of available agencies, to define agency as physical action, or in this case as violence, is unnecessarily to diminish women's access to agency in the culture. Similarly, women certainly achieved more passive, "covert," and therefore successful, forms of resistance than petty treason.[75] But I am interested here in how a discourse of criminality constructed the emergence of married women's subjectivity *into visibility* as violent.

Accounts of petty treason represent married women's subjectivity both as agency—words and deeds in the world and accountability for them—and as self-awareness. The accounts ally both to violent resis-

---

75. On wives' limited rights to passive disobedience, see the works cited above in note 37, as well as Margaret W. Ferguson, "Running On with Almost Public Voice: The Case of 'E. C'," in *Tradition and the Talents of Women,* ed. Florence Howe (Urbana: University of Illinois Press, 1991), pp. 37–67, esp. pp. 54–55; and Marie B. Rowlands, "Recusant Women, 1560–1640," in *Women in English Society, 1500–1800,* ed. Mary Prior (London: Methuen, 1985), pp. 149–80.

tance. In killing their husbands, early modern women transgressed the cultural boundaries that were supposed to delimit their subjectivity. Those texts that represent their actions, therefore, worry the relationships among female gender, subjectivity, and violence that such crimes enact and that threaten domestic and gender hierarchies.

The stories of women who plot against their husbands articulate and shape fears of the dangers lurking within the home, of women's voracious and ranging sexual appetites and capacities for violence, and of the instability of masculine privilege and power. In so succinctly articulating deep and complexly linked fears of disorder, these stories become a cultural resource for evoking and manipulating anxieties about that intersection of culturally determined boundaries and individual agency that is both the location of the subject and, in accounts of petty treason, a collision, a site of violence.

II. THE SUBORDINATE('S) PLOT: PETTY TREASON AND THE FORMS OF DOMESTIC REBELLION

The violently rebellious servant was as threatening a figure as the murderous wife; indeed, the two were feared to conspire in petty treason. In this chapter, I further investigate the relationship between the two kinds of dependents, servants and wives, and the two kinds of petty treason, examining how legal and literary narratives work to subordinate the story of insubordinate dependents within social and literary structures. While legal and literary narratives of petty treason suggest that, potentially, there are multiple subjectivities and stories within any household—as well as narratives alternative to the master's—social order and dramatic form both depend on the containment of those rival narratives.

I concentrate here on how aesthetic and social orders reinforce one another in three fairly well known texts: Shakespeare's *The Tempest*, *Arden of Faversham* (to which we pay a return visit), and printed transcripts of the earl of Castlehaven's infamous trial for rape and sodomy. Each constructs the story of murderous dependents as both the subordinates' plot against their master and as the plot formally subordinated to the master plot. In each of these texts, the story of petty treason focuses on the contradictions and fragilities of social status as seen in disobedient subordinates *and* in weak, flawed, or absentee masters. The texts focus on the ambiguous accountability of all parties to petty treason: the master, who is both authoritative and threatened, and the subordinates, who are constituted and recognized as agents through their violent resistance to their master's authority. Just as master and servant are interdependent, the plot of the insubordinate dependent and that of the implicated master imply and require one another.

The Tempest: The Servant-Monster's Foul Conspiracy

In act 4, scene 1, of *The Tempest* (first performed, so far as we know, in 1611 and first published in 1623), the elaborate masque that Prospero and Ariel present in order to show Ferdinand and Miranda "some vanity of [Prospero's] Art" and to celebrate the couple's betrothal suddenly dissolves; the dancing reapers and nymphs "heavily vanish" "to a strange, hollow, and confused noise."[1] As the moment of festivity and harmony fractures in dissonance, the artful, magical spectacle, which draws on prestigious classical and courtly traditions, disappears: "Our revels now are ended," says Prospero (l. 148). The disruption occurs because Prospero "starts suddenly, and speaks" about Caliban, the "servant-monster," and his brewing plot.

> I had forgot that foul conspiracy
> Of the beast Caliban and his confederates
> Against my life. The minute of their plot
> Is almost come.
> (ll. 139–42)

At the moment in which Prospero basks in self-congratulation, Caliban's plot—the scheming subordinate's subplot—which Paul Brown has identified as "a kind of antimasque," interrupts Prospero's master plan,

---

1. *The Tempest*, 4.1.41; and stage direction, in *William Shakespeare: The Complete Works*, ed. David Bevington, 4th ed. (New York: Harper Collins, 1992); subsequent citations are located in the text.

prompting him to ruminate on transience and mortality.[2] Although Prospero knows about, and even stages and manipulates, Caliban's plot, at this moment we sense briefly possible narratives other than that of Prospero's mastery. According to Peter Hulme and Francis Barker, "the sub-plot provides the only real moment of drama when Prospero calls a sudden halt to the celebratory masque." This "real drama" results from our sense that Prospero is not *completely* in control and that the outcome is not *wholly* predictable. As Hulme and Barker argue, this is the first moment in the play when it is possible to distinguish "between Prospero's play and *The Tempest* itself."[3] In this instant, we can imagine a play in which Caliban is the protagonist governing the main plot, a play in which he is once again his own king. The disruption reveals the fragility not only of the masque and the celebration but also of Prospero's power.

Caliban's disruptive intrusion is recognizably linked to the narrative of petty treason. Although Prospero rapidly recovers himself and consults with Ariel about how to curtail and punish Caliban's insubordination, Caliban's plot threatens to derail Prospero's elaborate schemes to regain his dukedom, marry off his daughter, and punish/educate his usurping brother. It threatens simultaneously the form and coherence of the play at its most gorgeous, most confident moment of aesthetic display. Like the petty traitor and his betrayal, the threats to Prospero and his agenda, to the patriarchal social and political order these represent, and to the form of *The Tempest* come from inside Prospero's household, from the character introduced as "my slave" (1.2.311).

Recent criticism connects *The Tempest* to various discourses of power in Renaissance culture. Focusing on Caliban's compelling narrative of how Prospero wooed then enslaved him and on how he was degraded from "mine own king" to "all the subjects that you have" (1.2.344–45), critics demonstrate brilliantly the play's relationship to discourses

---

2. Paul Brown, " 'This thing of darkness I acknowledge mine': *The Tempest* and the Discourse of Colonialism," in *Political Shakespeare: New Essays in Cultural Materialism*, ed. Jonathan Dollimore and Alan Sinfield (Ithaca: Cornell University Press, 1985), pp. 48–71, esp. pp. 64, 67.

3. Peter Hulme and Francis Barker, "Nymphs and Reapers Heavily Vanish: The Discursive Con-Texts of *The Tempest*," in *Alternative Shakespeares*, ed. John Drakakis (London: Methuen, 1985), pp. 191–205, esp. pp. 201, 203. On the interrupted masque, see also Julie R. Solomon, "Going Places: Absolutism and Movement in Shakespeare's *The Tempest*," *Renaissance Drama*, n.s. 22 (1991): 3–45.

of colonialism and the processes of exploration and exploitation in which they participate. In addition, Curt Breight articulates the relationship between *The Tempest* and discourses of treason. As he shows, the play includes two treason plots, one presented as a false accusation, the other as actual: Prospero accuses Ferdinand of being a traitor; Sebastian and Antonio plot to kill Alonso, king of Naples. The play's prehistory, which generates its plot, centers on Antonio's usurpation of his brother's dukedom and attempt to eliminate him.[4] From the perspective of recent critics, at the intersection of these discourses of power, Prospero, as sovereign and as imperialist, stands compromised by his power over others and the brutality with which he wields it. Yet the play also presents Prospero as compromised by his dependency on and vulnerability to those who serve him: first his brother, then his servants.

Just as *The Tempest* participates in discourses of colonialism and treason, it is also in dialogue with discourses of petty treason. Since Caliban acts both as Prospero's only subject and as his domestic servant, his plot against Prospero is both high and petty treason. The conflation of public and private, political and domestic, so evident in the legal construction of petty treason, particularly applies to the shrunken, enclosed world of *The Tempest,* in which Prospero's household *is* the commonwealth. He is master, father, and king, and his daughter and servants are his only subjects. Petty and high treason are so analogous in *The Tempest* that most readers and viewers have not distinguished between the two.

---

4. On *The Tempest* and discourses of colonialism, see Brown, " 'This thing of darkness' "; Hulme and Barker, "Nymphs"; and Deborah Willis, "Shakespeare's *Tempest* and the Discourse of Colonialism," *Studies in English Literature* 29 (1989): 277–89. See Anthony B. Dawson's response to such recent work in "*Tempest* in a Teapot: Critics, Evaluation, Ideology," in *"Bad" Shakespeare: Revaluations of the Shakespeare Canon,* ed. Maurice Charney (Rutherford, N.J.: Fairleigh Dickinson University Press, 1988), pp. 61–73. Ania Loomba explores the relationships among constructions of racial and gender difference in and around *The Tempest* in her *Gender, Race, Renaissance Drama* (Manchester: Manchester University Press, 1989), chap. 6. On reappropriations and reinterpretations of *The Tempest,* see Thomas Cartelli, "Prospero in Africa: *The Tempest* as Colonialist Text and Pretext," in *Shakespeare Reproduced: The Text in History and Ideology,* ed. Jean E. Howard and Marion F. O'Connor (New York: Methuen, 1987): pp. 99–115; and Rob Nixon, "Caribbean and African Appropriations of *The Tempest,*" *Critical Inquiry* 13 (1987): 557–77. On the play's relation to the discourses of treason, see Curt Breight, " 'Treason doth never prosper': *The Tempest* and the Discourse of Treason," *Shakespeare Quarterly* 41 (1990): 1–28.

Yet the relationship between Prospero and Caliban is first presented as a domestic one. When Prospero narrates his time on the island and his relationship to its original inhabitants in order to chastise Ariel and defer his request for freedom, he first identifies Caliban as the one "whom now I keep in service" (1.2.288). In this disciplinary narrative, Prospero characterizes himself as the good master by reminding Ariel what it was like to be tormented and imprisoned by a bad mistress, Sycorax.[5] Ariel clearly has the ability to irritate his master by requesting liberty and provoking a monthly reminder of his history, but he is presented as the good servant, as opposed to Caliban: the "villain" and "slave."

Although he is presented as monstrous and dangerous, Caliban is also presented as invaluable; Prospero and Miranda *depend* on him.

> We cannot miss him. He does make our fire,
> Fetch in our wood, and serves in offices
> That profit us.
> (1.2.314–16)

Stephen Greenblatt shows how many explorers of the new world depicted themselves as dependent on the natives to supply them with food, as entrusting basic subsistence needs to those they did not trust. They thus placed themselves in a relation of fearful dependency on those they violently subjugated as their inferiors and slaves. Greenblatt links this "determination to be nourished by the labor of others weaker, more vulnerable, than oneself" to a desire to distinguish one's self as a gentleman. By such means Europeans created a class hierarchy in the New World, a hierarchy in which virtually any European would be above the natives.[6] Like Europeans exploring the New World, then, Prospero needs a native to show him "all the qualities o' th' isle" (l.

5. Loomba argues that the play contrasts Prospero and Sycorax as the white and black, male and female, good and bad masters (*Gender, Race,* p. 152). Barbara A. Mowat points to the master-servant relationship between Prospero and Ariel in which Ariel operates as a sorcerer's apprentice ("Prospero, Agrippa, and Hocus Pocus," *English Literary Renaissance* 11.3 [1981]: 281–303). While Ariel and Caliban are both presented as servants, only Caliban is presented as domestic laborer and petty traitor.

6. See Stephen Greenblatt's "Invisible Bullets," in *Shakespearean Negotiations: The Circulation of Social Energy in Renaissance England* (Berkeley: University of California Press, 1988), pp. 21–65, esp. p. 29.

340); he also needs a slave so that he can proclaim himself a master. Just as Prospero and Miranda cannot survive on the island without Caliban, Prospero cannot be a king without a subject, or a master without his servants.

Such dependency motivates the fear of petty treason. Since Prospero's mastery depends on Caliban's and Ariel's subordination and his bodily life depends on Caliban's exertions, he must use force, threat, and magical torments to secure the submission of the subordinates on whom he depends and with whom he is so intimate. The danger of such dependency and intimacy is represented through Caliban's attempt to rape Miranda. As Prospero reminds Caliban: I "lodg'd thee / In mine own cell, till thou didst seek to violate / The honor of my child" (1.2.349–51). Only Caliban's attempt to rape Miranda convinces Prospero that Caliban, unlike most servants, cannot live in his house, cannot be a member of the family. As critics have noted, Prospero reminds Caliban of the rape and its relation to his "lodging" in order to construct Caliban as a bad servant, a betrayer of the household that has welcomed and included him, and therefore to sidestep Caliban's construction of Prospero as the betraying father/master and usurper of the island. Thus, to protect his own interests and displace blame, Prospero counters Caliban's narrative of tyranny and usurpation (a narrative too much like Prospero's own account of his lost dukedom) with a narrative of attempted rape.

Prospero also counters Caliban's claim that he is a victim with the charge that Caliban is a perpetrator and agent. Prospero holds Caliban accountable to the extent that this serves his own interests. In Prospero's view, Caliban is subhuman and monstrous, a ludicrous rival for rule. Yet Caliban is also responsible enough to work for Prospero and possesses enough agency to be held accountable and punished, first for the rape and later for the plot against his master. To manage the disturbing possibility that a Caliban could have legitimate claims to the kingship of his own island, a world "new" only to its invader, Prospero deploys the familiar, household discourse of master-servant relations.

Caliban's paradoxical position, which enables Prospero to manipulate his relation to Caliban and Caliban's accountability, is not particular to this amphibious inhabitant of an enchanted isle but corresponds, in part, to the status of the early modern household servant. As Michael MacDonald argues, "many households in early modern England harbored a Caliban, a 'servant-monster,' partly adult, partly child, partly domestic beast of burden."[7] MacDonald's vivid evocation of domestic servants as both familiar and strange, as monstrous in their conflation of categories, points to the difficulty of locating servants within early modern social order and the anxiety this could cause.

Those critics of *The Tempest* who have acknowledged class conflict in the play have oversimplified it as dualistic. They have not recognized the significance of Prospero's and Caliban's relationship as master and servant; nor do they address the complex, shifting relation of the roles of master and servant to social hierarchies. Brown, for instance, argues that the play defines the aristocracy against the masterless (Stephano, Trinculo, and Caliban) and that "the masterless therefore function to bind the rulers together in hegemony." Breight agrees that "Caliban's conspiracy appears to present a précis of Elizabethan fears regarding masterless men."[8] Yet, as Brown acknowledges at some points but disregards at others, Caliban is *not* masterless. Nor is the domestic hierarchy of master and servant quite the same as the social hierarchy of the aristocracy and the masterless (which elides the middle of the social order and the majority of the population) or the political hierarchy of governors and governed. Also, while the master-servant and king-subject relationships are analogous, as the definition of petty treason articulates, and while both of these hierarchical relations are associated with class hierarchies, the connections are complex. Excepting the king, each of the inhabitants of the realm is a subject; that subjection embraces every social class.

Like the category "subject" or "governed," "servant" incorporates many social and economic classes. As a result, historians argue that "servants did not understand themselves, and were not understood by early modern society, to be part of a labouring class, youthful prole- tarians."[9] Indeed, so many people, including aristocrats at court, spent

7. Michael MacDonald, *Mystical Bedlam: Madness, Anxiety, and Healing in Seventeenth-Century England* (Cambridge: Cambridge University Press, 1981), p. 85. On how a popular emblem depicts the domestic servant as "a monstrous anomaly," part beast and part man, see Mark Thornton Burnett, "The 'Trusty Servant': A Sixteenth-Century Eng-lish Emblem," *Emblematica* 6.2, forthcoming.

8. See Brown, " 'This thing of darkness,' " p. 53; and Breight, " 'Treason'," p. 17.

9. Ann Kussmaul, *Servants in Husbandry in Early Modern England* (Cambridge: Cam-bridge University Press, 1981), p. 9. In "The London Apprentices as Seventeenth-Century Adolescents," *Past and Present* 61 (1973): 149–61, Steven R. Smith argues that

some part of their life in service that it was considered a developmental phase more than a permanent social status. As Ann Kussmaul notes, "For most servants, it was a transitional occupation, specific to their transitional status between childhood and adulthood." Since most servants were youths, servants "constituted around 60 per cent of the population aged fifteen to twenty-four" in early modern England.[10] Furthermore, by Peter Laslett's calculation, "a quarter, or a third, of all the families in the country contained servants in Stuart times."[11] Integral members of the households in which they lived and worked, servants obtained their social status from their masters. They were thus woven into hierarchies that governed social order in early modern England and into households and families. Servants were neither distinguishable nor separable as a social group; because of their intimate relationship with their employers, servants were confusing, even threatening, figures.[12] The threat lay not in their stark opposition to their

seventeenth-century London apprentices "thought of themselves and were thought of as a separate order or subculture," but he goes on to point out that, "like the larger culture of which it was a part, the apprentice subculture was somewhat hierarchical" (p. 157). "Drawn from all levels of society," apprentices would also graduate out of this subculture to social positions and occupations that would divide them from one another (p. 150). They were thus connected by age, transition, and the shared experience of subordination; they were not a "class." On the master-apprentice relationship, also see Craig A. Bernthal, "Treason in the Family: The Trial of Thumpe v. Horner," *Shakespeare Quarterly* 42.1 (1991): 44–54, esp. pp. 45, 50–52; and Steven Rappaport, *Worlds within Worlds: Structures of Life in Sixteenth-Century London* (Cambridge: Cambridge University Press, 1989), pp. 291–322.

10. Kussmaul, *Servants in Husbandry*, pp. 4, 3. Ralph A. Houlbrooke points out that since service was a transitional phase for many throughout the social order, it shaped social relations by inculcating deference: "In a society in which service was the most important avenue of advancement at all levels, one of the most essential skills was the ability to make oneself acceptable to superiors" (*The English Family, 1450–1700* [London: Longman, 1984], p. 147).

11. Peter Laslett, *The World We Have Lost: Further Explored*, 3d ed. (London: Methuen, 1983), p. 13.

12. On master-servant relations, see also Mark Thornton Burnett, "Apprentice Literature and the 'Crisis' of the 1590s," *The Yearbook of English Studies* 21 (1991): 27–38, "Masters and Servants in Moral and Religious Treatises, c. 1580–c. 1642," in *The Arts, Literature, and Society,* ed. Arthur Marwick (London: Routledge, 1990), pp. 48–75, and *Authority and Obedience: Masters and Servants in English Literature and Society, 1580–1642* (Cambridge: Cambridge University Press, forthcoming); Houlbrooke, *English Family,* pp. 171–78; Laslett, *World We Have Lost,* pp. 1–21; MacDonald, *Mystical Bedlam,* pp. 85–88; Alan Macfarlane, *Marriage and Love in England: Modes of Reproduction, 1300–1840* (Oxford: Basil Blackwell, 1986), pp. 83–87; and Peter Stallybrass and Allon White, *The Politics and Poetics of Transgression* (Ithaca: Cornell University Press, 1986), esp. chap. 4.

masters or their demonized otherness but in their very familiarity and their insinuation into all social groups and situations. Furthermore, the role of service as a developmental phase reveals the dependency and deference that permeated social relations throughout early modern England.

Dependent yet depended upon, familiar yet not wholly known or controlled, a class yet not one, servants blurred boundaries and confused categories. To the complex positioning of the domestic servant in early modern England, the characterization of Caliban adds the further complication of racial difference; Caliban seems to occupy the same "curious outsider-within stance" that Patricia Hill Collins describes as typical of African-American women domestic workers in white upper-class households. In *The Tempest,* as in the situations that Collins describes, this position enables the servant to see the master/employer demystified and vulnerable.[13]

The story of the insubordinate dependent, the petty traitor, is the story of the outsider-within as told from the perspective of the threatened master; it articulates the fear that the other and the enemy might be the person who makes your fire, prepares your food, and lodges in your own cell. Pointing out that Ferdinand takes Caliban's place when Caliban is freed from log-toting to plot his rebellion, Breight argues that "in structural terms Prospero always needs a demonic 'other'."[14] It is important that Prospero needs not an *other* as much as a servant, a servant who, while he may be demonic, is also domestic. One of the threats Caliban offers as a servant is that he is not "other" enough: He once lived with Prospero; he remembers happier days of being petted; he is a thing of darkness whom Prospero feels compelled to acknowledge as his own.

Like the attempted rape that leads to Caliban's domestic exile and imprisonment, Caliban's plan to kill Prospero hinges on his role as the familiar, included member of the household as well as the estranged, monstrous "other." Displaying his knowledge of Prospero's habits and vulnerabilities, Caliban suggests to his confederates that they deprive Prospero of his power by "seiz[ing] his books" and then kill him during

13. Patricia Hill Collins, *Black Feminist Thought: Knowledge, Consciousness, and the Politics of Empowerment* (Boston: Unwin Hyman, 1990), p. 11.
14. Breight, " 'Treason'," p. 19.

his customary nap: "'Tis a custom with him / I'th'afternoon to sleep.
There thou mayst brain him" (3.2.87–89). Turning on the inside information that a servant would have, this plot constitutes a particularly
intimate, domestic betrayal. Prospero commands magical forces, but
his books and "brave utensils" are vulnerable to seizure and destruction
by one who knows their place and power.

Caliban is so consistently characterized as a servant that he appears
to internalize that characterization and to construe his actions as petty
treason rather than as the reclamation of his own usurped kingdom.
When he rebels against being reviled but depended on, included in the
household but excluded from the family—from the master who once
"strok'st me, and made much of me" (1.2.336) and the woman who
once pitied him and taught him to speak (ll. 356–61)—he does not
aspire to regain his status as "mine own king." Instead, he seeks a more
congenial master and a sense of belonging in the fellowship of "celestial
liquor." Gleefully subjecting himself to Stephano and never competing
with him or Trinculo for mastery, Caliban pursues a "freedom! high-
day! high-day, freedom!" that entails "a new master" who will not expect
him to perform domestic tasks such as food gathering or dishwashing
(2.2.178–84). The limited scope of Caliban's ambitions and the extent
to which, despite his eloquent nostalgia for lost autonomy, he seems
to agree with his positioning as a "servant-monster," neutralize the
threat that his plot poses, making him and his conspiracy not just
harmless but humorous.

Many recent critics have seen the humor of *The Tempest*'s subplot as
evidence of the play's complicity with discourses of colonialism and
treason and the forms of power these serve. Breight, for instance, expresses dismay that the display of chastened "lower-class conspirators"
can still be staged as comic.[15] If, as Hulme and Barker so suggestively
argue, "Prospero's play and *The Tempest* are not necessarily the same
thing," many contemporary viewers are ready and willing to imagine
Caliban's play, to empathize with the lower-class conspirators rather
than the aristocrats, to feel estranged from the exclusive and hostile
humor.[16]

The humor that disturbs so many contemporary readers and viewers

15. Ibid., p. 23.
16. Hulme and Barker, "Nymphs," p. 199.

may stem not only from the complicity of directors "with hierarchical discourse," as Breight argues, but also from the operations of dramatic form, which, itself constituting and constituted by hierarchical discourses, associates subordinates and their plot with the comic. This is also true in *Arden of Faversham*. Brown argues that the comic treatment of the conspiracy in *The Tempest* serves to restore social, political, and aesthetic orders; the aristocrats' "collective laughter at the chastened revolting plebians" enables them to displace responsibility for their own failures onto "the ludicrous revolt of the masterless" and to celebrate their reclaimed authority.[17] Addressing the social function of Renaissance dramatic forms more generally, critics such as Louis A. Montrose argue that Renaissance comedy performed social work by provoking and alleviating tensions.[18] According to such arguments, with which I agree, a play like *The Tempest* represents Caliban and his fellow conspirators in order to trivialize and overmaster them; it grants them their own plot in order to subordinate it to a plot structure and a larger cultural narrative that diminish their significance and locate power and prestige elsewhere—in the master and his story.[19]

Although *The Tempest,* in order to motivate the comedy, depends on "Prospero's anxious determination to keep the sub-plot of his play in its place," that anxiety always operates within carefully maintained boundaries.[20] However "anxious" he may be, Prospero remains at the center of the play. Few readers or viewers really fear or expect that Prospero will be displaced. He is never offstage for long; his agent Ariel is ubiquitous, observing and interfering; and Caliban himself, in the diminished forms that his rebellion takes, assures us that this will not become *Caliban: The Play.* In other words, in *The Tempest* the tension between subplot and main plot is scrupulously controlled and

17. Brown, " 'This thing of darkness'," p. 63. Hulme and Barker argue that both Prospero and *The Tempest* treat "Caliban's conspiracy in the fully comic mode." In the end, Prospero's "version of history remains *authoritative,* the larger play acceding as it were to the containment of the conspirators in the safely comic mode" ("Nymphs," p. 203).

18. See, for instance, Louis A. Montrose's " 'The Place of a Brother' in *As You Like It:* Social Process and Comic Form," *Shakespeare Quarterly* 32 (1981): 28–54.

19. Dawson argues that disunity and fragmentation are now privileged as standards of value, as unity and coherence once were ("*Tempest in a Teapot,*" pp. 70–71). I would argue that the critics whom Dawson discusses do not so much value disunity as they feel disturbed at the means of achieving cohesion in *The Tempest.*

20. Hulme and Barker, "Nymphs," p. 203.

the focus on the master and his plot is maintained through the subordination of Caliban and his attempt at petty treason.

Working to recover those alternative narratives that it was the project of colonialism to defeat or appropriate, some postcolonial critics stress the stark confrontation between two protagonists in colonial discourses.[21] This formulation refuses the hierarchy of master and slave, seeing instead a contest between two would-be protagonists for mastery, between two potential main plots. While *Arden of Faversham* dramatizes this formulation of domestic, not colonial, conflict, *The Tempest* does not. *The Tempest* owes the aesthetic orderliness for which it was once so praised and its lasting place in the literary canon to that refusal. That is, Shakespeare's masterful manipulation of form in *The Tempest* results from his privileging the master's story over the slave's. Caliban and Prospero are not equal protagonists but master and servant; the two plots are not alternative plays struggling for precedence but a master plot and a subplot that only briefly erupts into prominence. By identifying the rebellion of Caliban and his confederates with the antimasque, Brown suggestively conveys its relation to form. Like the carefully staged chaos in court masques, this outbreak of disorder is designed to be dispersed and contained; it is there to make the order and closure more orderly and beautiful. As other critics have noted, Caliban's rebellion is effectively subordinated, "an easily controllable insurrection," "a wholly containable plot."[22] In this play, aesthetic order reinforces a social order that depends on hierarchy. As Mary Beth Rose argues,

21. See the discussion in Loomba, *Gender, Race*, p. 157, regarding the relation of *The Tempest* to controversies among postcolonial theorists. See also Benita Parry, "Problems in Current Theories of Colonial Discourse," *Oxford Literary Review* 9.1–2 (1987): 27–58.

22. Hulme and Barker, "Nymphs," p. 202; Breight, "'Treason'," p. 19. Dawson argues that Northrop Frye is unable to readjust his categories in order to see Caliban as "repressed" rather than "included" ("*Tempest* in a Teapot," p. 65). Seeing Caliban, instead, as *subordinated* enables me to use a Renaissance category to mediate between the formalist analysis of scholars like Frye and the cultural materialism of scholars like Breight, Brown, and Hulme and Barker. In *The Tempest*, Caliban can be included because he is repressed; social order (at the domestic and political levels) and dramatic form laboriously achieve cohesion by acknowledging *and* subordinating the forces on whose energies they depend.

I am indebted to the work of Mary Beth Rose for a model of how to combine feminist, materialist, and formalist analyses. See, especially, her "Where Are the Mothers in Shakespeare?: Options for Gender Representation in the English Renaissance," *Shakespeare Quarterly* 42.3 (1991): 291–314. See also Fredric Jameson, *The Political Unconscious: Narrative as a Socially Symbolic Act* (Ithaca: Cornell University Press, 1981).

"given the variety of conceptual options available in Jacobean culture, [Shakespeare] often chooses the conservative ones"; the alliance of Shakespearean texts with the more traditional discourses has enabled their crucial role in the interrelated processes of shaping literary forms and maintaining social order.[23]

Although the plot of "the beast Caliban and his confederates" against Prospero disrupts the marriage masque and momentarily threatens to redirect the play, *The Tempest* reassures viewers that Caliban, however compellingly presented, will be remastered, and that Prospero will remain in charge of him, the island, and the main plot. While the play presents master and servant as interdependent, its plot does not work to reorder the relations within Prospero's household and on the island, between master and subordinate, and between main plot and subplot. The only changes it effects are magical restorations of aesthetic, social, and political order.

Arden of Faversham: The Master's Place and the Subordinates' Plots

It may seem an abrupt shift from *The Tempest* (1611) to *Arden of Faversham* (1592): from a magical island to a village in Kent; from the creation of a world of fantasy to the recreation of an actual crime; from monsters and airy spirits to carefully delineated participants in Elizabethan social order. It is the eruption of petty treason in the confining, stifling household, whether on an island or in Faversham, that links these two apparently unrelated plays. In moving from one play to the other, we not only shift from the fantastical to the realistic; we also move down the literary hierarchy from a play that self-consciously allies itself with the most prestigious literary and artistic traditions and depends on the most innovative technical resources to a play that, in its emphasis on the actual, the local, and the domestic, has been considered undistinguished and homely. In my discussion of *Arden of Faversham* in this chapter, I attend much more to its form and its relation to other plays than I did in Chapter 1. Although it achieved qualified, borrowed

23. Mary Beth Rose, *The Expense of Spirit: Love and Sexuality in English Renaissance Drama* (Ithaca: Cornell University Press, 1988), pp. 173ff., and "Where Are the Mothers," p. 313.

prestige as part of the Shakespeare apocrypha, *Arden of Faversham* has generally been attended to as an historical document more than a literary artifact. Yet it is a play peculiarly suited to blur the distinction between the two, providing insight into the complex relation between the documentation of social process and the operations of literary form, between a play described as "almost miraculous" and one described as leaving the viewer "positively irritated."[24]

While Shakespeare's subject in *The Tempest* enabled him to invent freely, the anonymous author of *Arden of Faversham* attempts to dramatize an actual murder that occurred in 1551. Recall that Arden's wife and her lover (a steward and her social inferior) as well as hired killers and various of Arden's dependents (servants and tenants) all conspired to murder him. The multiprotagonist, richly ambiguous, generically hybrid play leaves one wondering whose story it is: the tragedy of Arden, as the title page proclaims; or of his wife and her base lover; or of the multiple assailants who diffuse the focus and confuse the genre. As Alexander Leggatt argues, "The playwright keeps us guessing about what sort of play he is writing."[25] In its feverish activity and large, industrious cast of murderous subordinates, *Arden of Faversham*, refusing to be simply Arden's play, *acts out* petty treason. The result is a story that, because of its multiple voices and perspectives, is particularly suited to drama. Yet it is also a story that exists outside dramatic forms and that is not fully articulable within the conventions available.

With the figure of the master diminished from wizard and duke to landowning, upwardly mobile, gentle householder, with the subordinates multiplied and their relations to the master made more complex, and especially with the inclusion of the troublesome and unlocatable figure of the wife, *Arden of Faversham* presents the narrative of petty treason as less containable and more problematic than does *The Tempest*.[26] In *Arden* the subordinate plot does not know its place.[27]

24. Kermode quotes Coleridge's praise of *The Tempest* in the introduction to his Arden edition of the play ([London: Methuen, 1954], p. lxxxi); in his introduction to *The Tragedy of Master Arden of Faversham* (London: Methuen, 1973), M. L. Wine points out that "six external accidents save Arden, and a poor production could easily bear out M. C. Bradbrook's impression that 'the spectator feels positively irritated' after a while 'that the murderers do not succeed' " (p. lxxvi). All quotations of *Arden* are from Wine's edition; subsequent citations are located in the text.

25. Alexander Leggatt, "*Arden of Faversham*," *Shakespeare Survey* 36 (1983): 121–33, esp. p. 129.

26. *The Tempest* does not present us with a female petty traitor; it offers us the memory of a female mistress (Sycorax) and of a wife and mother, and a daughter who becomes

The presence of the wife particularly complicates the story of the plotting subordinates. Simultaneously holding the contradictory subject-positions of partner and dependent, the wife blurs the line between master and subordinate and moves between master plot and subplot. The story of a "foul conspiracy" against a master not only by his servants but also, more humiliatingly, by his wife, is more threatening and more difficult to tell. Focusing on petty treason rather than employing it as a comic subplot, *Arden of Faversham* grants central significance and scrutiny to the elements of complicity and weakness that haunt Prospero's story of his lost dukedom.

In *Arden of Faversham,* the narrative of petty treason is not an alternative or rival narrative because it has so little to supplant, compete with, or oppose. We have little sense of Arden himself prior to or apart from the challenges to him. Defined largely in relation to and response to his subordinates and their betrayals, he knows about his wife's adultery from the first scene of the play. Melancholy and defeatist, his response to his wife's adultery is to leave the household that defines relations and is the play's central arena of action and go to London. He is onstage most often as the potential or actual victim of assault (scenes 1, 3, 4, 9, 11, 13, and 14). We also see him being manipulated by Alice, lamenting his sad fate or reporting a bad dream (scenes 4 and 6), and being cursed by a displaced, resentful tenant (scene 13). In two scenes Arden threatens aggression against his wife's lover, Mosby (scenes 1 and 13), but he immediately backs down and becomes rec-

---

a bride, but it does not represent a wife. Stephen Orgel explores this point in "Prospero's Wife," in *Rewriting the Renaissance: The Discourses of Sexual Difference in Early Modern Europe,* ed. Margaret W. Ferguson, Maureen Quilligan, and Nancy J. Vickers (Chicago: University of Chicago Press, 1986), pp. 50–64. If, as Orgel argues, the day of Prospero's wife has come, it must be realized through other texts that, by including this troublesome figure, have departed from generic expectations and remained largely outside the canon. On the role of mothers in dramatic form, see Rose, "Where Are the Mothers?"

27. My work with *Arden of Faversham* here has been enabled by Wine's excellent Revels edition and informed by Catherine Belsey's path-breaking analysis of the play in relation to the many other representations of this crime and the contests for meaning in which these multiple representations engage, in *The Subject of Tragedy: Identity and Difference in Renaissance Drama* (London: Methuen, 1985); Frank Whigham's chapter on "Hunger and Pain in *Arden of Faversham*" in his *Seizures of the Will in Renaissance Drama: Identity and Violation* (Cambridge: Cambridge University Press, forthcoming); and Lena Cowen Orlin's "Man's House As His Castle in *Arden of Feversham,*" *Medieval and Renaissance Drama in England* 2 (1985), 57–89; and *Private Matters and Public Culture in Post-Reformation England* (Ithaca: Cornell University Press, 1994), which historically situate Arden as a landowning gentleman.

onciled with his rival. More important, even in these scenes he reacts to rather than initiates aggression. His plots, if they can be called that, are counterplots. Both in his threats and in his eagerness to reconcile with his rival, Arden cooperates in Alice's and Mosby's schemes, which depend on his having these responses.

Although he knows about his wife's adultery, he never knows that she, her lover, his servants, his tenants, and hired killers are all assiduously attempting to kill him. Unlike Prospero, who disrupts the betrothal masque at the memory of a "foul conspiracy," Arden never knows about the conspiracies against him until the moment when they at last succeed and he dies. Yet even if only as a target of assaults, Arden remains curiously central. When he retreats to London, for instance, the conspirators follow him there.

Nondramatic versions of the murder of Arden of Faversham had presented him as a compromised, even villainous, figure. As numerous critics have commented, the nondramatic accounts emphasize Arden's complicity while the play depicts Arden ambiguously.[28] Holinshed's account of the murder, for instance, presents Arden as condoning Alice's adultery because of his own greed and ambition. Although the play suppresses such overt condemnation of Arden, it offers no alternative explanation as to why he tolerates an adultery he suspects or why he simply abandons his wife and home. While Holinshed gives Arden his own agenda, a master's plot driven by acquisitiveness and ambition, the play suppresses that possible plot and the agency it would grant to Arden and instead plays out the multiple plots of the subordinates. In contrast to other versions of the story that make Arden an agent and a protagonist by making him culpable, the play enacts how a master can remain central without engaging in either positive or negative action, simply by holding the place that stands for privilege and power, the place for which his subordinates compete.

In the play, Arden remains a vaguely implicated figure. As a cuckold,

---

28. Leanore Lieblein observes that "while the dramatist . . . initially reinforces sympathy for the wronged husband, he takes other measures to qualify it" ("The Context of Murder in English Domestic Plays, 1590–1610," *Studies in English Literature* 23 [1983]: 181–96, esp. p. 184). Belsey argues that "two versions of Arden—as loving husband and as rapacious landlord—coexist equally uneasily in the play" (*Subject of Tragedy*, p. 132). Both Orlin's and Whigham's current works-in-progress, like Wine's introduction, attend to the particularities of the historical Arden's social status and the play's biting commentary on social and economic change. Their careful attention to detail frees me to direct my attentions elsewhere.

he, like the husbands who became targets of cuckold jokes and popular shaming rituals, is presented as responsible for his disordered household and his own humiliation, as diminished and compromised by his wife's insubordination. Arden's servant, Michael, ruminates on Arden's complicity and its role in his victimization: "Ah, harmless Arden, how, how hast thou misdone / That thus thy gentle life is levelled at?" (3.188–89). Michael considers Arden compromised by the very fact that his "gentle life is levelled at" by his own wife, servants, tenants, and inferiors. He is most compromised by the fact that he abandons his place in the household and the local community. Absenting himself from his "room" (4.29), his roles as husband, master, and landowning gentleman, and the physical locations through which those positions of power and prestige manifest themselves, he absents himself from the master plot to become the central figure of the subordinate plots, a "block [that] shall be removed" (1.137).

Since Arden remains central as an obstacle and the focus of prodigious murderous energies, the play emphasizes his significance simply as master. Even when absent, he is powerfully present at all times, represented by the chair at the head of the table and the place in the conjugal bed to which Mosby aspires. Even after his death Arden lingers, staking out a place of importance. His blood supernaturally asserts his presence and incriminates his killers: Susan worries that "The blood cleaveth to the ground and will not out," while Alice complains that "The more I strive the more the blood appears" (14.255, 257). In the Epilogue, Arden's friend Franklin reports the story of an incriminating print of Arden's body, a detail that also appears in Holinshed's account of the crime; Franklin uses the story to comment on the role that Arden's avarice played in his death.

> But this above the rest is to be noted:
> Arden lay murdered in that plot of ground
> Which he by force and violence held from Reede;
> And in the grass his body's print was seen
> Two years and more after the deed was done.
> (Epilogue 9–13)

By closing with this reference to Arden's lingering presence, and to a complicity that does not wholly fit with the previous characterization of him, the play thus presents Arden as both collaborator in his own death and victim of villainous subordinates, as both implicated and innocent.

This mysterious mapping of Arden's avarice on the land (like the stain of his blood that Susan and Alice cannot scrape from the floor even with their fingernails) demonstrates the tenacity of his presence and the impossibility of displacing him despite his failures and the extraordinary energy of his subordinates. Although Arden anguished over Mosby's usurpation of his "room" and various tenants' challenges to his ownership of the abbey lands, the stains that represent him reassert possession over both his lands and his house. Just as the "victim's body sometimes resisted" the control of public executions by means of its "magical reaction to death," as Karen Cunningham argues, the supernatural markings of Arden's place demonstrate the ability of the victim to assert himself even after death.[29] The play describes the limits both of Arden's power and of his subordinates' power, of social position and of determined, transgressive action. The blood stains and body print reveal that the subject position of the landowner and master remains powerful no matter how inadequate the holder of that position. Radiating into the ground, permeating the floor, the imprint of Arden's dead body suggests that his power was largely symbolic; Arden always marks out a spot, rather than acts. Exploring the gap between where he stood and who he was, the play scrutinizes the complexities of master status as well as those of subordinate status.

Around this "care-oppressed," often-absent master revolves an excess of frenzied, industrious, and inventive subordinates. By my count, eight attempts on Arden's life are made or contemplated: Mosby hopes to use a poisoned "counterfeit" or portrait; Alice poisons Arden's broth; Green, Black Will, and Shakebag attempt to kill him on a London street near Saint Paul's, then in his London lodgings, later on a road from Rochester, and then in a foggy mist; Mosby and Alice try to provoke Arden into violence so that they can retaliate; Black Will proposes that he, Shakebag, and Greene will dog Arden through the fair, stab him, and steal away; finally, all of the conspirators descend on Arden in his own home and kill him. In other scenes, Alice enlists Michael and, later,

---

29. Karen Cunningham, "Renaissance Execution and Marlovian Elocution: The Drama of Death," *PMLA* 105 (1990): 209–22, esp. p. 212.

Greene (whom she instructs to hire killers) in her plans to eliminate her husband. The subordinates' plots are thus *the* plot.

This staggering multiplicity contributes to the play's confusing genre. As either a tragedy, however domestic and thus diminished, or a document about social disorder and cultural anxiety, the play is deeply problematic. It takes so long to kill Arden that it is easy to root for the conspirators (Why won't he die?) rather than being appalled by their assault on their superior. Repeatedly foiled in their attempts, even the professional killers become exasperated, wondering, "Did ever man escape as thou hast done?" (9.134) and "When was I so long in killing a man?" (14.1). The attempts are also foiled in slapstick ways: Arden tastes the poison in his broth and spurns it; as Black Will lies in wait, a "prentice" accidentally drops a stall door on his head; Black Will and Shakebag cannot find their victim in the foggy mist.

The humor that creeps into the play and confuses its genre stems not only from these slapstick failures and endless deferrals, this frustrated industry, but from the traditional associations between lower-class characters—their aspirations and designs—and comic form.[30] As the lower-class characters and their numerous plots surge out of the substructure to take over the main structure (when they refuse to be subordinated), the play inherits from them an uneasily comic feel. The play moves outside of the genres that give shape to experience in its attempts to tell a true story about a local event, to represent life as confusing and generically mixed, and to describe the operations of Providence as disorganized and obscure. It questions the social order and dramatic forms that achieve cohesion by excluding or subordinating the story of petty treason.[31]

30. Renaissance critical theory ordained that tragedy should depict the public actions of royal figures who move from contentment to despair. In contrast, comedy was supposed to depict the private lives of "meaner" characters who move from confusion or danger to concord. The speech of the characters was to reflect their social position and moral prestige; tragic characters spoke in grandiloquent poetry, comic characters spoke in more familiar, unadorned prose. Domestic tragedies such as *Arden of Faversham* obviously defy such generic expectations. On Renaissance generic theory, see Madeleine Doran, *Endeavors of Art: A Study of Form in Elizabethan Drama* (Madison: University of Wisconsin Press, 1954); and Martin Mueller, *Children of Oedipus and Other Essays on the Imitation of Greek Tragedy, 1550–1800* (Toronto: University of Toronto Press, 1980).

31. Wine argues that the play's structure resembles "the episodic and unstructured quality of life itself" and compels the viewer to witness "how thin the boundary is between comedy and tragedy in men's lives" (*Arden of Faversham*, pp. lxxv, lxvii).

Despite its humor, *Arden of Faversham* is not a comedy; its plot revolves around petty treason, a crime against the social order. Nor is it Arden's tragedy; however implicated, he is a victim and, as we have seen, a social position, a spot, rather than an agent.[32] Nor is it the tragedy of Alice and Mosby, though both have the potential to be the play's protagonists. In enlisting collaborators and devising murder schemes, Alice so aggressively demands her role as protagonist that the hired killers, Black Will and Shakebag, have to remind her that they are the assassins: "Tush, get you gone! 'Tis we must do the deed" (14.140). As early as the first scene, Alice and Mosby quarrel over who is in charge of the murder plans. If Alice is a protagonist, she is not the only one, surrounded as she is with fellow subordinates and conspirators. Because all subordinates are not equal, as Alice's acrimonious exchanges with Mosby about the disparities in their social status reveal, the contests between the lovers are bitter and the outcome uncertain.

Since, in this play, to be the master is to be embattled, the only way that Mosby can attempt to distinguish himself from all the other plotting subordinates is by imagining them as plotting against *him* (scene 13). In his fantasy of assuming Arden's place and then killing Alice and the other conspirators, Mosby suggests a vision of a future without any resolution of conflict and violence.[33] Even for a prospective master as brutal as Mosby, the master's position can be construed only as insecure and defensive. Furthermore, the subordinates and conspirators can be understood as agents and protagonists only in negative, transient terms:

32. Most critics who work on Renaissance tragedy agree that, while conceptions of heroism were changing and diversifying in Renaissance England, the hero remained central to tragic form. On the shift from a heroism of public action in Elizabethan tragedy to a heroism of private endurance in Jacobean tragedy, see Mary Beth Rose, *Expense of Spirit*, chap. 3; on the problematization of human agency and the hero's increasing accountability for his own fate even in *de casibus* tragedy, see Doran, *Endeavors of Art*, esp. p. 121, and Willard Farnham, *The Medieval Heritage of Elizabethan Tragedy* (Oxford: Blackwell, 1963), esp. pp. 127–28; on the concepts of heroism available in the Renaissance, see Reuben A. Brower, *Hero and Saint: Shakespeare and the Graeco-Roman Heroic Tradition* (Oxford: Oxford University Press, 1971), and Richard S. Ide, *Possessed with Greatness: The Heroic Tragedies of Chapman and Shakespeare* (Chapel Hill: University of North Carolina Press, 1980); and on the disappearance of a central hero from Jacobean tragedy and the consequences for the form, see Franco Moretti, "The Great Eclipse: Tragic Form as the Deconsecration of Sovereignty," trans. David Miller, in *Signs Taken for Wonders: Essays in the Sociology of Literary Forms* (London: Verso, 1983), pp. 42–82.

33. See Belsey's discussion of the "new and insidious forms of control" that Mosby envisions (*Subject of Tragedy*, pp. 144–48).

Their authority resides only in violence. Having achieved protagonist status by killing the master, Alice and Mosby do not themselves achieve tragic heroism. Since *Arden* attempts to dramatize petty treason yet destabilize the hierarchical relations that define it, the result is a play with no hero, no master plot, and no identifiable form. The play suggests that when wife, husband, lover, and servants are all subjects with powerful stories and no one figure, subject position, or narrative is privileged, then in the battle that ensues, no one wins.

In *Arden of Faversham,* all of the characters' frenzied aspirations come to nothing; the conspirators accomplish only their own deaths. Although Mosby has imagined that, at last, he will be "sole ruler of mine own" (8.36) and Alice has imagined self-government and self-possession ("he shall be mine"; I "am to rule myself"), we last see them accusing one another ("Fie upon women!"; "but for thee I had never been strumpet" [18.34,14]) and heading for the scaffold, divided as much by their success in achieving their goal as by apprehension. With Arden dead, the cast has nothing left to do; the play's community has no purpose. Arden, it turns out, was important after all. But the fact that *eight* conspirators, including the innocent Bradshaw, go to the gallows for the murder of one implicated man casts doubt on such justice as excessive and lopsided.

The Castlehaven Trial: The Masterful Deployment of the Petty Treason Narrative

The unknown author of *Arden of Faversham* pushes the process of narrating petty treason as far as it will go by putting the subordinates at the center of the story. In another infamous case, which occurred almost one hundred years after the actual murder of Arden and which focused on a figure much farther up the social scale, the husband and master is at the center of a scandal and of the literary and legal attempts to narrate and redress it. The trial of Mervyn, Lord Audley, earl of Castlehaven, reveals that the same ideologies structuring dramatic plots also structure the dramas of the courtroom; it also shows how social structures and literary forms are mutually constitutive. Events, as they survive in texts, can follow scripts that, like the more conventionally literary texts they resemble (such as plays), participate in shaping and articulating ideologies of order.

In 1631, the earl of Castlehaven (1592–1631) was indicted for a variety of sexual offenses: for soliciting a servant, Giles Broadway, to rape his wife, the countess of Castlehaven, and helping Broadway to do so by holding the countess down; and for engaging in sodomy with another of his servants, Lawrence Fitzpatrick. In the course of the trial, Castlehaven was also accused of voyeurism, sodomy with other servants, and promoting sexual relations between his twelve-year-old stepdaughter, Elizabeth, and a favorite servant, Skipwith. Elizabeth was also Castlehaven's daughter-in-law, as the wife of his son and heir, James Touchet. In November 1630, this son, then aged fifteen, lodged a complaint against his father with the king and thus initiated the process of investigation that ended in the indictment, trial, conviction, and execution of his father. At the trial, the wife, stepdaughter/daughter-in-law, and servants all testified against the earl. The son, who did not testify but whom the earl accused of conspiring against him, ultimately inherited the estate; however, he never lived with his wife, Elizabeth, again. The two servants, Broadway and Fitzpatrick, who were indicted with the earl, were executed. Thus, the subordinates—son, wife, and servants—"won" the case, but those who supposedly participated in the indicted activities, whether consensually or not, and on whose testimony the prosecution depended were ultimately criminalized and resubordinated so that hierarchical, patriarchal order could be restored. While *Arden of Faversham* ends with an empty house, the story of the earl of Castlehaven concludes with one master replacing another, a son sitting in his father's place.

Like the humbler and less titillating story of Arden's murder, the story of this trial was retold for more than half a century after it took place. In the various accounts of the earl of Castlehaven's 1631 trial, the earl commands attention as the accused. According to his subordinates and accusers, the master's plot in this case is one of flagrant disregard for cultural norms of masculinity, heterosexuality, aristocratic privilege, property, and inheritance. In the narratives of Castlehaven's trial, his sexual transgressions, on which scholarship about the scandal has focused, are simultaneously represented as "unnatural" and as assaults on cultural constructions of masculinity and aristocracy. These narratives express particular concern over the earl's desire that his son's wife should conceive an heir not by his son but by Skipwith, the earl's favorite servant, and over his lavish gifts of money and land to his servants. By accusing the earl of opening the aristocratic female body to servants—by prising open his twelve-year-old daughter-in-law's body with oil and "art," holding his wife down as she is raped, or marrying his daughter to Amptil, one of his pages and lovers—the accounts of the trial expose the significant role of women's bodies in securing, or undermining, aristocratic masculinity.[34]

Dwelling as they do on Castlehaven's transgressions, the various accounts of the trial reveal the contradictions not only of subordinate status but of master status and the obligations and conditions under which even a figure as highly placed as the earl maintained his exalted social position and authority. Like *Arden,* the Castlehaven trial narratives explore the gap between social prestige and domestic authority, on the one hand, and the individual who attempts to fulfill the responsibilities of privilege, on the other. The attorney in the earl's trial articulates this gap for the peers who try him, reminding them that "the prisoner is honourable, the crimes dishonourable against which hee is indicted."[35] Like *Arden,* too, these trial narratives represent the chaos that emerges from that gap.

Focusing on the strategies that the earl of Castlehaven uses to defend himself, I explore how he attempts to challenge the legitimacy of the whole trial by drawing on the narrative of petty treason; he accuses his wife, servants, and son of plotting against him.[36] This narrative is so

34. As Bruce R. Smith points out, "What angered the lords most was not the *sexual* crimes that Castlehaven committed against the persons of his wife and servants but the *political* crime he attempted against the social order of which the lords were a part and over which they presided" (*Homosexual Desire in Shakespeare's England: A Cultural Poetics* [Chicago: University of Chicago Press, 1991], p. 52). See also B. R. Burg, "Ho Hum, Another Work of the Devil: Buggery and Sodomy in Early Stuart England," *Journal of Homosexuality* 6 (1980/81): 69–78, esp. pp. 72–74. On the complex cultural meanings of sodomy, see Gregory W. Bredbeck, *Sodomy and Interpretation: Marlowe to Milton* (Ithaca: Cornell University Press, 1991).

35. *The Arraignment and Conviction of Mervin Lord Audley* (London, 1642), p. 4, hereafter cited as *The Arraignment.* See also *Cobbett's Complete Collection of State Trials,* ed. Thomas B. Howell, 33 vols. (London: R. Bagshaw, 1809–1826), vol. 3, cols. 401–26, esp. col. 408; hereafter cited as *State Trials.*

36. Despite his privileged social status, the earl of Castlehaven, like anyone else tried for felony in this period, was denied the assistance of counsel and therefore was responsible

compelling that even a man perceived as a flamboyantly erring husband and master can attempt to marshall it to his own defense, playing on the fears of his auditors and judges.[37]

Throughout the proceedings, the earl challenges the prosecution's reliance on the testimony of his subordinates, mistakenly assuming that as subordinates they cannot incriminate him. When he attempts to discredit his wife as a witness on the basis of his subsumption of her and her sexual laxity, he is sharply informed that a wife can testify against her husband in criminal causes, "especially where she is the party grieved," that is, the victim of the crime. He is also informed that the crime against his wife is a rape even if she *is* "of evil fame": "If the party were of no chaste life but a whore, yet there may bee a ravishment"; "A whore may be ravished, and it is felony to doe it."[38] Furthermore, the lord chief justice and the lord high steward inform the earl that "persons of mean Extraction, and of no Estates" can give evidence against "a Baron" and that, unless they have been "convicted recusants," Catholics such as the servant Fitzpatrick may also testify.[39] The judges in this case thus grant the earl's wife and servants the legal status to make a case against him. Although his dependents' temporary authority must later be rescinded—the countess receives a pardon from the king and the servants who testify are executed—the earl expresses horrified disbelief at the inversions of class and gender hierarchies. Just as Prospero counters Caliban's accusations of usurpation with the accusation

---

for his own defense. See J. H. Baker, "Criminal Courts and Procedure in Common Law, 1550–1800," in *Crime in England, 1550–1800*, ed. J. S. Cockburn (Princeton: Princeton University Press, 1977), pp. 26, 36–37.

37. The texts purporting to record the earl of Castlehaven's trial that I have consulted are: *The Arraignment* (1642); *The Trial of the Lord Audley, Earl of Castlehaven, for Inhumanely Causing His Own Wife to Be Ravished and for Buggery* (London, 1679), hereafter cited as *The Trial*; *The Tryal and Condemnation of Mervin, Lord Audley Earl of Castlehaven* (London, 1699), reprinted in *Sodomy Trials: Seven Documents*, ed. Randolph Trumbach (New York: Garland, 1986), hereafter cited as *The Tryal and Condemnation*; and *State Trials*, ed. Howell. There are other printed accounts of the trial, as well as manuscript sources, that I have not consulted. For the most part, I quote from *The Arraignment* simply because it is the earliest published account; wherever possible I also cite in the notes parallel passages from other accounts. For my purposes, the disparities among the versions are not significant.

38. *The Arraignment*, p. 10; see also pp. 5, 11. Also see *The Trial*, p. 7; *The Tryal and Condemnation*, pp. 11, 23; and *State Trials*, ed. Howell, vol. 3, col. 414.

39. *The Tryal and Condemnation*, p. 24. See also *The Arraignment*, p. 11; *The Trial*, p. 6; and *State Trials*, ed. Howell, vol. 3, col. 415.

of rape, the earl of Castlehaven counters accusations of rape and sodomy with accusations of petty treason.

After attempting to challenge the right of his wife and servants to testify against him, Castlehaven finally protests his innocence and laments his situation by placing himself in the role of beleaguered patriarch familiar from accounts of petty treason.

1. Woe to that man, whose Wife should be a Witness against him!
2. Woe to that man, whose Son should persecute him, and conspire his death!
3. Woe to that man, whose Servants should be allowed Witnesses to take away his life!

And he willed the lords [his peers, before whom he was on trial] to take this into their consideration; for it might be some of their cases, or the case of any gentleman of worth, that keeps a footman or other, whose wife is weary of her husband, or his son arrived to full age, that would draw his servants to conspire his father's death.[40]

The earl here attempts to convince the jury of his peers to identify with him by attributing the accusations against him to a conspiracy against

40. *State Trials*, ed. Howell, col. 415. Also see *Historical Collections: The Second Part*, ed. John Rushworth, 2 vols. (London, 1721), 2: 100–101. Cynthia Herrup has pointed out to me that the 1679 account of the trial (*The Trial*) is the first to present a full-blown petty treason subplot. In *The Arraignment* (1642), the earl claims that his son "would have lands" and his wife "a younger husband, and therefore they plotted his death" (p. 11). In *The Trial* (1679), the earl claims that his wife and son "had plotted together against his Life" (p. 7) and, further, he emphasizes the implications of such a plot for a patriarchal order: "Lastly, He beseeched the Lords to consider what a dangerous preparative it was to this Kingdom, that a mans Wife and his Son, gaping after his Succession, the Devil and wicked Servants complotting together, might bereave the greatest Peer of his Life" (p. 8). In *The Tryal and Condemnation* (1699), the earl says that "if a Wife of such a Character, may be allowed to be a witness against her Husband, no Man is safe, when his Wife dislikes him, and would have a younger Husband" (p. 22). All these accounts, then, present the earl as using the same strategy of self-defense that I examine, although they do not all record his three "woes," which is the most elaborate articulation of a subordinates' plot and its implications. A 1708 text, *The Case of Sodomy, in the Tryal of Mervin Lord Audley, Earl of Castlehaven*, which went into multiple editions, including 1710 and 1719, also emphasizes the earl's insistence that his subordinates plotted against him.

Long after the earl's trial, in the 1640s and early 1650s, the earl's sister, Eleanor Touchet Davies, Lady Douglas, published a number of texts defending her brother. In one, *The Word of God, to the Citie of London, from the Lady Eleanor; of the Earle of Castlehaven* (1644), Lady Eleanor accuses the countess of Castlehaven and her own brother Ferdinando of conspiring against the earl.

patriarchal authority rather than to his own failures as a patriarch. The transgressions of which he is accused have already destabilized the hierarchies that he wishes to resurrect to defend himself.[41] In the view of those who try him, he has scandalously coerced his servants to take up the master's position and he cannot resume it.

Both the earl's machinations and the complex judicial process as represented in accounts of the trial manipulate the accountability of the subordinates in this case. According to the countess's testimony, her husband attempted to persuade her to have sex with various servants by arguing that, as a married woman, she was *not* an agent in her own right: He said that "her body was his, and that if she loved him, she must love *Antil* [Amptil, the servant who married the earl's daughter], and that if shee lay with any man with his consent, it was not her fault, but his."[42] The earl thus manipulates the logic of wifely coverture to construe sexual infidelity as a form of obedience. According to the trial narrative constructed out of the countess's testimony and the earl's rebuttals, the earl first absorbs all responsibility into himself, in order to enable complete sexual license—all his sexual partners are his subordinates, and not only can he make them do whatever he wishes in whatever combinations but he can watch. Then he attempts to reverse this process by displacing responsibility onto them once he is caught in the act. Although the peers find this shockingly unacceptable, the

41. I am grateful to Cynthia Herrup for clarifying many of the details of the case for me. Barbara Breasted first brought the Castlehaven case to the attention of scholars of seventeenth-century English literature in "*Comus* and the Castlehaven Scandal," *Milton Studies* 3 (1971): 201–24. Her essay remains the most thorough account of the many texts relating to the case, which included multiple accounts of the trial, poems, and correspondence. Other discussions of the case include: Alan Bray, *Homosexuality in Renaissance England* (London: Gay Men's Press, 1982); Caroline Bingham, "Seventeenth-Century Attitudes Toward Deviant Sex," *Journal of Interdisciplinary History* 1 (1971): 447–72; and Rosemary Karmelich Mundhenk, "Dark Scandal and the Sun-Clad Power of Chastity: The Historical Milieu of Milton's *Comus*," *Studies in English Literature* 15 (1975): 141–52. In her exploration of another topical controversy related to Milton's *Comus*, Leah Marcus also refers to the Castlehaven scandal ("The Milieu of Milton's *Comus*: Judicial Reform at Ludlow and the Problem of Sexual Assault," *Criticism* 25 [1983]: 293–327). None of the existing scholarship on this case delves into the rich insight the trial narratives provide of the complex interrelations of gender, class, and sexuality in this period. Herrup's work-in-progress on the trial, "Law, Sex, and Patriarchy: The Trials of the Second Earl of Castlehaven," will be the first to trace, through manuscript and printed versions, how the story changed over time in the process of retelling.

42. *The Arraignment*, p. 8. Also see *The Trial*, p. 4; *The Tryal and Condemnation*, p. 13; and *State Trials*, ed. Howell, vol. 3, col. 411.

trial itself follows a similar pattern of removing agency from the subordinates and then reconferring it on them. As in *Arden of Faversham,* the two plots imply one another: To dramatize insubordinate dependents, you need an implicated master; to prosecute an inadequate master, you need to construct implicated subordinates.

Castlehaven's strategies of self-defense reveal how the provocative, disturbing story—or plot—of petty treason might function as a cultural resource. Yet the courtroom so controls the proceedings, often silencing or ignoring the earl, that his account of a subordinate plot is contained by a more complex legal fiction that manipulates both the earl and the subordinates, their accountability, and their testimony in the interests of restoring order. The court briefly empowers the earl's subordinates in order to convict him and then immediately holds those very subordinates accountable. Although the narratives of the earl's trial construct the wife and servants as victims, once the desired closure has been achieved and order restored, they must be resubordinated to the order that they have helped to reconstitute. The countess's mother, Alice, countess dowager of Derby, spent months securing a pardon from the king for her daughter, actions which make nonsense of the trial's construction of the countess as a rape victim. Barbara Breasted recounts how the countess dowager held her daughter and granddaughter responsible for their roles in Castlehaven's sexual dramas: "From the first, she refused to take them into her home until the king had pardoned them, and until there was some hope of their reform."[43] In addition, the two servants who were co-defendants, indicted with the earl, and on whose testimony the trial depended, were also convicted. To their own amazement, Broadway was convicted for rape and Fitzpatrick for sodomy; both were executed. Paradoxically, the legal process resubordinates them by interpreting them as agents rather than victims and punishing them for their complicity in their master's social and sexual inversions. For instance, the lord chief justice informs Fitzpatrick that he is a "voluntary prostitute" because he "was not only of understanding and years to know the heinousness of the sin, but also of strength to have withstood his lord."[44] The servant is thus found guilty for not having disobeyed his master.

43. Breasted, "*Comus* and the Castlehaven Scandal," p. 214.
44. *State Trials,* ed. Howell, vol. 3, col. 420.

On the scaffold, Fitzpatrick confesses that "his lordship had both buggered him, and he his lordship." He thus undermines the fastidious decorum of the accusations in the earl's trial, during which both accused and witnesses insist that no penetration ever took place and that the sexual acts between. the earl and his male servants consisted only of "emission." The crime of sodomy is constructed as "the use of the body, so far as to emit thereupon," that is, the use of a man's body "as the body of a woman." By suggesting for the only time in the proceedings that the earl had allowed his own body to be used "as that of a woman," Fitzpatrick offers another perspective on how the earl abdicated the master's "position" (as heterosexual penetrator) and repositioned himself in sexually and socially subversive ways (as penetrated or as voyeur).[45]

The narrative of petty treason, which the accused evokes to displace blame onto his accusers, and which the court, with Prospero-like confidence and invention, temporarily and craftily imitates, is recuperated by criminalizing the subordinates: executing the servants and pardoning the wife. As in *Arden of Faversham,* the subordinates all go down with the master whether they are at the center or he is, whether they transgress or he does. These texts suggest that in early modern English culture it was only imaginable that masters and dependents could thrive within conventional social structures and literary forms and their subordinations. In these various representations of petty treason, any pressure from either above or below so destabilizes social structure and dramatic form that they collapse. However much Prospero's power is questioned and qualified, it is only in *The Tempest*'s representation of the supernaturally powerful master, who decisively subordinates the plot of his rebellious servant, that the story of attempted petty treason can end well for anyone, master or subordinate.

Although legal and theatrical texts represent the problematic figure

---

45. See ibid., vol. 3, cols. 422, 414, 413. Bruce R. Smith argues that, in Renaissance England, opprobrium attached particularly to the "passive" partner in homosexual acts, that is, the one placed in the "inferior" position associated with women, boys, and servants. On sexual relations between masters and servants, and how "Renaissance Englishmen, like the ancient Greeks and Romans, eroticized the power distinctions that set one male above another in their society," see Smith, *Homosexual Desire,* pp. 193–97; and Bray, *Homosexuality in Renaissance England,* pp. 48–51. See also David Halperin, *One Hundred Years of Homosexuality and Other Essays on Greek Love* (New York: Routledge, 1990), pp. 22–23, 29–35.

of the wife as both victim and agent as may suit social and dramatic structures, they acknowledge the irreconcilable contradictions of wifely status even as they exploit them. *Arden* constructs Alice as playing a victim when she wants to displace blame onto her husband or lover thereby acting to reshape her possibilities throughout the play. At its conclusion, the play, like the judicial process it reenacts, holds her accountable for her actions; she is an agent in order to be punished. More explicitly and unambiguously, the earl of Castlehaven, the king, the peers who try the earl, and the texts recounting that trial all construct the countess as a victim or agent as it suits them. In the statements attributed to the earl, he first enjoins her to be a grotesque caricature of the *feme covert,* a will-less puppet; then he accuses her of being a lustful, greedy schemer. The legal process that encompasses both the trial and her mother's subsequent suit for a pardon first positions the countess as a victim so that she can testify against and convict the earl, then as an agent so that she can be held accountable, pardoned, and reinscribed within social and sexual hierarchies.

The three texts I have discussed also explore the gap between positions of power and the weak, inadequate individuals who hold those positions: who withdraw into their studies rather than fulfill ducal obligations, retreat to London rather than manage their estates and govern their wives, or use sexuality to undermine rather than sustain lineage and inheritance. All three masters physically withdraw from their superior positions—on the throne and in receiving rooms, at the head of the table and in the conjugal bed, or as the heterosexual penetrator. Just as an empty chair could represent the king or queen at treason trials, these abdicated places represent the symbolic power of certain roles quite apart from the actions or character of those who fill them.[46]

Unlike the formalism that Carolyn Porter faults for "remarginaliz[ing]" both the social and the 'others' whose voices it should make

---

46. I am thinking particularly of Mary Stuart's trial for treason, at which two thrones were strategically placed to symbolize the relative power of the rival queens: "At the upper end of the chamber was placed a Chair of estate for the queen of England, under a cloth of estate. Over-against it, below and more remote, near the transom or beam that ran across the room, stood a chair for the queen of Scots" (*State Trials,* ed. Howell, vol. 1, esp. col. 1172). Although Mary Stuart occupied the chair provided for her, Elizabeth's chair remained empty, a vivid reminder that her authority eclipsed Mary's even in her absence.

audible," attention to the roles of social, domestic, and literary structures in privileging some stories and subordinating others helps us not to reproduce those hierarchies but to understand how and why they operated. In early modern England, there was not a "continuous, but continuously heterogeneous discursive field in which dominant and subjugated voices occupy the same plane" but rather structures that located certain groups and their stories upstairs and other groups and their stories downstairs. In order to move to the leveled social text to which Porter aspires, we must first understand the hierarchical social texts of the past, the complex ways in which they ascribe agency to figures such as wives and servants, and how these hierarchical social texts persist in the literary forms that we still value and use.[47]

In simultaneously narrating stories of irresponsible, brutal, or disaffected masters and of energetically insubordinate dependents, these three seemingly disparate texts suggest that social position is not wholly determining, that there is space for individual agency, although that agency is restricted and criminalized. These texts restore social and aesthetic order—on the scaffold, in the courtroom, and on the stage—by subordinating dependents and their stories through violent punishment and death, but they also grant a place to those subordinates and their plots. In doing so, these texts open up the possibility of other stories, other social structures, other literary forms.

47. Carolyn Porter, "History and Literature: 'After the New Historicism'," *New Literary History* 21 (1990): 253–72, esp. p. 265.

III. REVOLUTIONS, PETTY TYRANNY, AND THE MURDEROUS HUSBAND

The commonplace analogy of household and Commonwealth suggests that representations of domestic authority and obedience would change in the mid and late seventeenth century in tandem with reconceptualizations of the relation of citizen to government and of the subject's right to civil disobedience. Indeed, they did. Although murderous husbands remained two to three times more common than murderous wives throughout the century, popular representations shift their attention from the murderous wife to the murderous husband only in the second half of the century. While before 1650 representations of murderous wives outnumber those of murderous husbands, after 1650 the opposite is true. For instance, I have examined thirty-two accounts of wives who murder their husbands, only four of which were published after 1650. In contrast, I have examined twenty accounts of husbands who murder their wives, only two of which were published before 1650.[1]

1. In Chapter 1, I cite eleven pamphlets, two ballads, and one play about actual cases in which wives murder their husbands. In addition, I have consulted two ballads, one

Just as popular accounts construct a wife's murder of her husband as petty treason, they construct a husband's murder of his wife as petty tyranny. Yet petty tyranny was not a legal category, nor did the law distinguish wife murder from other kinds of murder. Even when pamphlets or ballads present husbandly excesses as irresponsible and analogous to tyranny, they do not represent this petty tyranny as threatening social order in the same ways that petty treason did. Certainly early modern culture did not encourage men to kill their wives, or dismiss the significance of such crimes: Men who were convicted of murdering their dependents paid for this crime with their lives, and pamphlets and ballads increasingly disseminated their stories as the century waned.[2]

---

play, and three tracts. The pamphlets have the following dates: 1583, 1591, 1592, 1604, 1609, 1635, 1641, [1675], 1678, [1687], 1688. The ballads date from 1616, 1628 (2), and 1629. The plays date from 1592 and 1599. There are also five prose accounts and a ballad about the Arden of Faversham case and five prose accounts and a ballad on the Sanders case, dramatized as *A Warning for Fair Women*. In contrast, I have found thirteen popular narratives about husbands who kill their wives, many of which are brief—broadsides rather than pamphlets—and seven ballads. Accounts of murderous husbands appear in fewer genres, are less detailed, and, most significantly, proliferate only in the second half of the century. The dates for the pamphlets I have consulted are: 1598, 1607, 1653 (2), 1655, 1677, 1679, 1680 (3), 1682, 1684, 1690. The ballads date from: 1685, 1690, 1695, 1697 (3), and circa late seventeenth century. Only two of the twenty accounts occur before 1650, while seven occur between 1680 and 1690 alone. In contrast, I have found twenty-eight plays, ballads, and pamphlets about wives killing their husbands written before 1650. I am not interested in attempting a statistical survey of these materials; the arbitrary survival of such ephemera would qualify any conclusions that could be drawn. Nevertheless, I want to convey a sense of what I have found.

In her own work on popular representations of spouse killing, Joy Wiltenburg sees the same trend. See her *Disorderly Women and Female Power in the Street Literature of Early Modern England and Germany* (Charlottesville: University of Virginia Press, 1992), chap. 9, esp. pp. 214, 221. By the eighteenth century, shaming rituals had similarly shifted their attention from disorderly women to wife-beaters. See Elizabeth Pleck, *Domestic Tyranny: The Making of Social Policy against Family Violence from Colonial Times to the Present* (New York: Oxford University Press, 1987), p. 233, n. 37, and chaps. 1 and 2; and David Underdown, "The Taming of the Scold: The Enforcement of Patriarchal Authority in Early Modern England," in *Order and Disorder in Early Modern England*, ed. Anthony Fletcher and John Stevenson (Cambridge: Cambridge University Press, 1985), pp. 116–36, esp. p. 121.

2. Since, according to Susan Amussen, the nonlethal "mistreatment of servants or wives created disorder through a failure of responsibility," church courts took such abuses seriously (*An Ordered Society: Gender and Class in Early Modern England* [Oxford: Basil Blackwell, 1988], p. 167). J. A. Sharpe, on the other hand, argues that *killing* servants was sometimes treated leniently. Sharpe's work with Essex assizes reveals that of the forty-four persons accused of killing servants or apprentices at those assizes, only five were found guilty (three men, two women), and only one seems to have been executed: "The explanation for this must be that judges and juries were convinced that if employers

However, neither the legal nor the literary representations of such crimes emphasize their significance outside of the home or beyond the lives of those involved. In contrast to the petty traitor, who overturns the hierarchy that is supposed to govern domestic relations, the domestic tyrant grotesquely caricatures his role, expanding the parameters of the patriarch's authority rather than openly challenging domestic hierarchy.

Revolution and Changing Domestic Ideologies

Before addressing the different concerns of narratives of murderous husbands, I would like to clarify that political upheaval and debates over tyranny, treason, and rebellion did not *immediately* generate reconsiderations of petty treason or endorsements of domestic revolution. Although all but the staunchest Royalists reconsidered the sources and implementations of authority during the 1640s and 1650s, those in power did not cease to value order. Parliament tried Charles I for treason; throughout the Protectorate, Cromwell and his council tried numerous people for sedition, libel, and treason.[3] As political upheaval made manifest changing conceptions of authority and obedience, domestic order seems to have become more rather than less important. Historians such as Christopher Hill and Lawrence Stone argue that the nonaristocratic Protestant household functioned both to subvert patriarchal structures and to support them. Familial Bible study promoted independent thought and dissension, and the "spiritualized" household could grow into the independent congregation. Empowering the male head of household with responsibility for his household's moral welfare increased his authority over his subordinates.[4] Wifely subordination

---

were deterred from beating their charges by death sentences when correction ended in fatality, godly discipline would be eroded" ("Domestic Homicide in Early Modern England," *The Historical Journal* 24.1 [1981]: 29–48, esp. p. 38). Although heads of household were expected to use their power responsibly, abuses could and did occur and, in most cases, Sharpe's research suggests that social order was better served by ignoring those abuses than by interfering with household governance.

3. See the proceedings from the Commonwealth in *Cobbett's Complete Collection of State Trials,* ed. Thomas B. Howell, 33 vols. (London: R. Bagshaw, 1809–1826), vol. 5; hereafter cited as *State Trials.*

4. Christopher Hill, *Society and Puritanism in Pre-Revolutionary England,* 2d ed. (New York: Schocken, 1967), p. 457. See also Lawrence Stone, "Family History in the 1980s:

remained, in Lawrence Stone's words, "the main guarantee of law and order in the body politic," a guarantee especially needed in a time of political and social upheaval, even by the minority involved in such radical sects as the Levellers.[5]

Although radical sects pursued the implications of the spiritual equality of all believers, Keith Thomas argues that "as soon as they took on institutional form even the most radical sects became conservative as regards the organisation and discipline of the family." For the most part, they also assumed that the franchise should be restricted to male householders, that women's participation in public speech and action should be limited, and that, according to Patricia Higgins, a married woman's political views "were included in, and became explicit only through her husband's."[6] Furthermore, even under the Protectorate the control of female sexuality and domestic order remained a concern; for instance, a 1650 act made adultery a capital offense.[7] The upheaval of the 1640s and 1650s enabled some married women to move beyond

Past Achievements and Future Trends," *Journal of Interdisciplinary History* 12 (1981): 51–87, and "The Rise of the Nuclear Family in Early Modern England: The Patriarchal Stage," in *The Family in History*, ed. Charles E. Rosenberg (Philadelphia: University of Pennsylvania Press, 1975), pp. 13–57; and Gordon J. Schochet, *Patriarchalism and Political Thought: The Authoritarian Family and Political Speculation and Attitudes* (Oxford: Blackwell, 1975), esp. chap. 4.

5. Lawrence Stone, *Family, Sex, and Marriage in England, 1500–1800* (New York: Harper and Row, 1977), p. 202; see also p. 195. Also see Ralph A. Houlbrooke on how political and social radicalism could accompany domestic conservatism in seventeenth-century England: "Even among the minority which experienced female religious radicalism it did not bring about a major redistribution of power within the family" (*The English Family, 1450–1700* [London: Longman, 1984], p. 114); see also David Underdown, *Revel, Riot, and Rebellion: Popular Politics and Culture in England, 1603–1660* (Oxford: Oxford University Press, 1985), esp. p. 286.

6. Keith Thomas, "Women and the Civil War Sects," *Past and Present* 13 (1958): 42–62, esp. p. 53; Patricia Higgins, "The Reactions of Women, with Special Reference to Petitioners," *Politics, Religion, and the English Civil War*, ed. Brian Manning (London: Edward Arnold Press, 1973), pp. 178–222, esp. p. 211. See also Phyllis Mack, "Women as Prophets during the English Civil War," *Feminist Studies* 8.1 (1982): 19–45, and *Visionary Women: Ecstatic Prophecy in Seventeenth-Century England* (Berkeley: University of California Press, 1992), esp. chap. 2; and Christopher Durston, *The Family in the English Revolution* (Oxford: Basil Blackwell, 1989), pp. 25–26.

7. Keith Thomas, "The Puritans and Adultery: The Act of 1650 Reconsidered," in *Puritans and Revolutionaries: Essays in Seventeenth-Century History*, ed. Donald Pennington and Keith Thomas (Oxford: Clarendon Press, 1978), pp. 257–82. Very few people seem to have been executed under this act, and it was soon repealed, due in part to the difficulty of securing admissible evidence of sexual offenses. See also Susan Staves, *Players' Scepters: Fictions of Authority in the Restoration* (Lincoln: University of Nebraska Press, 1979), p. 13; and Stone, *Family*, p. 632.

traditionally defined roles, whether they were aristocratic Royalists who managed their estates in their husbands' absence or proselytizing members of radical religious sects. Such women's activities, even when valued, were largely viewed as temporary, exceptional, or, in the case of female prophets, proof that God works through the humblest instruments.[8] They thus offered relatively little immediate challenge to dominant sexual and domestic ideologies.[9]

Contemplating rebellion themselves, heads of households exercised increasing control over their own dependents, those potential home-rebels and house-traitors. Even those men who were involved in what could be construed as treason—regicide—did not see their wives' and servants' positions as in any way analogous to their own.[10] For instance, when, in his *Doctrine and Discipline of Divorce* (1643/1644), Milton addresses Parliament seeking changes in divorce law, he asserts the necessity of reinforcing *domestic* patriarchal authority even as he formulates his radical arguments (which are even more radical in the 1644 edition) that a covenant is only legitimate and binding while it satisfies the terms under which it was proposed. Milton draws Parliament's attention to marital discord by stressing its public consequences; it is "unprofitable and dangerous to the Common-wealth, when the household estate, out of which must flourish forth the vigor and spirit of all publick enterprizes, is so ill contented and procur'd at home, and cannot be supported."[11] Milton thus uses the analogy between domestic and political life to authorize the legislative reform of marital relations and to validate the *husband's* claims to domestic happiness.

Although Milton insists that both domestic and political relations

---

8. See Mack, "Women as Prophets," pp. 28–29, 34–35, and passim.

9. See the essays on gender in the English Revolution, especially Rachel Trubowitz, "Female Preachers and Male Wives: Gender and Authority in Civil War England," in *Pamphlet Wars: Prose in the English Revolution*, ed. James Holstun, a special issue of *Prose Studies* 14.3 (1991): 112–33. See also Durston, *Family in the English Revolution*, chaps. 2 and 5. The assumption that change in traditional family structures was "deleterious" pervades Durston's otherwise useful book: "While *damage* was, therefore, done to some families, the serious *casualty* rate was very low" (p. 165, emphases added). I am also grateful to Sharon Achinstein for sharing her unpublished essay, "Allegories of Female Authority during the English Revolution: The *Parliaments of Ladies*."

10. See also Staves: "Men did not necessarily wish to pursue the implications of the analogies and impute to their wives and children rights like those they themselves claimed as subjects" (*Players' Scepters*, p. 116).

11. Milton, *Doctrine and Discipline of Divorce*, ed. Lowell W. Coolidge, in *Complete Prose Works of John Milton*, gen. ed. Don M. Wolfe, 8 vols. in 10 (New Haven: Yale University Press, 1959), 2:247 (1643/1644 eds.); subsequent citations are to this edition.

are contractual, and, in his discussion of divorce, first tests his arguments that a citizen can break a contract that no longer fills his needs, he never imagines that the wife also enters into a contract that she can break: "As a whole people is in proportion to an ill Government, so is one *man* to an ill mariage."[12] The husband thus contracts not with his wife, but with the institution of marriage, and "what ever the institution were, it could not be so enormous, nor so rebellious against both nature and reason as to exalt it selfe above the end and person for whom it was instituted."[13] Milton skews the analogy in favor of husbands;[14] if Milton took the analogy to its logical conclusion, he would have to argue that as a people is to ill-government, so is a wife to her abusive husband.[15]

As a result of his committed emphasis on the husband, his grievances, and his right to remedy them by means of "the liberty of second choice," Milton continues to depict the household, the seminary of revolution, as hierarchically organized.[16] In fact, he wants to increase the authority of the husband and father. Censuring the Roman Catholic church for "pluck[ing] the power and arbitrement of divorce from the master of family" and betraying what should be private to public scrutiny and intervention, Milton argues that the husband should be the judge of his own domestic concerns: "Shall then the disposal of that power return again to the maister of family? Wherfore not? Since God there put it, and the presumptuous Canon thence bereft it."[17] Thus, although Milton urges domestic reforms, even he does not seek domestic inversion or reordering. Some of Milton's contemporaries could imagine marriage

12. Ibid., 2:229 (1644 ed.), emphasis added.
13. Ibid., 2:245 (1644 ed.).
14. David Aers and Bob Hodge, " 'Rational Burning': Milton on Sex and Marriage," *Milton Studies* 13 (1979): 3–33, esp. p. 9. In skewing the analogy, Milton betrays an insight into how it worked to exclude women as parties to the contract as well as to deny their right to rebel against tyranny or initiate divorce proceedings. See the discussion of Carol Pateman's *Sexual Contract* below. See also Staves, *Players' Scepters,* pp. 155–56.
15. At least at the level of rhetoric, some of Milton's contemporaries could take the analogy to this conclusion, casting the challenge to political authority in feminine terms, as Phyllis Mack argues: "Parliament—the subject of the king—might be identified with the dutiful wife, who could justifiably abandon her ungodly husband" ("Women as Prophets," p. 21). But even those writers who employed such rhetoric might not be willing to pursue its implications for their own households.
16. Milton, *Doctrine and Discipline,* 2:345 (1644 ed.). See also 2:245–47, 324–26, 347.
17. Milton, *Doctrine and Discipline,* 2:343 (1643/1644 eds.); 2:353 (1643/1664 eds.).

as a partnership more successfully than he; in this, as in much else, he represents an exception and an extreme.[18] Carole Pateman's work suggests that, in his excess, Milton exposes how social contract theory established men's freedom by means of women's subjection, underwriting a social contract with a sexual one, yet repressing the crucial connection between these two contracts. Even in theory, a contractual model of marriage assumed and perpetuated, rather than replaced, a hierarchical relation between spouses.[19] Milton's arguments reveal that, at the domestic and national levels, the Revolution sought to enhance rather than curtail the male citizen's liberties and privileges. The results for dependents, in theory and in practice, were less than revolutionary.

The fact that Milton took up the issue of divorce at a time of profound political upheaval demonstrates, once again, that the domestic and political were understood through one another, and that those who argued for political change had to contemplate domestic change as well. As Mary Lyndon Shanley argues, the Royalists used the analogy between the marriage contract and the social contract to argue that both "established a relationship of irrevocable hierarchical authority between the parties." Parliamentarians, therefore, had to debate the Royalists' conception of marriage in order to rebut their claims for the permanence of the social contract.[20] Although even the most radical Parliamentarian

18. Critics of the divorce tracts agree that, despite Milton's attempts to imagine marital mutuality, he does not decenter *domestic* authority, he consistently blames wives for marital misery, and he lapses into misogyny and sexual disgust. See Aers and Hodge, " 'Rational Burning' "; essays by Stanley Fish, Stephen M. Fallon, and Annabel Patterson in *Politics, Poetics, and Hermeneutics in Milton's Prose,* ed. David Loewenstein and James Grantham Turner (Cambridge: Cambridge University Press, 1990), pp. 41–101; Mary Nyquist, "The Genesis of Gendered Subjectivity in the Divorce Tracts and in *Paradise Lost,*" in *Remembering Milton: Essays on the Texts and Traditions,* ed. Nyquist and Margaret W. Ferguson (London: Methuen, 1987), pp. 99–127; and James Grantham Turner, *One Flesh: Paradisal Marriage and Sexual Relations in the Age of Milton* (Oxford: Clarendon Press, 1987), pp. 106–23 and chap. 6.

19. Carole Pateman, *The Sexual Contract* (Stanford: Stanford University Press, 1988). Casting their arguments for change in misogynist terms, even the most radical seventeenth-century political theorists excluded women from their vision of the future, even defining that vision against women. On misogynist polemic, see Peter Stallybrass, "The World Turned Upside Down: Inversion, Gender, and the State," in *The Matter of Difference: Materialist Feminist Criticism of Shakespeare,* ed. Valerie Wayne (Ithaca: Cornell University Press, 1991), pp. 201–20, esp. p. 209; and Turner, *One Flesh,* pp. 223–25.

20. Mary Lyndon Shanley, "Marriage Contract and Social Contract in Seventeenth-Century English Political Thought," *Western Political Quarterly* 32.1 (1979): 79–91, esp. p. 81. See also Susan Dwyer Amussen, *An Ordered Society: Gender and Class in Early*

writers on marriage and social contracts assume that the husband is the authority figure in the household, the analogies that structure political debate force them to apply their arguments for the limits of authority to the domestic sphere. If the king holds his authority only on certain conditions, then, as Constance Jordan argues, "the husband cannot function as an absolute lawgiver within his family, nor can the exercise of his prerogative be unlimited." [21]

Despite Milton's insistence that a husband should arbitrate his own matrimonial causes, the household governor was not, in contrast to his dependents, autonomous and unconstrained; instead, he was himself limited by obligations and responsibilities. An abundant literature flourished to instruct the householder in the fulfillment of his duties. For instance, Edward Topsell, a London preacher, asserts in *The House-holder: Or, Perfect Man* (1609) that "a Housholder is not inferiour to the Governour of a Citty, and he that is not wise in Domesticall matters, shall never bee trusted in the Common-wealth." [22] Assuming that influence moves from the household to the Commonwealth rather than vice versa, William Gouge asserts a typical view: "Mariage is a kind of publike action: the well or ill ordering therof much tendeth to the good or hurt of family, Church, and common-wealth." [23] If church and state have only limited ability to control household government and domestic order is the foundation of political order, then the master and his domestic governance assume enormous significance.

> For although there bee never so good lawes in Cities: never so pure order in Churches, yet if maisters of families, do not practise at home catechising, and discipline in their houses, and joyne their helping hands to Magistrates, and Ministers: they may . . . complain that their children and servants were

Modern England (Oxford: Basil Blackwell, 1988), esp. chap. 2; and Staves, *Players' Scepters*, pp. 136–60.

21. Constance Jordan, *Renaissance Feminism: Literary Texts and Political Models* (Ithaca: Cornell University Press, 1990), p. 295. See also Staves, *Players' Scepters*, esp. chap. 3. On a master's authority, and its limits, see Mark Thornton Burnett, "Masters and Servants in Moral and Religious Treatises, c. 1580–c. 1642," in *The Arts, Literature, and Society*, ed. Arthur Maverick (London: Routledge, 1990), pp. 48–75, esp. pp. 53, 59.

22. Topsell, *The House-holder: Or, Perfect Man* (London, 1609), sig. A3v.

23. William Gouge, *Of Domesticall Duties* (London, 1622), p. 204.

disordered, and corrupted abroad, when in trueth, they were disordered, and are still corrupted, and marde at home.[24]

Thus, the household governor was not only powerful and influential but was responsible for his dependents even outside the home. While representations of murderous husbands reveal that domestic hierarchy remained largely unshaken by political upheaval, they also show that the domestic patriarch, like the royal one, was increasingly constrained in his exercise of power. Domestic tyranny was no more acceptable than political tyranny.

In her study of "fictions of authority" in Restoration drama, law, and political theory, Susan Staves argues that the subject's right to resist arbitrary rule did not become orthodoxy until the relative calm of the late seventeenth century, especially after the "glorious" Revolution of 1688. Only then did vigilance against abuses of authority extend to the family.[25] Staves sees this shift both in the law, which "long accustomed to punishing the petit treason of domestic inferiors, now takes an increased interest in curbing the exercise of authority by fathers and, especially, husbands," and in the drama, which no longer represents married women's self-assertion as inevitably violent and disorderly.[26] In Sir John Vanbrugh's *The Provoked Wife* (1697), for instance, the eponymous wife asserts that her husband Sir John Brute's mistreatment absolves her of her marriage vow: "The argument's good between the king and the people, why not between the husband and the wife? O, but that condition was not expressed. No matter, 'twas understood."[27] Yet despite her forthright justifications of rebellion, Lady Brute never cuckolds or leaves her carousing, violent husband, continuing to honor the vows whose binding force she questions. Restoration dramatiza-

24. John Dod and Robert Cleaver, *A Godly Forme of Houshold Government* (London, 1630), sig. A4.

25. See Staves, *Players' Scepters*, pp. 95, 114, 117, and chap. 3, passim; see also Durston, *Family in the English Revolution*, p. 173.

26. Staves, *Players' Scepters*, p. 159. Staves argues that late seventeenth-century drama portrays rebellious children even more sympathetically than it does provoked wives. Also see Staves's fascinating discussion of changes in treason law first after the Restoration and again after 1688 (pp. 60–63 and 94–100). For her survey of the many plays addressing "sovereignty in the family," see chap. 3.

27. Sir John Vanbrugh, *The Provoked Wife*, ed. Curt A. Zimansky (Lincoln: University of Nebraska Press, 1969), 1.1.69–72.

tions of spousal conflict, however common and however sympathetic to wives' frustration, tend to be comic. When, for instance, Aphra Behn rewrites George Wilkins's *The Miseries of Enforced Marriage* (1607), a play based on an actual case of enforced marriage, spousal conflict, and child murder, she transforms it into a comedy, *The Town Fop* (1676), in which divorce replaces murder as the means of resolving conflict and escaping miseries. Restoration audiences did not share earlier audiences' taste for all the details of domestic crime among the English nonelite. In the eighteenth century, George Lillo adapts *Arden* as a romanticized tragedy of ill-fated love—Alicia, coerced into making a promise she cannot keep, loves one man but is married to another;[28] Nicholas Rowe and others write tragedies about women's suffering and victimization.[29] But there is no counterpart to *Arden of Faversham,* that is, there is no play, based on an actual case, in which a husband kills his wife. In such absences, and in its ambiguous, usually comic, portrayals of rebellious wives, Restoration drama participates in what Margaret Hunt calls "a larger discourse that [is] simultaneously respectful of hierarchy and wary of potential abuses whether in government or domestic relationships." This larger discourse only tentatively explores the limits of a husband's authority, the responsibilities accompanying that authority, and a wife's rights.[30]

28. Lillo may have written his adaptation in 1736; it was performed in 1759 and published posthumously in 1762. See the introduction and appendixes to William H. McBurney's edition of Lillo's *The London Merchant* (Lincoln: University of Nebraska Press, 1965).

29. See Laura Brown, "The Defenseless Woman and the Development of English Tragedy," *Studies in English Literature* 22.3 (1982): 429–43. On Restoration drama, see also Laura Brown, *English Dramatic Form, 1660–1760: An Essay in Generic History* (New Haven: Yale University Press, 1981); and Robert D. Hume, *The Development of English Drama in the Late Seventeenth Century* (Oxford: Oxford University Press, 1976).

30. Margaret Hunt, "Wife Beating, Domesticity, and Women's Independence in Eighteenth-Century London," *Gender and History* 4.1 (1992): 10–33, esp. p. 16. Like Staves, Hunt perceives a "discursive shift" in the last quarter of the seventeenth century toward a more strenuous condemnation of domestic tyranny. For instance, Hunt argues that the 1682 reissue of William Heale's *An Apologie for Women* (1609) makes a stronger, less ambivalent case against wife-beating and more explicitly compares brutal husbands to tyrants, as its new title suggests: *The Great Advocate and Oratour for Women, or the Arraignment, Tryall and Conviction of All Such Wicked Husbands (or Monsters) Who Hold It Lawfull to Beate Their Wives, or to Demeane Themselves Severely and Tyrannically towards Them* (pp. 24–25). See also Anna Clark, "Humanity or Justice? Wifebeating and the Law in the Eighteenth and Nineteenth Centuries," in *Regulating Womanhood: Historical Essays on Marriage, Motherhood, and Sexuality,* ed. Carol Smart (London: Routledge, 1992), pp. 187–206.

Pamphlet Accounts of Murderous Husbands

Pamphlets and ballads do not make the parallels between domestic and political tyranny explicit; nor do they explore the implications of the parallel, particularly the possibility that a wife's or servant's active resistance might be justifiable. Yet in narratives about murderous husbands, as in those about murderous wives, domestic violence reveals the contradictions that undermine marriage from within. These narratives particularly expose the violence that underlies, and is even produced by, the fiction of subsumption, of two becoming one.

Rather than reproducing the "plots" most typical of actual instances of wife-killing—an angry husband who loses his temper, or "correction" (abuse) that escalates into murder—the pamphlets and ballads dwell on excessive, ingenious brutality. Detailing husbands' violent refusals to act as protectors, partners, or lovers, these texts present the murders of wives as abuses not only of authority but of intimacy. They thus join with the accounts of petty treason that we have seen to articulate deep fears of sexual and domestic familiarities. In both kinds of narratives, spouses employ the physical vulnerability of the conjugal relation to assault rather than solace their partners' bodies. Representing particularly grotesque acts—throttling a bedridden invalid, clandestinely inserting poison into the vagina, roasting the murdered body as if it were meat—accounts of wife-murder depict husbands as enemies, rather than protectors or partners.[31]

In presenting such intimate betrayals, many texts follow the model of the Judas kiss. After pretending to be reconciled to his pregnant wife, John Marketman, for instance, "took her about the neck *Judas* like as if he intended to kiss her, and all on a sudden thrust his accursed knife into, if not through her poor Heart, so that she fell down dead upon the spot."[32] Another jealous husband, William Tite, perched his

---

31. The account of Henry Robson's bizarre murder of his wife, discussed below, is the only account I have discovered of a husband who employs poison, the wife's preferred method. Robson's act brings together a feminized transgression (poisoning) and a masculinized one (rape/sexual assault).

32. *The True Narrative of the Execution of John Marketman . . . for Committing a Horrible & Bloody Murther upon the Body of His Wife, That Was Big with Child When He Stabbed Her* (London, n.d.), sig. A2. For another direct reference to a "*Judas* kiss," see "The

wife on his knee, kissed her and spoke lovingly to her, then "put his hand under her Apron, and ript up her bowels and belly, insomuch that the child which was in her womb, fell out on the ground, and sprawled before him."[33] Thomas White, sitting close beside his wife, slowly and secretly maneuvered the point of his "scimiter" into his "pocket-hole" and "as he sate close by Her, he forc'd it in at her right Breast, and through her Body" to the amazement of others present in the room.[34] In all these cases, the husband not only exploits his wife's trust and physical proximity but acts out his betrayal in an unseemly way. Hunt reviewed consistory court wife-beating cases from 1711 to 1713 and relates: "One often gets the sense, reading these cases, of acts designed specifically for an audience. Men persistently abused their wives in front of relatives."[35] Similarly, representations of those husbands who kill their wives depict the murders as simultaneously intimate and theatrical. Pornographically conjoining violence, eros, and performance, the murders force into visibility a disturbing connection between marital sex and violence against women.

The Examination, Confession, and Condemnation of Henry Robson Fisherman of Rye, Who Poysoned His Wife in the Strangest Maner That Ever Hitherto Hath Bin Heard of (1598) explores this connection in even more extreme terms than the popular texts that begin with conjugal caresses and end with the wife's disembowelment. In this pamphlet, the profligate Robson sees his wife's life as an obstacle to his release from debtor's prison. To eliminate her, another prisoner advises Robson to mix ratsbane and ground glass, and wrap this mixture "in the skinne

---

Bloody-Minded Husband" (circa 1685) in *The Pepys Ballads,* ed. Hyder E. Rollins (Cambridge: Harvard University Press, 1929–1932), 3:202–6.

33. Lawrence Price, *A Ready Way to Prevent Sudden Death* (London, 1655), sigs. A5–A5v. After William Barwick drowned his pregnant wife (whom he had been constrained to marry), he could still see the fetus quickening inside her (*A Full and True Relation of the Examination and Confession of W. Barwick and E. Mangall, of Two Horrid Murders* [London, 1690]). Thomas Laret also beat then stabbed to death his pregnant wife (Lawrence Price, *Bloody Actions Performed* [London, 1653]). Two ballads, "The Bloody-Minded Husband" (1690) and "The Inhuman Butcher" (1697) refer to the murder of pregnant wives (see *Pepys Ballads,* ed. Rollins, 5:287–90 and 6:257–61). In all these texts, since the murder of the wife is also an act of infanticide, the husband betrays his responsibilities as both spouse and parent. On the fascination with pregnant victims, see Wiltenburg, *Disorderly Women,* p. 196.

34. *A True Relation of the Most Horrible Murther Committed by Thomas White . . . upon the Body of His Wife* (London, 1682), p. 4.

35. Hunt, "Wife Beating," p. 23.

of a shoulder of mutton, to the quantity of a hasle nut, or lesse, and in the night when his wife should next come to lie with him, [Robson] should convey it into her privie parts, which hee would warra[n]t without danger to him shuld kill her."[36] When Robson's wife next pays him a conjugal visit, by "a dissembling shew of friendship" he "constrain[s] her to stay all night," during which time she enjoys "the dearest nights pleasure that ever woma[n] had."[37] Those scholars who have commented on this text sanitize Robson's act. One describes Robson's method as "filling his wife's genitals with a mixture of ratsbane and ground glass while she slept," although the text suggests that she was having sex with her husband, not sleeping; another describes Robson as "introducing rat poison into her vagina," decorously evading the means by which Robson "introduces" his carefully prepared depository.[38] Clearly, Robson uses sexual penetration to poison his wife. Although the wife expects "pleasure" from sexual intercourse, physical intimacy empowers her husband to kill her "without danger to him," rather than mystically transforming husband and wife into "one flesh."

An account of a less devious murder, *A True Relation of the Most Horrible Murther Committed by Thomas White ... upon the Body of His Wife Mrs. Dorothy White* (1682), reveals a similar concern with the complexities and dangers when spouses become one flesh occupied by antagonistic wills. Citing Genesis ("This is now Bone of my Bone, and Flesh of my Flesh"), the title page asserts the husband's obligation to love his wife as he loves himself. The text then recounts the breakdown of this marital ideal; through his "vitious Practices" and "the Abuse of Himself with lewd Women," Thomas White contracts "that Disease which commonly is the Consequence of Uncleanness" and transmits it to his wife: "Thus you see a Man, who by the Laws of God and Common Natural Duty, was Bound by all lawful means to take Care for the Welfare and Preservation both of the Souls and Bodie, of his Wife and Children, Contriving and Resolving the Ruine of both."[39] After White

---

36. *The Examination, Confession, and Condemnation of Henry Robson Fisherman of Rye* (London, 1598), sig. A4.

37. Ibid., sig. A4v.

38. Sharpe, "Domestic Homicide," p. 41, n. 51; John H. Langbein, *Prosecuting Crime in the Renaissance: England, Germany, France* (Cambridge: Harvard University Press, 1974), p. 51, n. 77.

39. *A True Relation*, pp. 2–3.

infects his wife, he proceeds to threaten her against disclosure so that she does not seek adequate medical attention; the text presents his subsequent murder of her as the logical consequence of neglecting to cherish her flesh as his. In some accounts of the murder of husbands, a wife's infidelity leads to her husband's death; in these two texts, a wife's fidelity enables her husband to kill her, suggesting the dangers of "due benevolence" for women.

Like discussions of wife-beating, then, these texts explore what it means to be one flesh when the occupants of this shared body are at odds. The construction of husband and wife as one flesh, like the legal fiction that the husband subsumes his wife, assumes that the husband's and wife's interests correspond. In a vivid, often-cited image, Milton explicitly links the failed ideal of one flesh to tyranny. When husband and wife are incompatible, "instead of beeing one flesh, they will be rather two carkasses chain'd unnaturally together; or as it may happ'n, a living soule bound to a dead corps, a punishment too like that inflicted by the tyrant *Mezentius*."[40] While Milton assumes that the husband is the victim of tyranny, writers more concerned that husbands themselves may act as tyrants similarly insist that the degeneration of "one flesh" into "two carkasses chain'd unnaturally together" subverts constructions of the subject and the couple as stable, self-preserving, cohesive: "The wife is as a mans selfe. *They two are one flesh*. No man but a frantike, furious, desperate wretch will beat himselfe"; "What man will be so wicked as to strike, and beate, and ban, and curse his own flesh which is his lawful and absolute wife[?]"[41]

Yet accounts of wife-beating and wife-killing suggest that the masculine subject, and therefore the corporate subject forged when he subsumes his wife, could be fragile, fragmented, and self-destructive. Examining cases brought against brutal husbands in church courts, Martin Ingram argues that the community judged such men's domestic violence as a symptom of uncontrol and abnormality. For instance, in

---

40. Milton, *Doctrine and Discipline*, 2:326–27 (1643/1644 eds.).
41. Gouge, *Of Domesticall Duties*, p. 395; Lawrence Price, *Bloody Actions Performed: Or, A Brief and True Relation of Three Notorious Murthers, Committed by Three Bloud-Thirsty Men, 2 upon Their Wives* (London, 1653), sig. A6v; see also *A Caution to Married Couples: Being a True Relation How a Man in Nightingale-lane Having Beat and Abused His Wife, Murthered a Tub-man That Endevoured to Stop Him from Killing Her* (London, 1677), sig. A2v.

five cases of excessive, life-threatening wife-beating in Wiltshire, "all of the husbands involved showed signs of mental disturbance or instability."[42] One account of a husband's murder of his wife suggests that legal, literary, and moral texts so consistently attributed murderous husbands' actions to madness that husbands themselves might have exploited this convention. *The Bloody Husband* (1653) presents Adam Sprackling as dispassionately calculating his own insanity defense immediately after murdering his wife. According to a servant's testimony, Sprackling, who "loved his Dogs better than he loved his Wife," enjoined the servant to help him slaughter them: "Now let us kill the Dogs, and then they'l say we are mad indeed."[43] Subsequently, Sprackling pleads in court "that he was mad when he kill'd his Wife; and that he knew not what he did."[44] According to *The Bloody Husband,* Sprackling manipulates the convention of the mad husband, and even his public persona ("He loved his Dogs better than he loved his Wife."), to defend himself. The servant's testimony that Sprackling calculated the effect of slaughtering the dogs combined with testimony that Sprackling "was of an habitual bloody disposition and practise" undermined the strategy and led to Sprackling's conviction.[45] The narrative framing here (the story of the story that Sprackling devises) and the function of the courtroom as an arena of competing narratives draw attention to a cultural perception, produced and transmitted through popular accounts of actual crimes, that a man who would murder his wife was no longer a representative of order or authority.[46]

42. Martin Ingram, *Church Courts, Sex, and Marriage in England, 1570–1640* (Cambridge: Cambridge University Press, 1987), p. 183.

43. Price, *Bloody Actions,* sig. A3v; *The Bloody Husband, and Cruell Neighbour* (London, 1653), sig. A4v.

44. *Bloody Husband,* sig. A4v.

45. Ibid., sig. B.

46. On other cases of those who mimic insanity to avoid criminal prosecution, see Michael MacDonald, *Mystical Bedlam: Madness, Anxiety, and Healing in Seventeenth-Century England* (Cambridge: Cambridge University Press, 1981), pp. 123–25.

Other pamphlet and broadside accounts of wife-killing include: *A Strange and Wonderful Relation of a Barbarous Murder Committed by James Robison . . . upon the Body of His Own Wife* (London, 1679); *The Sufferer's Legacy to Surviving Sinners . . . Edmund Kirk's Dying Advice to Young Men* (London, 1684); and the multiple accounts of John Marketman's murder of his wife, including (in addition to the account cited in n. 32) *A Full and True Relation of All the Proceedings Holden at Chelmsford* and *A Full and True Account of the Penitence of John Marketman* (both 1680). Ballads include: "The Murtherer Justly Condemned" (1697) and "Strange and True News from Westmoreland" (n.d.) in *The*

Like the emphasis on their instability, the emphasis on murderous husband's tyranny suggests that their actions bear no relation to acceptable assertions of domestic authority and reveal nothing about the distribution of power in marriage. *Two Horrible and Inhumane Murders Done in Lincolneshire* (1607; fig. 2), for instance, describes how John Dilworth silences his wife's justifiable complaints with several blows to her head, makes a fire, and then, "like a terrible torturing tyrant, tooke uppe the dead carcase, and laide it thereon, clothes and all, not forgetting to hang uppe blankets and coverlids before the windowes, to the end to hide the light this great fire did cast."[47] By offering the demonic image of Dilworth reveling before his wife's smoldering corpse, "as it were rejoycing at that his most hatefull, horrible, and hellish fact, like a most gracelesse and mercilesse miscreant," the text sidesteps the issue of the husband's responsibility; at the same time it qualifies his claims to authority.[48]

Such exaggerated, grotesque characterizations evade the relationship between wife-murder and the dominant ideology of male supremacy. Although murderous husbands refuse responsibility for their wives' welfare (a crucial part of the husband's role), their extreme assertions of their authority, like the earl of Castlehaven's scandalous avowal that he can pimp for his wife, reveal how much power marriage affords them. Like Castlehaven, some violent husbands appeal to domestic and sexual ideologies to justify their actions: "No man can judge between man and wife, but God alone";[49] or, "If he cripled her, *he* must keep her, if he kild her, *he* must be hanged for her."[50] While a wife's violence

---

Ewing Collection of English Broadside Ballads (Glasgow: University of Glasgow Publications, 1971); and "The Unnatural Husband" (1695) and "The Mournful Murderer" (1697) in *Pepys Ballads,* ed. Rollins, vol. 7. Accounts of masters or mistresses who kill their servants, which are fairly rare, include *Three Bloodie Murders . . . The Second, Committed by Elizabeth James, on the Body of Her Mayde* (London, 1613); and *An Exact Relation of the Bloody and Barbarous Murder, Committed by Miles Lewis and His Wife . . . upon Their Apprentice* (London, 1646).

47. *Two Horrible and Inhumane Murders Done in Lincolneshire, by Two Husbands upon Their Wives* (London, 1607), sig. B4.

48. *Two Horrible,* sig. B4. On Renaissance conventions for representing tyrants, see Rebecca Bushnell, *Tragedies of Tyrants: Political Thought and Theater in the English Renaissance* (Ithaca: Cornell University Press, 1990), esp. chap. 2.

49. *Bloody Husband,* sigs. B2v–B3.

50. Price, *Bloody Actions,* sig. A5v, emphasis added. In *A Caution to Married Couples,* a husband pursues his wife out into the street, and kills the man who intervenes for "hindring him to correct his wife" (sig. A4v).

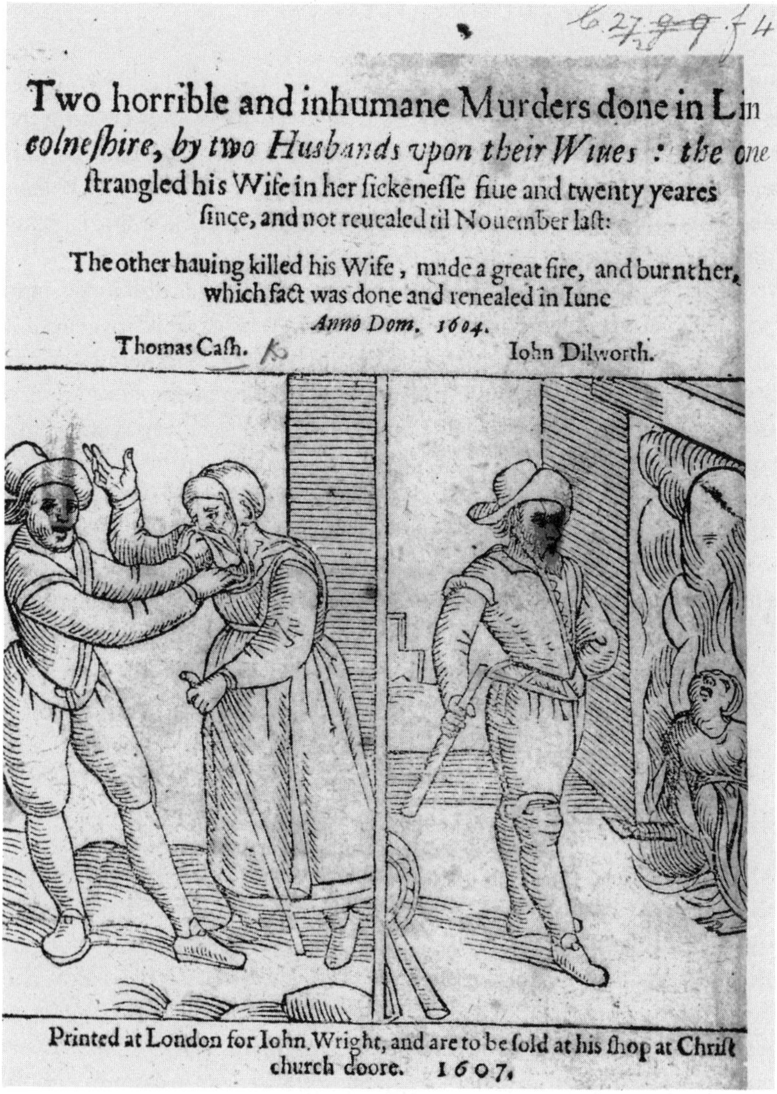

Two horrible and inhumane Murders done in Lincolneſhire, by two Husbands upon their Wiues: the one ſtrangled his Wife in her ſickeneſſe fiue and twenty yeares ſince, and not reuealed til Nouember laſt:

The other hauing killed his Wife, made a great fire, and burnt her, which fact was done and renealed in Iune

Anno Dom. 1604.

Thomas Caſh. Iohn Dilworth.

Printed at London for Iohn Wright, and are to be ſold at his ſhop at Chriſt church doore. 1607.

Figure 2. Petty tyrants: one husband smothers his invalid wife; another bludgeons his wife, then throws her on the fire. Title page from *Two Horrible and Inhumane Murders* (1607). By permission of the British Library.

refutes the logic of coverture by resisting and deconstructing her role, a husband's violence exploits the logic of coverture by exaggerating the power of his role. Like the peers who tried Castlehaven and the narratives circulating about his trial, however, most pamphlets and ballads deny transgressive husbands' attempts to justify their actions, labeling their interpretations of coverture as criminal and crazed.[51]

By the eighteenth century, conduct literature, legal discourses, and popular literature demonized wife abuse and "rhetorically" displaced it onto the lower classes, so that "wife beating became, for literate people, a particular mark of the inferiority and animality of the poor."[52] Anticipating this trend, pamphlets remove "terrible, torturing tyrants" like John Dilworth from the continuum of husbandly authority, foreclosing the interrogation of husbandly power and its limits. While Heywood's *An Apology for Actors* (1612) suggests that murderous wives lurk everywhere in the disguise of the familiar and innocuous, a text such as *Two Horrible and Inhumane Murders* suggests that murderous husbands are monstrous exceptions, not husbands whose "legitimate" correction of their wives gets out of hand.

Competing Perspectives on Spouse Murder: Rereading a Wife's Treason as a Husband's Tyranny

Most texts about spouse killing focus either on the murderous wife or the murderous husband; that focus is largely historically contingent. In some texts, however, such as Gilbert Burnet's 1679 account of Anne Boleyn's trial and execution in 1536, the narratives of petty treason and domestic tyranny compete, revealing the profound cultural changes in which the shift from one to the other participates. What Tudor court culture treated as an instance of wifely betrayal with treasonous ramifications, Burnet's *History of the Reformation of the Church of England* recasts after the Restoration as an instance of tyranny, domestic and political. Layering two distinct interpretations of the same event, texts

51. See my discussion of the Castlehaven case in Chapter 2. My argument here is informed by Cynthia Herrup's work-in-progress on Castlehaven.

52. Hunt, "Wife Beating," p. 27; see also p. 25. Wiltenburg argues that in the course of the seventeenth century, English popular literature increasingly depicted wife-beating as a lower-class, vulgar activity (*Disorderly Women*, p. 128).

such as Burnet's can be read as palimpsests, texts in which one narrative has been erased to make room for another, yet a shadow of the earlier narrative lingers. By analyzing how one narrative supersedes but does not quite cancel out the other in Burnet's text, I offer a model for reading *Othello,* which stubbornly refuses to fit into my discussions of murderous wives, or insubordinate servants, or murderous husbands, yet is affiliated with all of them.

In April 1536, Henry VIII began to investigate charges that Anne, his second wife, had been unfaithful to him; in May, Anne and five men purported to have been her lovers (including her brother) were executed.[53] One of only two English queens to suffer execution (the other was Henry's fifth wife, Catherine Howard), Anne was the first convicted of high treason. Since a queen's adultery jeopardizes the succession, all of the parties to Anne's alleged adultery were indicted for treason. The treason statute of 1352, which also defines petty treason, makes it treason to "violate" the king's wife, his unmarried eldest daughter, or the daughter of his eldest son. Although, according to Margery Stone Schauer and Frederick Schauer, "it does not... state that it is treason for the King's wife to allow herself to be violated[,] ... if she consented to the treasonous act, she was an accomplice, or at least an accessory, and thus equally guilty of treason."[54] The construction of a queen's adultery as high treason and of a housewife's murder

53. Many historians connect Anne's downfall to her miscarriage of a fetus identified as male on January 29, 1536, the very day on which Catherine of Aragon was buried. Given the controversy surrounding Henry's divorce from Catherine, the marriage to Anne would never be viewed as legitimate by many inside as well as outside England. Catherine's death made another, more acceptable marriage possible; the miscarriage gave Henry an additional reason to find a new queen. See E. W. Ives, "Faction at the Court of Henry VIII: The Fall of Anne Boleyn," *History* 57 (1972): 169–88; and Retha M. Warnicke, "Sexual Heresy at the Court of Henry VIII," *The Historical Journal* 30.2 (1987): 247–68.

54. In addition, Anne's adultery and consequent "slandering" of her issue were treason under a statute of 1533 that provided that "anyone slandering the issue of the King by writing, printing, or other overt act would be guilty of treason" (Margery Stone Schauer and Frederick Schauer, "Law as the Engine of State: The Trial of Anne Boleyn," *William and Mary Law Review* 22 [1965]: 49–84, esp. pp. 67–68). As Gilbert Burnet explains, "The law that was made for her, and the issue of her marriage, is now made use of to destroy her" (*The History of the Reformation of the Church of England,* ed. Nicholas Pocock [Oxford: Oxford University Press, 1865], pt. 1, book 3, p. 324). See also *State Trials,* ed. Howell, vol. 1, cols. 409–34, esp. col. 418; and Ives, "Faction at the Court," p. 172. The account of the proceedings reprinted in Howell is based largely on Burnet, as well as some manuscript material and J. Strype's *Ecclesiastical Memorials* (1721).

of her husband as petty treason are parallel; by conflating the private and the public, both see women's betrayals of their husbands as having political significance. In either case, the legal construction of a married woman's crime emphasizes the consequences of her actions, maximizes her accountability, and justifies her elimination.

Burnet registers but does not conspire in this process, focusing instead on how Henry and his counselors reshaped the law to suit their needs.

> It was also added in the indictment, that she and her complices, *had conspired the king's death;* but this, it seems, was only put in to swell the charge, for if there had been any evidence for it, there was no need of stretching the other statute; or if they could have proved the violating of the queen, the known statute of the twenty fifth year of the reign of Edward Third, had been sufficient.[55]

In his vivid, corporeal language of "swelling" the charge and "stretching" the statute, Burnet shifts attention from Anne's transgressions to Henry's manipulations of the law. He cites the indictment's attribution of conspiratorial agency to Anne ("She had conspired the king's death.") yet himself presents her as the possible victim of conspiracy, as well as "violation."

Burnet's post-Restoration concerns most explicitly inflect his interpretation of Henry's simultaneous insistence that Anne was adulterous *and* that their marriage should be annulled and its issue (Elizabeth) illegitimated.[56]

> The two sentences ... did so contradict one another, that it was apparent, one, if not both of them, must be unjust; for if the marriage between the king and her was null from the beginning, then, since she was not the king's wedded wife, there could be no adultery: and her marriage to the king was either a true marriage, or not; if it was true, then the annulling of it was unjust; and if it was no true marriage, then the attainder was

55. Burnet, *History of the Reformation,* ed. Pocock, pt. 1, book 3, p. 324; *State Trials,* ed. Howell, vol. 1, col. 418.

56. Burnet, *History of the Reformation,* ed. Pocock, pt. 1, book 3, p. 325. The annulment was sought on the grounds that Anne had entered into a pre-contract prior to her marriage to Henry. Anne confessed to this, although never to the adulteries with which she was charged. See Burnet, *History of the Reformation,* ed. Pocock, pt. 1, book 3, p. 326.

unjust; for there could be no breach of that faith which was never given; so that it is plain, the king was resolved to be rid of her, and to illegitimate her daughter, and in that transport of his fury did not consider that the very method he took discovered the injustice of his proceedings against her.[57]

Burnet here "discovers" the tyranny of Henry's proceedings, which he locates in the fictiveness of the charges and the "transport of his fury." Burnet's interpretation reveals how the post-1650 perspective questions authority and assumes and champions the subject's rights; the contours of the event he narrates remind his readers that the pre-1650 perspective identifies with and privileges authority, casting a suspicious eye on subordinates, domestic and political, who assert their "rights."

Competing Perspectives on Spouse Murder: *Othello* as Palimpsest

Like Burnet's account of Anne Boleyn's trial and execution, Shakespeare's *Othello* can be read as a palimpsest, simultaneously the story of treason and that of tyranny, here played out in more claustrophobically domestic terms, yet retaining political implications.[58] Burnet's historical location explains the palimpsestic quality of his work. Writing

57. Burnet, *History of the Reformation*, ed. Pocock, pt. 1, book 3, pp. 325–26; *State Trials*, ed. Howell, vol. 1, col. 419. By the time Anne was beheaded, sixteen days after her arrest, she was no longer either queen or wife. In a special hearing on May 17, Thomas Cranmer had secretly annulled the marriage. Retha M. Warnicke, "The Fall of Anne Boleyn: A Reassessment," *History* 70 (1985): 1–15, esp. p. 12.

58. On the play's domestic focus, see Emily Bartels, "Making More of the Moor: Aaron, Othello, and Renaissance Refashionings of Race," *Shakespeare Quarterly* 41.4 (1990): 433–54, esp. p. 452; G. K. Hunter, "*Othello* and Colour Prejudice," *Proceedings of the British Academy* 53 (1967): 139–63, esp. pp. 161–62; and, especially, Michael Neill, "Unproper Beds: Race, Adultery, and the Hideous in *Othello*," *Shakespeare Quarterly* 40.4 (1989): 383–412; and Mary Beth Rose, *The Expense of Spirit: Love and Sexuality in English Renaissance Drama* (Ithaca: Cornell University Press, 1988), chap. 3. Although Stanley Cavell insists that "there can be no argument . . . with the description, compared with the cases of Shakespeare's other tragedies, that this one is not political but domestic," the play, like other early modern discourses, presents the domestic ("house affairs" [1.3.149]) and the political ("state affairs" [1.3.193]) as inextricably linked (*The Claim of Reason: Wittgenstein, Skepticism, Morality, and Tragedy* [Oxford: Clarendon Press, 1979], p. 485). I am grateful to my colleague, Mitchell Greenberg, for drawing my attention to this passage in Cavell, and for sharing his own work on *Othello*, chap. 1 of his *Canonical States, Canonical Stages: Oedipus, Othering, and Seventeenth-Century Drama* (Minneapolis: University of Minnesota Press, forthcoming).

in 1679 and actively engaged in securing a constitutional monarchy and a Protestant succession, he mobilizes a usable past to protect subjects' rights and enforce limits on secular authority. Performed in 1604, *Othello* anticipates the post-1650 pattern in part because the protagonist's race prepared its original audience to question his authority.[59] On the one hand, Othello is the victim of a plotting subordinate (Iago), a "curse'd slave" (5.2.300) who "poisons" him with the fiction of another subordinate's plot (his wife's adultery).[60] On the other hand, Othello is a domestic tyrant who murders his wife on spurious grounds.[61]

If in *Othello,* as in so many representations of domestic conflict, danger

59. On Othello's race, and its crucial significance, see Michael D. Bristol, "Charivari and the Comedy of Abjection in *Othello,*" *Renaissance Drama,* n.s. 21 (1990): 3–21; Ruth Cowhig, "Blacks in English Renaissance Drama and the Role of Shakespeare's Othello," in *The Black Presence in English Literature,* ed. David Dabydeen (Manchester: Manchester University Press, 1985), pp. 1–25; Hunter, "*Othello* and Colour Prejudice"; Arthur Kirsch, *Shakespeare and the Experience of Love* (Cambridge: Cambridge University Press, 1981), chap. 2; Ania Loomba, *Gender, Race, and Renaissance Drama* (Manchester: Manchester University Press, 1989), chap. 2; Karen Newman, " 'And wash the Ethiop white': Femininity and the Monstrous in *Othello,*" in *Shakespeare Reproduced: The Text in History and Ideology,* ed. Jean E. Howard and Marion F. O'Connor (New York: Methuen, 1987), pp. 143–62, also found in Newman's recent book, *Fashioning Femininity and English Renaissance Drama* (Chicago: University of Chicago Press, 1991); and Valerie Traub, *Desire and Anxiety: Circulations of Sexuality in Shakespearean Drama* (London: Routledge, 1992), pp. 33–41. See also Anthony Gerard Barthelemy, *Black Face, Maligned Race: The Representation of Blacks in English Drama from Shakespeare to Southerne* (Baton Rouge: Louisiana State University Press, 1987), pp. 150–62; and Jack D'Amico, *The Moor in English Renaissance Drama* (Tampa: University of South Florida Press, 1991), pp. 177–96.

60. In the tradition of petty traitors, Iago "poisons" his master's "delight" (1.1.70): "I'll pour this pestilence into his ear" (2.3.350); "Dangerous conceits are in their natures poisons" (3.3.342). All citations of *Othello* are from *William Shakespeare: The Complete Works,* ed. David Bevington, 4th ed. (New York: Harper Collins, 1992).

61. Peter Stallybrass argues that sometimes Othello can be seen as "the master of an insubordinate servant" ("Patriarchal Territories: The Body Enclosed," in *Rewriting the Renaissance: The Discourses of Sexual Difference in Early Modern Europe,* eds. Margaret W. Ferguson, Maureen Quilligan, and Nancy J. Vickers [Chicago: University of Chicago Press, 1986], pp. 123–42, esp. p. 140); Emily Bartels argues that Brabantio casts Desdemona as "a traitor" ("Making More of the Moor," p. 450). But no one I know of has connected the play to the popular discourses about domestic tyranny and petty treason. Also, although many scholars have connected the play to discourses about marriage and sexuality, they have not explored its relation to those about master-servant relations. Patricia Parker's analysis of "structures of 'following' and their 'preposterous' inverse" identifies what I would call a rhetorical analogue to petty treason ("Preposterous Events," *Shakespeare Quarterly* 43.2 [1992]: 186–213, esp. p. 187).

lies in the familiar, Othello stands both as the victim of those dangerous familiars and as one himself—in the state, as well as the household. Like Caliban, Othello is the "outsider-within," "more familiar than strange," as Emily Bartels argues.[62] Because, as "both monster and *hero,*" he has more power and dignity than Caliban, he poses more of a threat to those who employ him and to his own dependents and intimates.[63] He is "an extravagant and wheeling stranger, / Of here and everywhere" (1.1.139–40), who was yet loved and oft invited by Brabantio (1.3.130). A "bond slave" (1.2.101) to his "masters" (1.3.79) in the signiory, he is also a valued general whom the senate "cannot with safety cast" (1.1.153); he is depended on yet distrusted in a way characteristic of servants.[64] Critics have long noted Othello's ambiguous social positioning: Because of his racial difference from the Venetians, Othello does not hold his authority securely and confidently, especially at home; because he is a successful, trusted general, he is not really a servant. Like Caliban, Othello internalizes the racist assessments of his worth, ultimately accepting the role that grants him the least amount of dignity and authority, in this case, that of cuckold.

Despite what G. K. Hunter calls the play's "claustrophobic intensity," *Othello* does not fit neatly into "the critical category domestic tragedy," as Karen Newman points out when she urges us to "reread *Othello* from another perspective, also admittedly historically bound, that seeks to displace conventional interpretations by exposing the extraordinary fascination with and fear of racial sexual difference which characterizes Elizabethan and Jacobean culture."[65] My interest is in the complex interrelations between discourses of domesticity and those of difference, between the familiar and the strange in the play. It is not only that, as Emily Bartels argues, discourses of racial difference themselves targeted "not the outsider but the insider, the population that threatens by being

---

62. Bartels, "Making More of the Moor," p. 435.

63. This is Karen Newman's phrase, emphasis added (" 'And wash the Ethiop white'," p. 150).

64. On Othello's multiple, contradictory positions, see Bartels, "Making More of the Moor," pp. 433, 435, 451, and passim; Loomba, *Gender, Race,* pp. 41, 48–49, 54; Neill, "Unproper Beds," p. 412; Newman, " 'And wash the Ethiop white'," pp. 150, 153; Rose, *Expense of Spirit,* p. 132; and Stallybrass, "Patriarchal Territories," p. 140.

65. Hunter, "*Othello* and Colour Prejudice," p. 161; Newman, " 'And wash the Ethiop white'," pp. 156–57.

too close to home, too powerful, too successful, or merely too present";[66] it is also that, in focusing on a black hero, *Othello* draws on several distinct, even competing, cultural constructions of domestic threat, of the difference that can undermine domesticity from within. A crucible of cultural fears and anxieties, the play anticipates later cultural obsessions as well as confronting its audience with the full range of contemporary fears: the racial other; the traitor who schemes against the nation from within; the witch; the plotting subordinate; the abusive authority figure. Granting Othello the prestige and sympathy of protagonist status, the play yet allies him with each of these specters of disorder.

Although the most discussed domestic conflict in the play is that between Othello and Desdemona, the play begins as Iago describes a conflict between himself and Othello that is both professional and domestic; Iago first presents himself as a *servant* and Othello as his *master*. Iago's malignity seems more motivated and comprehensible in the context of other representations of scheming subordinates, which similarly criminalize subordinates' ambition. Iago "attends on himself" by fostering Othello's suspicions and "engender[ing]" a plot against his master that exploits both Othello's distrust of his wife and his trust in his ensign (1.1.53; 1.3.404). In the first scene of the play, Iago complains about arbitrary preferment as "the curse of service" and he also proposes a solution to that curse.

> I follow him [Othello] to serve my turn upon him:
> We cannot all be masters, nor all masters
> Cannot be truly followed.
> (1.1.36, 44–46)

By this strategy, Iago cunningly transforms obedience into self-promotion and pursues his master's interests only to the extent that they overlap with his own: "In following him, I follow but myself" (1.1.60). As opposed to "duteous and knee-crooking" servants, Iago links himself with those who "have some soul" (ll.47, 56); that soul is found in the scandalous separation between the servant's interest and the master's interest.

66. Bartels, "Making More of the Moor," p. 433.

> others there are,
> Who, trimmed in forms and visages of duty,
> Keep yet their hearts attending on themselves.
> (1.1.51–53)

In Iago's view, presented as villainous, "outward action" and "the native act, and figure of my heart" cannot correspond for a servant (ll.63–64). While self-interest is too dangerous a livery to wear, the master's livery should also not shape the servant too much, because, in Iago's view, a servant's "soul" exists only in resistance. Iago makes service bearable by so redefining the verbs "serve," "follow," and "attend" that they are no longer recognizable.

Iago's reinvention of service decisively defeats Desdemona's attempt to reinvent marriage to allow both spouses to be subjects and heroes.[67] In contrast to the prevalent representations of conspiring wives and servants, here the treacherous servant works *against* the wife. As critics have noted, Desdemona dwindles when the play abandons the romantic comic structure of the first acts; she is lost without the roles of romantic heroine and loving wife that the play's first generic movement affords her.[68] By act 4, her diminishment accrues greater significance when we see that the play oscillates between competing plots of domestic violence, neither of which offers Desdemona an acceptable role. In both plots, husband and wife are antagonists; each offers her a role that violates what Mary Beth Rose calls her "visionary construction of marriage." She can be either an adulterous wife or a murdered wife. If, as Rose argues, Desdemona aspires to be a heroine of marriage, embarking on a shared adventure,[69] Iago defeats her by drawing on the deeply entrenched, reactionary cultural interest in insubordinate wives, which associates female self-assertion with betrayal, adultery, and violence. First, Iago manipulates Brabantio's fears by interpreting Desdemona's elopement as "a gross revolt" (1.1.137). Then Brabantio and Iago use this "revolt" to warn Othello to anticipate duplicity and to construe

---

67. On the "heroics of marriage" in *Othello*, see Rose, *Expense of Spirit*, pp. 131–55. See also the discussions of marital eroticism in Kirsch, *Shakespeare and the Experience of Love*, passim; and Stephen Greenblatt, *Renaissance Self-Fashioning from More to Shakespeare* (Chicago: University of Chicago Press, 1980), chap. 6.

68. On Desdemona's fracturing and diminution, see Loomba, *Gender, Race*, pp. 57–59; Rose, *Expense of Spirit*, pp. 151–54; and Stallybrass, "Patriarchal Territories," p. 141.

69. Rose, *Expense of Spirit*, esp. p. 138.

Desdemona's self-determination as criminal: "She has deceived her father, and may do thee" (1.3.296; cf. 3.3.211). Othello's doubts about
his own worth and the depth of his love for Desdemona prepare him
to experience her infidelity as a fatal assault. By seeing how Iago deploys
the fiction of the traitorous wife, and remembering how pervasive that
fiction was, we gain one more perspective on the endlessly interesting
question of why Othello so readily distrusts Desdemona.

While the play begins as a romantic comedy, it also has affinities to
darker, crueller comic traditions, such as the cuckold joke and charivari.
In this, it resembles *Arden of Faversham,* with the additional twist that
Othello's race helps to position him as the butt of a mean joke.[70] Like
Arden, he is, in his subordinate's view, "the impediment most profitably
removed" (2.1.279–80), trapped into being what he most fears, "a fixèd
figure for the time of scorn / To point his slow and moving finger at"
(4.2.56–57). Iago and Emilia offer a farcical perspective on adultery,
trivializing what Othello experiences as the most intimate and fatal of
betrayals as a "small vice," not even "peculiar" to him (4.3.72f.; 4.1.68–
70). Also in the tradition of cuckold jokes and shaming rituals, Iago
casts Desdemona as the woman on top: "Our general's wife is now the
general" (2.3.308–9); "She may make, unmake, do what she list"
(l.340).[71] If Iago successfully deploys the structures of inversion and
exaggeration to humiliate and punish those who challenge domestic
norms, the play's central action follows him. As Michael Bristol argues,
playwright and audience are both implicated: "The play as a whole is
organized around the abjection and violent punishment of its central
figures."[72] Even Thomas Rymer, outraged at the absurdity of a black
hero and fully complicit in the trivialization of Othello, censures the
playwright's cruelty toward his characters. In fact, Rymer depicts Shakespeare as himself a tyrant, who "in a barbarous arbitrary way, executes
and makes havock of his subjects, *Hab-nab,* as they come to hand."[73]

Several of Shakespeare's doomed subjects themselves respond "in a

70. See Bristol's provocative argument ("Charivari").
71. On the play's affinities to comedy, see Bristol, "Charivari"; Greenblatt, *Renaissance
Self-Fashioning,* p. 234; Neill, "Unproper Beds"; and Susan Snyder, "*Othello* and the
Conventions of Romantic Comedy," *Renaissance Drama,* n.s. 5 (1972): 123–41.
72. Bristol, "Charivari," p. 3.
73. Thomas Rymer, "A Short View of Tragedy" (1692) in *The Critical Works of
Thomas Rymer,* ed. Curt A. Zimansky (New Haven: Yale University Press, 1956),
pp. 162–63.

barbarous arbitrary way" to their subordinates' self-assertions ("revolts"): Brabantio fears that Desdemona's "escape would teach [him] tyranny" if he had another child (1.3.200); suspicion turns Othello's love to "tyrannous hate" (3.3.464). When Othello acts on these feelings, he anticipates the popular representations of violent, murderous husbands. After Othello publicly slaps and insults his wife, Lodovico assumes that he has lost his mind: "Are his wits safe? Is he not light of brain?" (4.1.274). Othello justifies his murder of Desdemona by casting himself not as a jealous, vengeful husband but as a domestic governor who "proceed[s] upon just grounds" (5.2.143). In this role, he collects the evidence, forms a judgment, and carries out the punishment best suited to the crime, strangling Desdemona in the very "bed she hath contaminated"; "Good, good! The justice of it pleases. Very good" (4.1.208; cf. 5.1.37).[74] Although, as Mary Beth Rose argues, Othello "construes his murder of Desdemona as an execution of justice and revenge undertaken (dispassionately) as a public service,"[75] he finally murders Desdemona, as Richard S. Ide observes, "*in propria persona: as a base, selfish, passionately jealous husband.*"[76] Othello himself comes to see his action as unjust and unjustified, the act of an abused master and an abusive husband, too weak and foolish to overmaster his ensign and his own fears, yet so brutal and tyrannical that he would murder his own wife on a rumor.

As Iago joins the two plots, Emilia disentangles them. Choosing her role as loyal servant over her role as wife, she identifies Iago as a pretty traitor, Othello as a domestic tyrant, and Desdemona as the victim of them both. Proclaiming that "the Moor hath killed my mistress!" (5.2.174), not that "Othello has killed his wife," she privileges her own relation to Desdemona as that least compromised by betrayal and violence. While Emilia bravely chooses among competing alliances, identifies conspiracies, and places blame, the two distinct plots, of petty treason and domestic tyranny, remain in tension. Iago plotted against Othello, but Othello murdered Desdemona.

74. On Othello's murder/execution of Desdemona, see Greenblatt, *Renaissance Self-Fashioning*, p. 250; Rose, *Expense of Spirit*, p. 142; and Rymer, "Short View," pp. 134, 160, 162–63.

75. Rose, *Expense of Spirit*, p. 142.

76. Richard S. Ide, *Possessed with Greatness: The Heroic Tragedies of Chapman and Shakespeare* (Chapel Hill: University of North Carolina Press, 1980), p. 69.

A comparison to Elizabeth Cary's *The Tragedie of Mariam* (1613) can elucidate how both the structure of *Othello* and the characterization of the hero remain persistently dual even in the last act. Like *Othello*, *Mariam* anticipates later interest in domestic tyranny by demonizing and racializing the tyrannous husband as a dark "other." Further, as a play written by a woman, with an outspoken female protagonist, *The Tragedie of Mariam* is particularly well positioned to question not only the limits on a husband's authority but the possibility of a wife's resistance. Compared to *Othello*, *Mariam* more obviously structures the action around antagonistic plots of a wife's treason and a husband's tyranny, linking the two with a false accusation. In *Mariam*, Herod, the tyrannous king and husband, has his wife executed on the false charges that she committed adultery and plotted to poison him, the two wifely transgressions so conventionally linked. It is easier to recognize and separate the two distinct "plots" of spousal conflict in *Mariam* than in *Othello*. When we first meet Mariam, ruminating on the (false) news of Herod's death, she confides how "oft" she has "wished his Carkas dead to see."[77] Mariam; Doris, Herod's bitter ex-wife; and Salome, his sister, whose hand is "ever readie lifted . . . to aime destruction at a husbands throat" dominate the first three acts of the play until Herod returns (2.4.884–85). With Herod's arrival, the play shifts its focus from angry, rebellious, and murderous wives to an angry, repressive, and vengeful tyrant.

In contrast to Desdemona, Mariam is implicated in the false charges

---

77. Elizabeth Cary, *The Tragedie of Mariam,* ed. A. C. Dunstan (The Malone Society Reprints; Oxford: Oxford University Press, 1914), 1.1.20; subsequent references to this edition are located in the text. Recent analyses of the play's ambivalences and contradictions include: Elaine Beilin, *Redeeming Eve: Women Writers of the English Renaissance* (Princeton: Princeton University Press, 1987), chap. 6; Sandra K. Fischer, "Elizabeth Cary and Tyranny, Domestic and Religious," in *Silent But for the Word: Tudor Women as Patrons, Translators, and Writers of Religious Works,* ed. Margaret P. Hannay (Kent, Ohio: Kent State University Press, 1985), pp. 225–37; and Betty S. Travitsky, "The *Feme Covert* in Elizabeth Cary's *Mariam*," in *Ambiguous Realities: Women in the Middle Ages and Renaissance,* ed. Carole Levin and Jeanie Watson (Detroit: Wayne State University Press, 1987), pp. 184–96. Margaret W. Ferguson suggests that "an overdetermined topical allegory in *Mariam*" draws parallels between Henry VIII and Herod as tyrants ("Running On with Almost Public Voice: The Case of 'E. C.'," in *Tradition and the Talents of Women,* ed. Florence Howe [Urbana: University of Illinois Press, 1991], pp. 37–67, esp. p. 66, n. 48); such a topical allegory points to the similarities between *Mariam* and Burnet's account of Anne Boleyn's trial and execution as "palimpsests."

brought against her: She has wished her husband dead; she has resisted him and his authority; she has participated in a kind of adultery, simply by displacing his first wife and children. Until the fifth act, when Mariam is safely dead, the play dramatizes Mariam's conflicts ambivalently, exploring her justifications for resistance, yet presenting that resistance as "a subversive political act that defies Herod's authority as King, as well as husband."[78] Since the play is Mariam's tragedy rather than Herod's, it concludes with a relatively unambiguous indictment of the tyrannous husband. Herod censures himself as a tyrant who deserves his subjects' rebellion: "Why graspe not each of you a sword in hand, / To ayme at me your cruell Soveraignes head" (5.1.2115–16). The concluding Chorus also condemns him as one who "hath his power so much betraide" and who "lunatickly rave[s]" (5.1.2228, 2230).

The characterization of Herod is less sympathetic and nuanced than that of Othello, but he, too, is racialized, his tyrannical behavior presented as that of a man against a woman who "was so white": "If she had bene like an *Egiptian* blacke, / And not so faire, she had bene longer livde" (5.1.2092; 2181–82).[79] Herod, like Othello, "transgresses the norms associated with the idea of a husband" while he reveals the potential for tyranny inherent in those norms.[80] By emphasizing the "fairness" of the murdered wives, most lovable when silent, pallid, and dead, and presenting the murderous husbands as foreign, duped, and dark, both *Mariam* and *Othello*, like the later depictions of murderous husbands, avoid holding the available conceptions of marriage and spousal roles accountable for the tragic outcome. Each play deflects much of the blame for domestic tyranny onto racialized difference between the husband and wife, which undermines the husband's authority, and onto malevolent schemers like Iago and Salome.

Seeing *Othello* as a palimpsest, like Emilia's plain speaking, does not resolve all conflicts: The representation of Iago's schemes is indebted to

78. Nancy Gutierrez, "Valuing *Mariam*: Genre Study and Feminist Analysis," *Tulsa Studies in Women's Literature* 10 (1991): 233–51, esp. p. 245.

79. I depend here on Dympna Callaghan's illuminating analysis of the significance of race in the play: "Re-reading *The Tragedie of Mariam, Faire Queen of Jewry*," in *Women, "Race," and Writing in the Early Modern Period,* ed. Margo Hendricks and Patricia Parker (London: Routledge, forthcoming).

80. Bristol, "Charivari," p. 9, see also p. 15; see also Rose, *Expense of Spirit,* p. 131 and passim.

depictions of traitorous servants, but he is a military subordinate, not a domestic servant;[81] Iago fatally casts Desdemona as an adulterous wife, but he accuses her falsely; Othello is simultaneously more and less powerful than his white, Venetian ensign, a master and a servant of the state, insider and outsider, the victim of conspiracy, and a man who murders his wife. Connecting *Othello* to these two narratives of domestic conflict, each of which locates the threat so differently, offers additional evidence of the play's complexity, particularly of the ways in which it casts each of its central characters in conflicting roles. In its last act, *The Tragedie of Mariam* excludes "the slaughtered Mariam" from view and leaves both Herod and Salome unpunished for Mariam's death; it closes with an uncluttered, less ambivalent emphasis on the tyrant's arbitrary and unchecked power as the cause of the tragedy. In contrast, *Othello* concludes with the unseemly image of the bloody, crowded conjugal bed. Like other representations of wife murder, this image shockingly conjoins marital sex and violence; yet it is also grotesquely adulterous and comic. Piling one body on top of another, forcing spectators to look at all the casualties at once, the play's final act also piles one plot on top of another, refusing to disentangle them even at the end. Focusing on the play's palimpsestic structure also reveals that Othello's race crucially informs the play's form and its relation to other popular materials. By making his protagonist black, Shakespeare prepared his original audience to question Othello's authority, to suspect that he might misuse it groundlessly, and to explore the interrelations of different and domestic, dangerous and familiar.

Comparing *Othello* and *Mariam* suggests that early seventeenth-century drama could anticipate later inquiries into domestic tyranny only under unusual conditions: when a playwright racializes the differences between spouses and thus somewhat distances them from the conflict in most English marriages, or when a female playwright focuses on a wife's subjectivity. Furthermore, in these two plays the analogies between the household and the Commonwealth have a particular force, since both focus on the actions of public men—a general and a king—in domestic situations. Indeed, both men conflate "state affairs" and

---

81. On the significance of the fact that Iago is an ensign who covets a lieutenancy and how lieutenancy "collapses military and domestic structures," see Julia Genster, "Lieutenancy, Standing In, and *Othello*," *ELH* 57 (1990): 785–809, esp. p. 786.

"house affairs" with disastrous results, approaching "private and do-mestic quarrels" with all of the violence and dispatch required to defeat the Turks in bloody battle or murder one's way to the throne (*Othello*, 1.3.193; 1.3.149; 2.3.209). Blurring the distinction between Othello's and Herod's acts as husbands and as public authority figures, the two plays cast them as dangerous familiars—untrustworthy "others" un-dermining order from within—in both spheres. The analogy between household and Commonwealth thus operates in these plays to dissociate tyranny from English patriarchal authority, political and domestic.

Although our culture focuses much of its anxiety about domestic order on the threat of abusive authority, British culture prior to the Civil War focused its anxieties on the threat of the insubordinate or murderous dependent. Before 1650, and a collective act of treason, the domestic ramifications of that anxiety were explored through represen-tations of the murderous wife. After 1650, however, while the mur-derous wife remained a focus of anxiety, the murderous husband attracted increasing attention. Interest shifted from the treacherous sub-ordinate to the irresponsible, even lunatic, authority figure. Husbands and masters may have been reluctant to draw parallels between their rebellion as citizens and their wives' and dependents' frustrations, but they found the story of abused authority—of tyranny—on domestic and political levels increasingly compelling as they justified and instan-tiated their rebellions. After the 1688 Revolution, when representations of murderous husbands are especially numerous, the limits on and responsibilities of power were once again of particular concern.

By telling the stories of household governors who fail to fulfill the responsibilities accompanying their authority, representations of do-mestic tyranny suggest the dangers of trusting husbands not to abuse their power. Francis Barker contends that a new form of masculine subjectivity, the self-regulating "private and judicious individual," emerged in the second half of the seventeenth century. This individual, the propertied male head of household, enjoyed considerable power over others, power that was ambiguously defined and beyond official regulation except in the most extreme instances. Representations of those extremes explore the dangers for dependents and for the social order when the household governor is not self-regulating but arbitrary, not private but inscrutable, not judicious but a brutal lunatic, not individual but estranged from and irresponsible toward his dependents.[82] Yet by dwelling on murder—the most extreme abuse of authority—and demonizing it as the work of tyrants, lunatics, and Moors, the representations of wife-killing avoid implying that marriage is arbitrary, tyrannous, and exploitative, or that wives' rebellion might be justified.

82. Francis Barker, *The Tremulous Private Body: Essays on Subjection* (London: Methuen, 1984), p. 55 and passim.

IV. FINDING WHAT HAS BEEN "LOST": REPRESENTATIONS OF INFANTICIDE AND *THE WINTER'S TALE*

In *The Winter's Tale,* Perdita's name identifies her as "she who has been lost." The process by which she is "lost" is neither accidental, nor mysterious; she is "lost" through her father's violent, purposeful action. After her father, Leontes, referring to her only as "the bastard" or "it," threatens to dash out her "bastard brains with these [his] proper hands," and unsuccessfully attempts to persuade various members of his court to throw the baby into the fire, he orders Antigonus to abandon the baby where she will have small chance of being found.[1]

>   carry
> This female bastard hence, and ... bear it
> To some remote and desert place quite out
> Of our dominions, and ... there ... leave it,
> Without more mercy, to its own protection,
> And favor of the climate. As by strange fortune

---

1. *The Winter's Tale,* 2.3.140. All quotations from *The Winter's Tale* are from *William Shakespeare: The Complete Works,* ed. David Bevington, 4th ed. (New York: Harper Collins, 1992); subsequent references are located in the text.

> It came to us, I do in justice charge thee,
> On thy soul's peril and thy body's torture,
> That thou commend it strangely to some place
> Where chance may nurse or end it. Take it up.
> (2.3.174–83)

Amazingly, John Boswell uses this passage as the epigraph of his book *The Kindness of Strangers,* in which he argues that infant abandonment was a benevolent practice, since parents depended on charitable strangers to find and adopt abandoned babies. Although Boswell argues persuasively that abandonment did not equal murder and literary representations from antiquity through the eighteenth century tend to give foundlings happy endings, most foundlings left in "remote and desert places" probably died.[2] This passage from *The Winter's Tale,* especially when read in context, explicitly describes a father's "horrible" and "bloody" desire to dispose of a child he is (wrongly) convinced is a bastard. Other members of the Sicilian court assume that abandonment will only be a less direct and thus less merciful means of murder than "present death" (2.3.184–85); Hermione accuses Leontes of ripping her newborn from her breast and haling it out to "murder" (3.2.101). Focusing on the cruelty of parents rather than the kindness of strangers, I connect *The Winter's Tale* to the profuse, varied early modern discourses on child murder and the ways that these work to focus blame on murderous mothers yet privilege the stories of murderous fathers.[3]

Although nonfatal forms of violence against children have left little record, assize and quarter sessions documents suggest that when children were murdered, it was usually by members of their families or by

2. John Boswell, *The Kindness of Strangers: The Abandonment of Children in Western Europe from Late Antiquity to the Renaissance* (New York: Vintage, 1988), pp. 41–45 and passim. See also R. W. Malcolmson, "Infanticide in the Eighteenth Century," in *Crime in England, 1550–1800,* ed. J. S. Cockburn (Princeton: Princeton University Press, 1977), pp. 188–89.

3. On the importance of tracing the relations among high, popular, and mass culture and tracing differences across genres and media, see Dominick LaCapra, *History and Criticism* (Ithaca: Cornell University Press, 1985), esp. pp. 71–94; and Richard Johnson, "What Is Cultural Studies Anyway?" *Social Text* 17 (Fall 1987): 38–80. On the importance of rereading canonical texts from the perspective of less familiar works, see Christine Froula, "When Eve Reads Milton: Undoing the Canonical Economy," *Critical Inquiry* 10.2 (1983): 321–64; and Paul Lauter, *Canons and Contexts* (New York: Oxford University Press, 1991), among others.

members of households in which they worked as servants and apprentices. Based on his work with Essex assizes for the period from 1560 to 1709, J. A. Sharpe claims that "the victims of family killings, if we exclude servants and apprentices, were predominantly the offspring of the accused. In nearly half the cases, the person killed was either a child or a stepchild." According to J. S. Cockburn, "A surprisingly high number of family killings in Essex—ten of the nineteen recorded—involved the murder of sons, daughters or step-children."[4] These statistics do not include neonatal infanticide, the murder of newborns in the first twenty-four hours of life, the incidence of which historians debate. Peter C. Hoffer and N.E.H. Hull, for instance, argue for a very high incidence: "Over 25 percent of all murders heard in the early modern English courts [home circuit assizes, circa 1558–1650] ... were infanticides."[5] In contrast, Cockburn argues that indictments for neonatal infanticide were relatively uncommon. From Essex, Herts, and Sussex, "only sixty-two survive from the reign of Elizabeth, an average of less than one a year in each county"; indictments were even rarer in the early seventeenth century.[6] Yet Cockburn warns that the data are unreliable, and elsewhere contends that the available evidence may seriously underestimate the levels of incidence.[7]

Whatever the incidence of neonatal infanticide, increasingly rigorous infanticide legislation culminated in a particularly harsh statute of 1624. Ignoring the many ways of and motives for eliminating children, this statute expressly criminalized only one: unmarried women's murder of their illegitimate newborns. Neonatal infanticide generated new legis-

4. J. A. Sharpe, "Domestic Homicide in Early Modern England," *The Historical Journal* 24.1 (1981): 29–48, esp. p. 37; J. S. Cockburn, "The Nature and Incidence of Crime in England, 1559–1625: A Preliminary Survey," in *Crime in England,* ed. Cockburn, pp. 49–71, esp. p. 57.

5. Peter C. Hoffer and N.E.H. Hull, *Murdering Mothers: Infanticide in England and New England, 1558–1803* (New York: New York University Press, 1981), p. xviii.

6. Cockburn, "Nature and Incidence," p. 58. Angus McLaren also argues that neonatal infanticide was never very common (*Reproductive Rituals: The Perception of Fertility in England from the Sixteenth Century to the Nineteenth Century* [London: Methuen, 1984], pp. 129–35).

7. J. S. Cockburn, "Patterns of Violence in English Society: Homicide in Kent, 1560–1985," *Past and Present* 130 (1991): 70–106, esp. pp. 95–97. Cockburn questions many commentators' decision to exclude infanticide when they chart patterns of violence. When infanticide is included in discussions of violence in early modern England, Cockburn argues, domestic violence emerges as more widespread than many historians have conceded; women also begin to figure more significantly as perpetrators (p. 96).

lation and increased prosecution in the seventeenth century; indictments and guilty verdicts peaked in the late Tudor and early Stuart periods and remained high until the early eighteenth century.[8] I am less interested here in the incidence of various forms of child murder, than in the extensive legal and popular representations of child murder and how these displaced blame for the neglect and elimination of children onto mothers, especially unmarried ones.

Some early modern women do seem to have killed their children. Although women were generally unlikely to perpetrate violence, when they did they killed intimates—husbands, servants, or children. Indeed, by Hoffer's and Hull's calculation, "90 percent of all murderous assaults by women were directed at infants."[9] Women may have been more likely to kill or fatally neglect their newborns than to engage in any other kind of murderous violence. While acknowledging women's significant role in violence against children, it is important to remember that women were more often the victims of domestic violence than the assailants. Those women who did commit infanticide were so reluctant to use force that suffocation and exposure were the most popular methods of killing infants and small children.[10] Furthermore, women were certainly not solely responsible for all lethal assaults on children.

If abandonment could operate as a widespread practice of deferred, displaced violence, it was one in which fathers, in practice as in fairy tales, may often have taken the initiative. In addition, Keith Wrightson

8. Hoffer and Hull, *Murdering Mothers,* p. x; see also Cockburn, "Patterns," pp. 96–97. Susan Dwyer Amussen sees prosecution and conviction rates declining even earlier, by the late seventeenth century (*An Ordered Society: Gender and Class in Early Modern England* [Oxford: Basil Blackwell, 1988], p. 115). According to J. A. Sharpe, infanticide was a "distinctive new offence" in the late sixteenth century (*Crime in Early Modern England, 1550–1750* [London: Longman, 1984], pp. 170; see also pp. 60–62).

9. Hoffer and Hull, *Murdering Mothers,* pp. xviii–xix. This percentage is almost the reverse of the case in murders and manslaughters of adult victims, in which men far outnumber women as perpetrators (p. 98); also see Sharpe, "Domestic Homicide," pp. 37–38; and Cockburn, "Nature and Incidence," p. 57.

10. Court records and popular representations correspond here. See Keith Wrightson, "Infanticide in Earlier Seventeenth-Century England," *Local Population Studies* 15 (1975): 10–22, esp. p. 15. In *Murther Will Out, or, A True and Faithful Relation of an Horrible Murther Committed Thirty Three Years Ago, by an Unnatural Mother, upon the Body of Her Own Child* (London, 1675), for instance, the mother first tries to smother her infant by leaving a pillow over his face; she finally kills him by placing him under a tub and leaving for an hour.

argues that fathers engaged in a subtle method of disposing of bastard children to which he refers as "infanticidal nursing," that is, fostering out newborns to impoverished, overworked wet nurses who would neglect them.[11] Wrightson describes how some fathers gave their bastard children to vagrant nurses, even strapping the babies on the backs of unwilling women. Themselves destitute, these women could be depended upon to abandon or starve the babies. Under such circumstances, as Valerie Fildes suggests, blame should rest "not on the women involved in nursing, but on the men who employed, supervised, and, ultimately, exploited them."[12] Although fathers were rarely prosecuted

11. Wrightson, "Infanticide," p. 16. On abandonment as a displaced form of infanticide, see Lawrence Stone, *The Family, Sex, and Marriage in England, 1500–1800* (New York: Harper and Row, 1977), pp. 474–76. When foundling hospitals emerged to enclose and conceal the social phenomenon of abandonment and to assuage parental guilt, they became a form of institutionalized infanticide, sacrificing as much as 87 percent of those in their care to disease (Boswell, *Kindness of Strangers*, pp. 421–22 and passim; and Malcolmson, "Infanticide in the Eighteenth Century," p. 189). On babies left in urban locations where they were likely to be found and how this kind of abandonment is not necessarily infanticidal or associated with illegitimacy, see Valerie Fildes, "Maternal Feelings Re-Assessed: Child Abandonment and Neglect in London and Westminster, 1550–1800," in *Women as Mothers in Pre-Industrial England: Essays in Memory of Dorothy McLaren*, ed. Fildes (London: Routledge, 1990), pp. 139–78, esp. pp. 151–53. Boswell (*Kindness of Strangers*) also focuses on urban abandonments.

Some opponents of wet-nursing also considered it potentially infanticidal because it might tempt nurses to sacrifice their own children's welfare to that of their paying charges. See Gail Kern Paster's brilliant work on "a rich, somatic discourse about nursing, nurses, and weaning almost entirely lost to us" and its relation to Renaissance drama (*The Body Embarrassed: Drama and the Disciplines of Shame in Early Modern England* [Ithaca: Cornell University Press, 1993], chap. 5, esp. p. 229).

On the father's role in eliminating an illegitimate newborn, see Thomas Brewer, *The Bloudy Mother, or The Most Inhumane Murthers Committed by Jane Hattersley* (London, 1609); *A True and Perfect Relation of the Tryal and Condemnation, Execution and Last Speech of That Unfortunate Gentleman Mr. Robert Foulks Late Minister . . . for Murder and Adultery* (London, 1679); and *An Alarme for Sinners: Containing the Confession, Prayers, Letters, and Last Words of Robert Foulkes* (London, 1679).

12. Fildes, "Maternal Feelings," p. 168; see also pp. 162–68. Not all wet-nursing was covertly infanticidal. Many families selected wet nurses with care; wet-nursing also offered employment at good wages to women and functioned as a "cottage industry." See Valerie Fildes, "The English Wet Nurse and Her Role in Infant Care, 1538–1800," *Medical History* 32 (1988): 142–73; Linda A. Pollock, *Forgotten Children: Parent-Child Relations from 1500 to 1900* (Cambridge: Cambridge University Press, 1983), pp. 24–25, 50; and Keith Wrightson, *English Society, 1580–1680* (New Brunswick, N.J.: Rutgers University Press, 1982), p. 108. In several accounts of infanticide, wet nurses preserve the lives of suckling children, simply by keeping them out of the house. See for instance, *A Pitilesse Mother That Most Unnaturally at One Time, Murthered Two of Her Owne Children* (London,

as the principals in infanticide, they played important roles in eliminating unwanted infants while yet avoiding the direct, violent action that would expose them to criminal prosecution.[13]

In this chapter, I chart the distinctly different trajectories of legal and literary representations of child murder in the seventeenth century and the interrelations between the two. Legal discourses participate in the criminalization of women and of poverty; they define infanticide as the crime of indigent, unmarried women against newborns. Some pamphlets, ballads, and plays purporting to represent actual instances of child murder correspond to the statutes in focusing on a particular kind of criminalized maternal agency. Most, however, exceed the statutes' limits; they scrutinize all of the circumstances, perpetrators, and motives for which the law cannot account. These diverse texts describe fathers as well as mothers, wives as well as spinsters, the murder of legitimate older children of both genders as well as bastard newborns; parents who kill all of their children at once; parents who smother, drown, and stab; parents motivated by poverty, depression, or insanity. These numerous, diverse texts suggest that child murder and, most important for my purposes, the obsession with representing it pervade the culture. As these representations move up literary hierarchies from pamphlets to romances and up social hierarchies from indigent spinsters to kings, they increasingly displace the violence and distance representation from concrete depictions of English domestic life; by means of these two kinds of detachments the focus shifts to the father as the perpetrator and protagonist. Thus, legal representations—those with the most direct material consequences—dwell on women's power over their children, assuming and criminalizing their agency and holding them

---

1616); accounts of the Calverley murders; and *Blood for Blood, or, Justice Executed for Innocent Blood-Shed* (London, 1670). I am grateful to Douglas B. Patton for directing me to *Blood for Blood*.

Regardless of the "intentions" of parents or nurses, wet-nursing increased infant mortality by depriving babies of the immunological properties of collostrum and by introducing them to unfamiliar, often unsanitary, environments. On infant feeding practices, how class shaped these practices, and popular debate over breast-feeding, see Valerie A. Fildes, *Breasts, Bottles, and Babies: A History of Infant Feeding* (Edinburgh: University of Edinburgh, 1986), and *Wet Nursing: A History from Antiquity to the Present* (Oxford: Basil Blackwell, 1988); and Pollock, *Forgotten Children*, pp. 212–22.

13. "Fathers were included in indictments as accessories and conspirators in the concealment of births, but women bore the brunt of the prosecution" (Hoffer and Hull, *Murdering Mothers*, p. 103).

accountable for its consequences. Pamphlets and plays also associate mothers' authority and agency with violence and crime, depicting a destructively intimate mother-child relation with fatal consequences for the child. In contrast, they present fathers' authority over their children more positively and euphemize their agency in disposing of children.

In connecting the fantastic story of how Leontes loses his daughter to the dismal chronicles of spinsters who toss their newborns in the privy, I argue that suppressing that connection has been crucial to the process of canon-formation. In this process, itself dependent on abandonments, exclusions, and violence, *The Winter's Tale* has become one of the best known early modern stories of child disposal; yet it is rarely acknowledged as such.

Legal Constructions of Infanticide

In England prior to Elizabeth I's reign, neonatal infanticide was dealt with primarily by the church courts, which could assign penances but not capital punishments.[14] Thus, infanticide was not considered homicide in this period, and it did not result in execution for the convicted.[15] Although "coroners were charged with the examination of all corpses, and an inquest into the cause of death of an infant could lead to an indictment for homicide in the king's courts," infanticide cases rarely appeared in the secular courts and rarely resulted in convictions.[16] In addition, surviving records of infanticide in the Middle Ages, from penitentials to church court records, suggest that this crime was not yet associated only with women or with illegitimate children.

As the regulation of personal conduct shifted from the church courts to the secular courts, infanticide came under secular control. Increasingly rigorous legislation against infanticide was interwoven with leg-

14. On infanticide in the Middle Ages, see Boswell, *Kindness of Strangers;* Barbara Hanawalt, *Crime and Conflict in English Communities, 1300–1348* (Cambridge: Harvard University Press, 1979), and "The Female Felon in Fourteenth-Century England," *Viator* 5 (1974): 253–68; and R. H. Helmholz, "Infanticide in the Province of Canterbury during the Fifteenth Century," *History of Childhood Quarterly* 2.3 (1975): 379–90.

15. Barbara A. Kellum, "Infanticide in England in the Later Middle Ages," *History of Childhood Quarterly* 1.3 (1974): 366–88, esp. p. 375; and Helmholz, "Infanticide in Canterbury," pp. 383–84.

16. Hoffer and Hull, *Murdering Mothers,* p. 5, see also pp. 4–7.

islation controlling the poor and the sexually incontinent and linking the two.[17] In the secular courts, infanticide was treated as homicide and thus as a capital offense. Although the murder of children older than a few hours or days was not distinct from other forms of homicide in terms of how it was punished, the statutes increasingly associated the murder of newborns with social and sexual disorder, singling it out as an important target of regulation. In this process, statutes under Elizabeth and James (Acts 18 Eliz. c. 3 [1575/76] and 7 Jac. 1 c. 4 [1609]) that attempted to control the rates of illegitimacy and to hold parents responsible for supporting bastards played an important role. According to the first statute, parents who could not support their bastard infants could be imprisoned in the House of Correction.[18] The later law, which focuses on the *mothers* of bastards, connecting them with "rogues, vagabonds, sturdy beggars, and other lewd and idle persons," empowers magistrates to set unwed mothers "on work" or to imprison them indefinitely for repeat offenses. Both statutes thus focus on bastards "which may be chargeable to the Parish."[19]

In trying to control one form of social disorder, this legislation may have produced another. Hoffer and Hull argue that these poor laws so fiercely punished the parents of illegitimate children, especially mothers, that they might even have motivated infanticide: "With the same force that the poor law urged magistrates to ferret out bastardy among the poor and punish it severely, the law counselled the poor to conceal bastardy pregnancy and perhaps to murder their bastard newborns."[20] Probably because of both increased rates of infanticide and increased vigilance in hunting down the mothers of bastards and the indigent, after the poor law [1576], indictments for infanticide increased 225

17. On personal conduct laws, see Hoffer and Hull (ibid., pp. 13–19) and Joan R. Kent, "Attitudes of Members of the House of Commons to the Regulation of 'Personal Conduct' in Late Elizabethan and Early Stuart England," *Bulletin of the Institute of Historical Research* 46 (May 1973): 41–71. On the role of ecclesiastical courts in regulating conduct and legislating morality, see Martin Ingram, *Church Courts, Sex, and Marriage in England, 1570–1640* (Cambridge: Cambridge University Press, 1987).

18. See the statute in Ferdinand Pulton, *A Collection of Sundry Statutes, Frequent in Use* (London, 1636), sig. Ccccc; see also Wrightson, "Infanticide," p. 21, n. 22.

19. Edward Coke, *The Second Part of the Institutes of the Laws of England,* 6th ed. (London, 1681), sig. Aaaaa3; see also Pulton, *Sundry Statutes;* and Hoffer and Hull, *Murdering Mothers,* p. 13.

20. Hoffer and Hull, *Murdering Mothers,* p. 17.

percent.[21] Later in the seventeenth century, legislation about bastardy and other forms of sexual irregularity (for example, the short-lived 1650 act making adultery and incest felonies) may have continued to prompt violent forms of concealment.

Because of the increase in indictments for infanticide following the poor laws, and the concomitant interest in regulating the conduct of the socially and sexually ranging and disruptive, Parliaments of 1606–1607 and 1610 debated bills dealing with infanticide; Parliament passed new legislation in 1624 (repealed in 1803).[22] These debates and the legislation they produced, like other legal strategies for social control in the period, reveal more about the processes of defining and addressing threats to order than about the actual incidence of particular transgressions. The infanticide statute of 1624 definitively associated the crime with women, bastardy, and poverty and attempted to remove concealment as either a motive for infanticide or a barrier to prosecution. Since "many lewd women that have beene delivered of Bastard Children, to avoid their shame, and to escape punishment, [did] secretly burie or conceale the death of their Children," it was impossible to tell whether a child was born dead or was murdered by the "lewd mother" if a corpse was found. A mother who had just given birth under traumatic circumstances, working alone and in secret, usually could not get very far away from her residence; often she buried the infant's body at night, hid it in a cupboard or laundry hamper, or discarded it in a ditch or privy. Therefore, the primary evidence against her was rarely hard to find. The statute seeks to eliminate the confusion attending the discovery of an infant's corpse, especially if it had no marks of violence upon it. "If any woman . . . [was] delivered of any Issue of her body, Male or

21. Ibid., pp. 17–18. For an extended discussion of Elizabethan legal constructions of infanticide, see Hoffer and Hull's discussion of the "kite case" that debated a mother's responsibility for the death of her infant, which she had abandoned, when it was struck by a kite in 1560 in the Welsh border shire of Chester (ibid., pp. 8–11). On the denial of pardons to women who committed infanticide in sixteenth- and seventeenth-century France, see Natalie Z. Davis, *Fiction in the Archives: Pardon Tales and Their Tellers in Sixteenth-Century France* (Stanford: Stanford University Press, 1987), pp. 85–87.

On the criminalization of poverty, see A. L. Beier, *Masterless Men: The Vagrancy Problem in England, 1560–1640* (London: Methuen, 1985); Kent, "Attitudes"; Sharpe, *Crime in Early Modern England*, pp. 176–77; and Paul Slack, "Vagrants and Vagrancy in England, 1598–1664," *Economic History Review*, 2d ser. 27 (1974): 360–79.

22. Wrightson, "Infanticide," p. 11.

Female, which being borne alive, should by the Lawes of this Realme be a Bastard," and she tried to conceal the miscarriage or stillbirth by hiding the corpse, she would suffer death unless she could produce at least one witness to testify that the infant had been born dead.[23]

The 1624 statute, which one statute book summarizes as "murther for a mother to conceale the death of her Bastard child," generated increased prosecutions, as had the Elizabethan poor law. While the poor law of 1576 boosted prosecutions by creating "a new class of potential infanticidal offenders," the 1624 statute quadrupled prosecutions by fostering "increased vigilance on the part of magistrates." Under newly authorized surveillance, concealment of a stillbirth and purposeful murder became indistinguishable for legal purposes.[24]

This legislation so successfully constructed the crime of infanticide that, according to Wrightson, in fifty-nine of sixty cases of infanticide prosecuted at the Essex assizes between 1601 and 1665, the mother was the accused. Of these, fifty-three are described as spinsters, six as widows. Of sixty-two victims, fifty-three were "unambiguously described as bastards."[25] Such identifications of victims are found mostly after the 1624 legislation. Even in the eighteenth century, when the 1624 statute was seen as excessively severe and many accusations ended in acquittal, the obsolete legislation continued to define the crime and the criminal. R. W. Malcolmson finds that those accused of infanticide were usually unmarried mothers from "labouring, mechanic or farming backgrounds" who were servant maids or had recently retired from service; most infanticides occurred directly after birth, as an attempt to conceal it.[26] Thus, the law discovered what it was designed to discover,

---

23. Pulton, *Sundry Statutes,* sig. Dddddd3.

24. Hoffer and Hull, *Murdering Mothers,* pp. 19–31; and Wrightson, "Infanticide," p. 15.

25. Wrightson, "Infanticide," p. 12.

26. Malcolmson, "Infanticide in the Eighteenth Century," p. 192; see also Hoffer and Hull, *Murdering Mothers,* pp. 102–3. On the associations between servants and bastardy, see Peter Laslett, *The World We Have Lost: England before the Industrial Age,* 3d ed. (New York: Scribners, 1984), esp. pp. 178–79; and G. R. Quaife, *Wanton Wenches and Wayward Wives: Peasants and Illicit Sex in Early Seventeenth-Century England* (New Brunswick, N.J.: Rutgers University Press, 1979), pp. 89–123, 202–42. Cockburn argues that the victims of neonatal infanticide were "typically, conceived on the fringes of the biological family—as the result of relationships with masters—or within the household—during affairs with fellow servants" ("Patterns," p. 95).

and it created and enforced a profile of the murderous unmarried mother.

Joining with other statutes such as those criminalizing witchcraft and vagrancy in locating threats to order in marginalized and powerless community members, the infanticide statutes articulated fears about women's capacity for violence rather than accurately describing their behavior. Although arbitrary record survival and the relative ease of concealing this crime make it difficult for us to recover actual numbers, there was probably always a gap between these and the perceived frequency of the crime.[27]

Furthermore, there was a gap between legal theory and legal practice, between statutes and juries, regarding neonatal infanticide. Juries attended to the "exceptional circumstances" that might drive a mother to dispose of her newborn; they were also reluctant to convict for infanticide, even after changes in legislation made it easier to do so, seeing it as a lesser evil than charging a bastard to the parish.[28] Thus, although the statutes rigidly defined the killing of illegitimate infants as criminal, the slippery processes of investigation and prosecution reveal that the value of infant life was disturbingly relative. Wrightson finds that,

> while it was certainly not a generally tolerated practice, infanticide would appear to have had a considerable currency in the disposal of a minority of unwanted, predominantly illegitimate, children.... The discussion of infanticide thus uncovers a perplexing relativity in popular attitudes to-

27. In the eighteenth century, for instance, Malcolmson sees a gap between popular representations, which suggest that infanticide was widespread, and legal records, which suggest that it was not very common ("Infanticide in the Eighteenth Century," pp. 190–91). See also Michael MacDonald, *Mystical Bedlam: Madness, Anxiety, and Healing in Seventeenth-Century England* (Cambridge: Cambridge University Press, 1981), p. 83; Wrightson, "Infanticide," esp. p. 19; and McLaren, *Reproductive Rituals*, pp. 129–35.

28. Amussen, *Ordered Society*, p. 115; see also McLaren, *Reproductive Rituals*, p. 131. In her work-in-progress on cases of infanticide in Scotland, Deborah Symonds argues that extenuating circumstances—such as the mother's status and the amount of force used in the murder—significantly shaped how courts treated particular instances of infanticide. I am grateful to Professor Symonds, of the Drake University Department of History, for sharing her manuscript, "The Baby Killers: Mary Hamilton, Jeanie Deans, and the Economic and Juridical Transformation of Scotland, 1690–1820."

wards the value of infant life which contrasts markedly with the clear prescriptions of contemporary official morality.[29]

The mother's criminality was also relative, as the very wording of the statutes targeting unmarried mothers reveals. Denying the possibility that unmarried women who concealed their pregnancies might suffer stillbirths, the statute yet left stillbirth open as a possible defense for married women. Married women were also more likely to be pardoned as insane at the time that they murdered their infants, while unmarried women were more often found sane and thus criminal and accountable. Unless undeniable signs of violence were found on the victim's body, a married suspect was rarely convicted of infanticide.[30] In short, then, unmarried mothers of infants found dead were guilty until proven innocent, while married mothers were innocent until proven guilty.[31] Here again, the legal system exonerated women only by denying their agency; it attributed agency to women largely when it criminalized that agency and held women fatally accountable for it. The legal construction of infanticide thus participated in the criminalizations of poverty and of women outside of the familial and social structures designed to control them. It also participated in contests over women's control over and responsibility for their bodies and their offspring. In this process, the nonelite female body became an object of inquiry and social control.

Murder or Miscarriage? Negotiating the Boundary between Mother and Fetus

Pamphlets, ballads, and plays tend to ignore infanticide as the statutes defined it—as if there is not much of a story in it. They direct their attention instead to instances of child murder for which the statutes

29. Wrightson, "Infanticide," p. 10. See also Catherine Damme, "Infanticide: The Worth of an Infant under Law," *Medical History* 22 (1978): 1–24.

30. See Hoffer and Hull, *Murdering Mothers,* pp. 146–47, 106–7; and McLaren, *Reproductive Rituals,* p. 131.

31. When the statute was reformed in 1803, the burden of proof was shifted from the mother to the prosecution, as in other felonies. See McLaren, *Reproductive Rituals,* pp. 129–35.

cannot account.[32] Although some pamphlets string together terse accounts of infants' bodies discovered in privies and ditches, those relatively rare texts that actually try to tell the story of neonatal infanticide
dwell on the exceptional—a mother who slaughters countless infants
in order to continue in sexual incontinency or a convicted mother who
miraculously survives her execution.[33] Richard Watkins's *Newes from
the Dead* (1651), a learned account of the "miraculous" survival of Anne
Greene, a woman hanged for neonatal infanticide, parallels the statutes
by intervening in a legally and morally ambiguous area to fix a boundary
between the mother's body and the fetus. Watkins's text is an anomaly—
a learned treatise on the medical, theological, and legal issues raised by
the case as well as a sensational account of "miraculous" "news" that
was sure to appeal to a wide audience. Neonatal infanticide is only
represented under such exceptional circumstances.

In 1650, when Anne Greene was hanged, her friends thumped her
on the breast and pulled on her legs, hoping to make her death faster
and less painful. Despite these efforts, once Greene was cut down, put
in a coffin, and taken to be dissected by physicians, she revived. This
startling revival attracted a great deal of attention from both elite and
popular audiences. Scholars at Oxford, where Greene was executed,
contribute pages of dedicatory poems to Richard Watkins's volume
about her "miraculous deliverance," in which they reflect on the philo-
sophical and theological implications of Greene's experience. The physicians who were to dissect her and later worked, invasively and
aggressively, to revive her evince a professional/scientific interest.
Greene also attracted popular interest: "In the same Roome where her
Body was to have beene dissected for the satisfaction of a few, she
became a greater wonder, being reviv'd, to the satisfaction of multitudes

32. Noting that popular literature generally depicts the most sensational murders,
Bernard Capp argues that "the mundane crime of an unmarried servant girl who smoth-
ered her new-born baby to escape disgrace was a very untypical subject" ("Popular
Literature," in *Popular Culture in Seventeenth-Century England,* ed. Barry Reay [London:
Croom Helm, 1985], p. 224). Betty Travitsky points out that the drama depicts neo-
naticide only rarely ("Child Murder in English Renaissance Life and Drama," *Medieval
and Renaissance Drama in England* 6 [1993]: 63–84).

33. For a pamphlet that strings together many brief accounts of murderous mothers,
see *Natures Cruell Step-Dames: Or, Matchless Monsters of the Female Sex, Elizabeth Barnes
and Anne Willis* (London, 1637); for an account of a mother who murders several of
her illegitimate infants, see Brewer's *The Bloudy Mother.*

that flocked thither daily to see her."[34] Greene became, in fact, such a popular attraction that her physicians wished to limit access in the interests of her still fragile health. To protect Greene yet cater to the curious, the authorities decided on a combination of entrepreneurship and charity.

> Yet because those of the better sort could not altogether be denied admission, they thought it a seasonable opportunity, for the maid's behalfe, to invite them either to exercise their Charity, or at least to pay for their Curiosity. And therefore (themselves first leading the way) they commended it to those that came in, to give every one what they pleas'd, her Father being there ready to receive it.
> (sigs. B4–B4v)

Cut down from the scaffold, Greene remains an edifying spectacle for a mixed audience, but she metamorphoses from a cause of her father's shame to one of his pride and profit, from a negative to a positive example.

Watkins's text plays an important part in this process. Sure that God spared Greene because she was innocent, Watkins takes his readers through a reconsideration of the evidence against her; although it was standard practice to acquit automatically those rare convicts who survived execution, legal and medical authorities reviewed the evidence in order to acquit Greene.[35] This process of review, as represented in Watkins's text, translates the fetus from a person deserving legal protection to a discharge of its mother's body. A midwife testifies that the stillborn infant was small, hairless, its sex indistinguishable. Fellow servants testify that Greene had been hemorrhaging for seven weeks prior to the birth, that she was only seventeen weeks pregnant, and

34. Richard Watkins, *Newes from the Dead. Or, A True and Exact Narration of the Miraculous Deliverance of Anne Greene, Who Being Executed at Oxford . . . Afterwards Revived* (Oxford, 1651), sig. B4; subsequent references are located in the text.

35. Angus McLaren cites one example from the late seventeenth century that remarkably resembles Greene's case, yet demonstrates that those who survived execution were not *always* acquitted. In 1658, "a woman had been hanged for infanticide but when taken to be anatomized was revived by the doctors. The bailiffs seized her and hanged her again. 'The Women,' a contemporary report read, who 'were exceedingly enraged by it, cut downe the tree whereon shee was hanged'" (McLaren, *Reproductive Rituals,* p. 132, quoting *The Life and Times of Anthony Wood,* ed. A. Clark [Oxford: Oxford University Press, 1891–1895], 1:250–51).

that heavy work preceded the "birth." Thus, the reproductive event becomes a miscarriage rather than the birth and murder of a live infant. According to Greene, she did not know for certain that she was pregnant and the fetus "fell from her unawares as she was in the house of office" (sig. B4v). Although Greene could not then distinguish the miscarriage from the preceding hemorrhaging, Watkins can subsequently conclude that "the child which fell from her unawares, was nothing but a lump of the same matter coagulated" (sig. C), that matter being "suppressed" menstrual flow. In order to exonerate Anne Greene, Watkins reabsorbs the fetus-as-victim into its mother's body, presenting the mother as "unaware" of and therefore not responsible for her body and its discharges. Like the many mothers who disposed of their illegitimate newborns, dead or alive, in privies, including Greene herself, the experts who review the evidence define as lifeless matter, excrement, the fetus who was defended in the first trial.[36]

The relationship between the mother's body and the fetus it carries was the focus of moral and legal debate in the period, which centered on the point at which the fetus becomes a separate entity and on the mother's responsibility for preserving fetal life. Until the Infant Life Preservation Act of 1929, a mother was not legally accountable for killing a child during the birth process, and before it was fully detached from her body.[37] As William L. Langer rather gruesomely clarifies, before 1929, "to kill a child by crushing its head with a hairbrush or hammer, or cutting its throat was technically not a crime, so long as its lower extremities were still in the body of the mother."[38] Given the invasive, violent forms of birth assistance sometimes employed in the early modern period, children often died during difficult births; some

36. For accounts of women who throw their newborns into "houses of office," see *Deeds against Nature, and Monsters by Kinde* (London, 1614), and *Natures Cruell Step-Dames,* among others. Virtually all historical accounts of infanticide discuss how often infant corpses were found in privy vaults, and how often women were accused of having dumped their newborns in privies.

37. See Wrightson, "Infanticide," p. 20, n. 15; and Hoffer and Hull, *Murdering Mothers,* p. 155. In his discussion of pleading the belly, or seeking to defer execution by means of pregnancy, Oldham also addresses debates regarding "quickening" as the point at which the fetus began to be legally protected (James C. Oldham, "On Pleading the Belly: A History of the Jury of Matrons," *Criminal Justice History* 6 [1985]: 1–64, esp. pp. 6, 17–19, 24–25).

38. William L. Langer, "Infanticide: A Historical Survey," *History of Childhood Quarterly* 1.3 (1974): 353–65, esp. p. 360.

of these deaths may have been deliberate. Although midwives took an oath to preserve and protect the infant's life, there were those who maintained houses for clandestine lying-in and the convenient disappearance of newborns.[39]

In addition to this confusion about when the fetus was separate from its mother and thus a person deserving legal protection, abortion had an unclear legal and moral status in this period. Like the value of a newborn infant's life, the moral status of abortion was interpreted according to the circumstances. If abortion enabled an unmarried woman or adulteress to conceal and continue illicit sexual activity, it was wrong; if it occurred before quickening and enabled a married woman to control her fertility, it was acceptable.[40] Although abortion was condemned, and canon law equated infanticide and abortion, it had no clear legal status in England until it was made a statutory offense in 1803.[41] Women who attempted to induce their own miscarriages, as women traditionally had, were still not targeted by the 1803 statute.

Abortifacients (such as the herbs ergot of rye, pennyroyal, and savin) were known and available, and, although moralists and medical practitioners condemned abortion, women collected and circulated recipes.[42] Countering Lawrence Stone's claim that methods of inducing

39. See Thomas R. Forbes, "The Regulation of English Midwives in the Sixteenth and Seventeenth Centuries," *Medical History* 8.3 (1964): 235–44; Hoffer and Hull, *Murdering Mothers,* pp. 155–57; and McLaren, *Reproductive Rituals,* pp. 98–100. Also see ballads concerning Mary Compton, a midwife accused of killing newborns and children left in her care by neglecting and starving them (ballads 428–31 in vol. 7 of *The Pepys Ballads,* ed. Hyder E. Rollins, 8 vols. [Cambridge: Harvard University Press, 1929–1935]).

40. See McLaren, *Reproductive Rituals,* p. 107. Abortions were perceived as so dangerous in the early modern period that they were construed as suicidal by many writers (pp. 93–94). It is hard to tell whether this perception was accurate or a way of articulating moral censure and of insisting that the mother's welfare and the fetus's could *never* be dissociated.

41. See Ingram, *Church Courts,* p. 159; Hoffer and Hull, *Murdering Mothers,* p. 157; Kellum, "Infanticide in England," pp. 374–75; and McLaren, *Reproductive Rituals,* passim, esp. chap. 5. Cornelia Hughes Dayton shows how documents concerning a woman who died after a botched abortion reveal widespread knowledge of abortifacients, but do not exhibit "either outrage over the destruction of a fetus or denunciations of those who would arrest 'nature's proper course' " ("Taking the Trade: Abortion and Gender Relations in an Eighteenth-Century New England Village," *William and Mary Quarterly,* 3d ser. 48.1 [1991]: 19–49, esp. p. 23).

42. Amussen, *Ordered Society,* pp. 114–15; Linda A. Pollock, "Embarking on a Rough Passage: The Experience of Pregnancy in Early Modern Society," in *Women as Mothers,* ed. Fildes, pp. 39–67, esp. p. 55.

miscarriage were not widely known or used, Linda Pollock argues that "these remedies were not hidden in 'obscure medical treatises' but were kept by women in their private medical books, presumably because they thought they might require recourse to such knowledge."[43] Prior to "quickening," usually in the fourth month, women felt that inducing a miscarriage, or provoking a resumption of menstruation, as they described this, was unobjectionable. Angus McLaren concurs with Pollock's emphasis on women's common knowledge of abortifacients: "In seventeenth- and eighteenth-century women's receipts books...one finds extensive suggestions on how to 'provoke the terms,' 'purge the courses,' 'bring down the flowers' and deal with 'menses obstructed'."[44] Historians of contraception and women's bodies thus conclude that abortion was one form of family limitation available to early modern women.[45] Women bravely took control of their own fertility in consultation with other women and by depending on traditional knowledge of the herbs in their gardens.

Throughout the early modern period in England, the mother's responsibility for her own fertility and the fetuses she carried was uncertain, contested. Traditionally, mothers assumed considerable control over reproduction; legally, even if certain actions were seen as morally questionable, there was no basis for interfering in a married mother's control over an unborn child until it was fully detached from her body. As Anne Greene's case demonstrates, medical and legal interpretation of the evidence could reattach the fetus to the mother even then. At the point that mother's and infant's bodies separated, infanticide legislation intervened, attempting to distinguish mother and child and hold the mother, especially the socially dislocated mother, accountable for her infant's life.

If the unclear distinction between the mother's body and the fetus caused moral and legal debate as well as anxiety and confusion, the mother's relation to her own body was also problematic. When women in the neighborhood suspected an unmarried woman of having concealed a birth, they searched her and her residence for evidence—milk

---

43. Pollock, "Embarking," p. 56; Stone, *Family,* pp. 415–24.
44. McLaren, *Reproductive Rituals,* pp. 102, 111.
45. Audrey Eccles, *Obstetrics and Gynaeocology in Tudor and Stuart England* (Kent, Ohio: Kent State University Press), pp. 67–70; McLaren, *Reproductive Rituals,* chap. 4; Pollock, "Embarking," pp. 55–58.

in her breasts; hemorrhaging; soiled sheets; an infant, dead or alive. In *Fair Warning to Murderers of Infants* (1692), "2 or 3 Neighbours suspecting the matter, came to her [a suspected woman], and upon search, presently discovered by her Breasts, &c. that she had had a Child."[46] In *The Bloudy Mother* (1609), a neighbor, suspecting that a woman who has concealed numerous bastard births is in labor again, "peep[s] through the key-hole of the doore." Seeing evidence of childbirth, the prying neighbor goes downstairs for awhile. On her return, "her eye and eare were busie, to find that she sawe through the key hole; but she could neither see what she had seene, nor heard what she had heard; for all was most cunningly cleard [away]."[47] Just as juries of matrons searched the bodies of accused witches for damning evidence of witches' or devil's marks, so neighborhood women searched the bodies of suspected unwed mothers; in both cases, suspected women's bodies could expose them to criminal prosecution. In the case of neonatal infanticide, neighborhood women actively participated in policing the indistinct, contested border between the mother's body and the fetus.

In Watkins's view, Anne Greene deserves a pardon because she had no control over her body, and indeed was hardly present during her rather spectacular bodily adventures. She remembers neither her execution nor the vigorous means used to revive her: "Shee remembered nothing at all that had been done unto her" (sig. B3), despite the fact that she spoke "very sensibly" on the gallows. Upon her revival, she seemed "there to go on where she had so long time left off; like to a Clock whose weights had been taken off a while, and afterwards hung on againe" (sig. B3v). An automaton, a machine that was temporarily turned off rather than a human agent struggling for life, "she . . . was so farre from knowing anything whilst she was dead, that she remembred not what had happened to her even when she was yet alive" (sig. Cv). In short, there is very little news from the dead. From the pregnancy, to the miscarriage, to the execution and revival, she was not fully present and never really knew what was going on. Her body is presented as powerful and mysterious; but that power and mystery are made more tolerable by estranging Greene as subject from them and

46. *Fair Warning to Murderers of Infants: Being an Account of the Tryal, Condemnation and Execution of Mary Goodenough* (London, 1692), sig. A4.
47. Brewer, *The Bloudy Mother*, sig. B2v.

closing the boundary around her body and her self.[48] Associating awareness, self-knowledge, and memory with guilt, Watkins participates in the diverse legal, moral, popular, and medical discourses that link women's agency to transgression. To prove a suspected woman's innocence, Watkins insists not only that she did not perform the act for which she was convicted but also that she utterly lacked self-consciousness. *Newes from the Dead* and the events it narrates are extraordinary; this strategy of criminalizing women's subjectivity and agency is not.

Blood and the Maternal: Loving Your Children to Death

Even long after birth, after a child was physically and legally distinct from its mother, both parents' relation to and responsibility for their offspring remained uncertain and contested. Depicting a range of perpetrators and circumstances for which infanticide legislation cannot account—widows, wives, and prodigal gentlemen who murder their older, legitimate children—pamphlets and plays participated in these contests. Both parents were assumed to be responsible for their children and were held accountable for *fatally* neglecting or injuring them. Yet far from simply condemning the murder of one's own child, these texts exhibit startling empathy for many murderous parents' predicaments, especially in their interrogation of how material conditions contribute to violence against children and how gender and class shape parents' investment in and authority over their children.

Accounts of child murder differ markedly from accounts of other kinds of domestic crime, especially regarding the subjectivities they create for the murderers and how they depict the relationship between perpetrator and victim. One unrepresentative account of a murderous mother—*Murther Will Out,* which was written in 1675 about a murder that occurred thirty-three years earlier—should help to clarify the dif-

---

48. See Hoffer and Hull on the "dissociative reaction" of some contemporary mothers who kill their newborns. Such mothers deny their pregnancies and forget or repress "what was done to the child and by whom" (*Murdering Mothers,* p. 147). Even in the early modern period, such "distraction" could sometimes succeed as a defense. On how "street literature" dwells on the mysteries of the reproductive female body, see Joy Wiltenburg, *Disorderly Women and Female Power in the Street Literature of Early Modern England and Germany* (Charlottesville: University of Virginia Press, 1992), pp. 143, 177, 233–38.

ferences between most of the texts about murderous parents and those about petty treason. First, most texts about parents who murder their children do not present the parent as defining him or herself against the child. In contrast to such texts, *Murther Will Out* explores a mother's resentment of her infant and her sense that she must secure her own prosperity over his dead body. The mother, a young widow, struggles to care for her "froward" baby, whose "pining away" of a "lingering distemper" and "continual crying a nights made its Mothers life very uncomfortable."[49] The devil harrasses her by preying on her sleeplessness, articulating her frustrations, and suggesting that the baby impairs her own prospects.

> For now says he you are unhappy onely in this child of yours, which as long as it lives you will never enjoy a good day: and besides it hinders your preferment; you are young and handsome, and might have a husband or two more if this childs head was but laid, but who do you think will come to wooe you as long as this froward child is with you: and therefore it is your best way to rid your hands of it.[50]

Using Satan to portray the voice of self-interest and practical concern, this text presents self-assertion as violent and as prompted by demonic possession.[51] *Murther Will Out*, then, like representations of petty treason, constructs a woman's subjectivity in and through violence, as a severing of relations and an assertion of the self against others.

Yet this construction of maternal subjectivity is unusual in accounts of infanticide, in which the difference, let alone antagonism, between murderer and victim remains unclear. *Murther Will Out* also stands out among accounts of child murder in its depiction of children as burdens and provocations as well as victims. Virtually every other account of

49. *Murther Will Out*, sig. A2v. See Hoffer and Hull on Chief Justice Hale's account in 1668 of a married woman who "not having slept many nights" and "under a phrenzy ... by reason of her late delivery and want of sleep" killed her infant and was found not guilty (*Murdering Mothers*, pp. 146–47).

50. *Murther Will Out*, sigs. A3–A3v.

51. Michael MacDonald also sees this strategy in murderous mothers' accounts of their violent impulses in the early modern period: "Mothers who wanted to kill their children frequently found the thought so troubling that they believed it had been implanted into them by the Devil or by witchcraft" (*Mystical Bedlam*, p. 83).

child murder I have seen presents the victims as innocent lambs, sub-missive sacrifices who prattle and smile at the parents who are about to kill them.[52] Accounts of child murder rarely imagine subjectivities for children and do not represent a violent struggle between parent and child that ends in murder. Children do not fear or resist their parents; parents do not respond to their children's personalities or behavior, killing them because they are fretful or disobedient; nor do fatalities result because parental correction goes too far, or even by accident.[53] Instead, these texts present parents who, motivated by poverty, shame, despair, and isolation, intend to eliminate their children "for their own good." Far from acting out of anger against their children, parents often assert their attachment to them rather than attempting to dissociate themselves through violence. Murderous parents instead direct their anger at other family members, social/economic circumstances, God, or themselves. The contrast to *Murther Will Out* reveals how this more prevalent way of representing child victims works to distinguish parents' murderous urges from the frustrations of all parents. When sympathy arises for murderous parents, it focuses on isolation and poverty rather than on the undoubtedly more widespread, indeed unavoidable, frus-trations of caring for a dependent, demanding, inescapable little creature.

Parents are, of course, positioned much differently in relation to their vulnerable, wholly dependent offspring than are servants and wives in relation to masters and husbands who are both powerful and dependent. On the one hand, accounts of child murder represent parents as having considerable power over their children. But they are powerful only in relation to their children and only in negative, destructive ways, only as givers and takers of life. On the other hand, these texts present parents, especially mothers, as constrained and vulnerable in relation to their social and economic circumstances. By locating the motivation

---

52. On the aestheticization of children in aristocratic culture, to the point that they were perceived and treated as ephemeral, exchangeable ornaments, as "domestic pets," see Patricia Fumerton, *Cultural Aesthetics: Renaissance Literature and the Practice of Social Ornament* (Chicago: University of Chicago Press, 1992), chap. 2.

53. Hoffer and Hull link early modern infanticide to "baby battering syndrome" (*Murdering Mothers*, see chap. 6). This link does not exist in popular accounts of the crime in early modern England.

for child murder in social circumstances largely beyond parents' control, these texts are less censorious than we might imagine; they are as much about social breakdown as they are about parents' agencies.

Always linking the parent's survival in a carefully reproduced social world to the child's, popular representations explore the fluid boundaries between parent and child by associating child murder and various forms of parental self-destruction.[54] The connection between child murder and self-consumption is gender- and class-inflected. Representations of murderous mothers focus on wives or widows, presenting their murder of their children as a form of suicide, the destruction of a part of the self, rather than on unmarried women whose elimination of their newborns is an attempt at self-preservation. Such mothers do not pursue self-interest at their children's expense; instead, their attachment to their children is itself deranged, consuming, and dangerous. The few representations of murderous fathers, which focus on married heads of households, construe their murders of their children as acts of social suicide, as assaults on the family's collective identity. Equating children and property from the perspective of elite families, these texts place fathers' murders of their children at the extreme end of a continuum of prodigality and self-consumption. Fathers, like mothers, take responsibility for their children through murder. While sparing readers the spectacle of parents' hostility toward their children, these texts suggest the equally disquieting possibility that parental (especially maternal) "love" and responsibility can have as destructive consequences for the child as parental anger.

54. On parent-child relations, see Ralph A. Houlbrooke, *The English Family, 1450–1700* (London: Longman, 1984), chap. 6; Laslett, *World We Have Lost,* chap. 1; Alan Macfarlane, *Marriage and Love in England, 1300–1840* (Oxford: Basil Blackwell, 1986), chap. 4; Pollock, *Forgotten Children,* chaps. 1 and 2; Stone, *Family,* pp. 105–14, 159–95, and chap. 9; and Wrightson, *English Society,* pp. 108–18. Each of these historians (except Stone) emphasizes continuity rather than change. On the disparity between advice regarding child-rearing and actual practice, see Pollock, *Forgotten Children,* pp. 43–46, 199; Houlbrooke, *English Family,* p. 156; and Robert V. Schnucker, "Puritan Attitudes towards Childhood Discipline, 1560–1634," *Women as Mothers,* ed. Fildes, pp. 108–21, esp. p. 112.

In all of the stories that are told, the parents are caught and executed. Whatever the motive, such parents' murder of their children *is* self-destructive. See also Natalie Zemon Davis, "Boundaries and the Sense of Self in Sixteenth-Century France," *Reconstructing Individualism: Autonomy, Individuality, and the Self in Western Thought,* ed. Thomas C. Heller, Morton Sosna, and David E. Wellbery (Stanford: Stanford University Press, 1986), pp. 53–63.

Figure 3. A mother who has killed her children commits suicide. The frontispiece of Thomas Brewer, *The Bloudy Mother* (1609). The case described in the text does not correspond to this woodcut, which may be recycled from another pamphlet or ballad. By permission of the Houghton Library, Harvard University.

The very poor might well have felt that their infants were in competition with them for life. Unmarried poor or servant women, for instance, might have felt that their own economic survival depended on concealing their pregnancies and deliveries, even if this meant murder or murderous neglect. In addition to poor laws that could lead to fines and imprisonment, the shame of illegitimacy could socially and economically imperil women. As Hoffer and Hull argue, "for the poor female servant who could not afford to lose her job, much less feed another mouth, just as for the overburdened cottager family with perhaps one too many offspring already, infanticide might have seemed a matter of survival."[55] In such cases, a mother could only survive shame and poverty, and maintain her socially and economically precarious place in the world, by eliminating her newborn.

Although popular accounts of infanticide suggest that even married women or widows who are heads of families might lack the resources to provide for their children, they insist that such mothers murder out of responsibility toward their starving children, not to facilitate their own survival. Vividly depicting the isolation and desperation of poverty, such texts position murderous mothers as victims as well as victimizers. In *A Distressed Mother: Or Sorrowful Wife in Tears* (n.d.), for instance, Katherine Fox struggles to care for her children despite her drunken husband's waste of his estate through "riotous Living," absence from home, physical abuse, and irresponsibility.[56] Frantic because she has no way to feed her children, she decides "better it is [*for them*] to Die with one Stroke, than to languish in a continual Famine" and cuts their throats. When her husband returns home drunk, she slits his throat, too, in retribution for the "ill government" that has ruined her and her children. This text, its title revealing its sympathy for this woman's "distress," presents her more as the victim of her husband's violence and irresponsibility than as a "monster."

Similarly, in *Fair Warning to Murderers of Infants*, a widowed moth-

---

55. Hoffer and Hull, *Murdering Mothers*, p. 115. See also Malcolmson's claim that servants would lose their livelihoods by bearing bastards ("Infanticide in the Eighteenth Century," pp. 192–93, 203). For infanticides motivated by shame and poverty, see *Natures Cruell Step-Dames; Deeds against Nature; Fair Warning;* Watkins's *Newes from the Dead;* and "No Natural Mother, but a Monster" (1633) in *A Pepysian Garland,* ed. Hyder E. Rollins (Cambridge: Cambridge University Press, 1922), pp. 425–30.

56. This is a single-page broadside, so there are no page numbers.

er, Mary Goodenough, becomes involved with a married baker who promises to help her feed her children. When this liaison produces not relief for the existing children but another mouth to feed, Goodenough allows the newborn to die. The writer of this pamphlet dwells on the community's failure to support Goodenough and the dilemma of the "modest poor" who struggle in obscure poverty.[57] Castigating irresponsible husbands, heartless lovers, and uncharitable neighbors (the failures of paternalism), both *A Distressed Mother* and *Fair Warning* construct the mothers as taking responsibility for their children *by means of violence* because they feel that they have no other option. By placing some of the blame for these murders on the many people who should have assisted the mother and by emphasizing her suffering and helplessness, such pamphlets qualify and therefore somewhat decriminalize the mother's agency.

Texts that less explicitly qualify the blame of murderous mothers still position them simultaneously as murderers and victims. *A Pitilesse Mother* (1616) describes "a Tygerous Mother" who "wolvishly" kills her children but herself is a "sweete Lambe" who falls into the clutches of "Romaine Wolves." *Blood for Blood* (1670) describes a murderous mother on a scaffold: "Excepting the guilt of murder that lay on her conscience, her constant carriage was more like a Lamb going to the slaughter, than a Murderer going to the Gallows."[58] In her work on child welfare in the American Progressive Era, Linda Gordon charts the same difficulties in identifying the victim in cases of child abuse because mothers are "simultaneously victims and victimizers, dependent and depended on, weak and powerful."[59] Gordon emphasizes that women are not simply victims in cases of domestic violence. Conversely, since early modern accounts of domestic crime so disproportionately emphasize the role of women as perpetrators of violence, I wish to draw attention to how they are also represented as victims. Like the mothers whom Gordon studies, these women are doubly positioned: threateningly powerful in relation to their children, they are yet vul-

57. On compassion for poor mothers and the Mary Goodenough case, see Patricia Crawford, "The Construction and Experience of Maternity in Seventeenth-Century England," in *Women as Mothers,* ed. Fildes, pp. 3–38, esp. p. 15.

58. *Blood for Blood,* sigs. A3, A2v, C7v.

59. Linda Gordon, "Family Violence, Feminism, and Social Control," *Feminist Studies* 12.3 (1986): 453–78, esp. p. 458.

nerable to poverty, exploitation, and depression; guilty of murder, they are yet curiously innocent, lambs going to the slaughter rather than convicted killers facing execution.

Both *A Pitilesse Mother,* a text about a woman who kills her two children before attempting to kill herself, and *Blood for Blood,* another text about a mother who plans to kill herself and her children, portray married mothers as just as isolated and desperate as the impoverished, ashamed, resourceless women whose stories I have examined, despite the fact that they are married, prosperous, and well-placed socially and economically.[60] These two texts reveal that a gendered, class-inflected division of labor that shifted the burden of childcare onto women also made them more likely than men to fantasize or act out violence against a child.[61] They also grant significance to women's depression and the possibilities for marginalization even within the structures that are supposed to protect them. In *A Pitilesse Mother,* Margaret Vincent's Catholicism is described as separating her from others and motivating her to unite with her children against her family and community by means of death. *Blood for Blood* depicts thirty-seven-year-old Mary Cook, married for twelve years and the mother of eight, as melancholy because of what she perceives as her husband's and relations' neglect.

60. Michael MacDonald has made it possible to think of a social history of suicide and its changing medical, legal, and moral constructions, which he sees as following a trend toward secularization in the early modern period. See MacDonald's recent book, with Terence R. Murphy, *Sleepless Souls: Suicide in Early Modern England* (Oxford: Clarendon Press, 1991), and his various articles on the subject, especially "The Secularization of Suicide in England, 1660–1800," *Past and Present* III (May 1986): 52–70, and the ensuing debate in *Past and Present.*

When scholars discuss the relation of women to suicide in the early modern period, they usually present Lucretia as the only model for female suicide and all female suicides as motivated by sexual shame. Murderous/suicidal mothers, especially those who are married, are obviously outside of the Lucretia paradigm. On retellings of the Lucretia story, see Ian Donaldson, *The Rapes of Lucretia: A Myth and Its Transformations* (Oxford: Clarendon, 1982); and Simon Shepherd, *Amazons and Warrior Women: Varieties of Feminism in Seventeenth-Century Drama* (New York: St. Martin's, 1981), chaps. 12 and 13.

61. According to Pollock, "It seems that parental views on discipline are not so much shaped by class and religion, but by daily involvement with and intimate knowledge of the parent's *own* children" (*Forgotten Children,* p. 155). Michael MacDonald argues that among physician Richard Napier's patients, "men in general were sufficiently remote from their sons and daughters to be...seldom troubled by urges to murder them" (*Mystical Bedlam,* p. 84). In contrast, see Hoffer and Hull's claim that infanticide is "a crime rooted in indifference for infants" (*Murdering Mothers,* p. ix).

Depicting Cook's violence as directed first against herself, *Blood for Blood* censures suicide as a blasphemous form of self-determination; those who kill themselves "resolve not to be at all, because they may not be what they would be themselves, not submitting themselves to what God will have them to be."[62] The text links Cook's plan to kill her child to her many thwarted plans to kill herself and to get her husband's and her neglectful relations' attention, portraying both child murder and suicide as self-destructive self-assertions: "Now the Devil puts her upon a fresh consultation what should become of that child, which she so dearly loved, after she was dead; upon this she concludes, she had better rid that of life first, and then all her fears and cares for it would be at an end, and so she should put an end unto her own miserable life, which was so burdensome unto her" (sig. B5). Determined to protect her child from the uncertainties of having to live without her, Cook, "laying aside all Motherly Bowels," slits her baby's throat. By killing her child, she secures her own death: "She then appeared not relenting, at all, but said, *it was done because she was weary of her life,* her Relations slighting her and lest that child being most in her affection, should come to want when she was gone, she killed it first, knowing that way would also bring her to her desired end" (sig. B6v; emphasis added).

In both of these statements, Cook confuses herself with her child. She kills the child, Betty, because she is weary of her own life. Furthermore, her own sense of neglect leads her to believe that her relations will neglect her beloved child as they have her. Since, for Cook, to kill her youngest, most dependent child was to sever her last connection to life, the prattling, adorable Betty "became the Mothers sinful sacrifice" (sig. B5v). This, like most representations of murderous parents, depicts the child from the parent's perspective as an extension of him or her self, never imagining a distinct, separate subjectivity for the child.

---

62. *Blood for Blood*, sig. Bv; see also sig. B; subsequent citations are located in the text. MacDonald argues that the conception of suicide as a sign of complete alienation from God and concession to the Devil's temptations "was ubiquitous, surfacing in the formal language of the coroner's inquisitions and in Star Chamber suits, in the explanations that Napier's patients gave for their suicidal emotions, and in the confessions of spiritual autobiographies" ("The Inner Side of Wisdom: Suicide in Early Modern England," *Psychological Medicine* 7 [1977]: 565–82, esp. p. 574).

If a wife's subjectivity is threatening when it violently draws a boundary between husband and wife, maternal subjectivity is threatening when its boundaries expand to include—even consume—the offspring.

Michael MacDonald's work with the casebooks of Richard Napier, an astrological physician who treated patients between 1597 and 1634, suggests that representations such as *A Pitilesse Mother* and *Blood for Blood* disseminate and inform a conception of motherhood that women may actually have experienced. Among Napier's patients, some mothers were

> so strongly attached to their children that when they became depressed and suicidal they thought of their youngsters as extensions of the identity they wished to exterminate. Twenty women were tormented by urges to kill themselves *or* their children. . . . twelve other women . . . also wanted their children to die with them. Thus, even the hostility disturbed women expressed toward their children betrays their involvement with them.[63]

Women who experience such a vexed connection to their offspring might perceive murder as a positive action on behalf of their children. Hoffer and Hull describe a pattern that they call "altruistic suicides" in which child murderers, "mainly women because they spend more time rearing children than men, may conclude that they cannot abandon their children when they commit suicide, or delude themselves that the child is suffering so much that it has to be killed, or believe themselves and their children persecuted."[64] Like the "distressed mother" who killed her children rather than watch them starve; or Mary Cook, who killed her most beloved child because she assumed that it would suffer as she did; or Margaret Vincent, who killed her children to make them "saints in heaven," such mothers think that they are helping their children by ending their lives. Popular representations of murderous mothers in early modern England suggest that child-rearing practices and domestic divisions of labor promote identification between mother and child, creating conditions in which murder can be interpreted as part of good mothering.[65]

63. MacDonald, *Mystical Bedlam*, p. 84.
64. Hoffer and Hull, *Murdering Mothers*, p. 149; see also p. 135.
65. In Marlowe's *2 Tamburlaine* and Fletcher's *Bonduca*, mothers kill their children to spare them suffering and slavery. As Betty Travitsky argues, both plays emphasize the

Such pamphlets suggest that the ideologies and practices that assiduously reinforce a "natural" identification between mother and child could themselves contribute to domestic violence.[66] Rather than oppose or transgress against the ideal of "natural" maternal care, such violence represents maternal solicitude at its most extreme. Representations of murderous mothers thus suggest that violence against children is not unnatural or strange, but is, instead, familiar. The author of *A Pitilesse Mother* offers a typical delineation of natural parental affection and behavior in both human and animal societies.

> Oh that the blood of her owne body should have no more power to pearce remorse into her Iron naturd heart, when Pagan women that know not God nor have any feeling of his Deity will shun to commit bloodshed, much more of their owne seede: the Caniballs that eate one another will spare the fruites of their owne bodies, the Savages will doe the like, yea every beast and fowle hath a feeling of nature, and according to kinde will cherish their young ones, and shall woman, nay a Christian woman, Gods own Image, be more unnaturall then Pagan, Caniball, Savage, Beast or Fowle[?].[67]

Although this text insists that animals, cannibals, and savages have "a feeling of nature" that protects their offspring, it also suggests that some English mothers lack this feeling. Their behavior thus makes such terms of opprobrium as "bestial," "savage," and "pagan" meaningless, for it is the English mothers who are vicious, unfeeling, and unnatural, not those groups to which they are compared unfavorably.

A Pitilesse Mother offers the pelican as an image of a positive identification between mothers and children, a model of how mothers *should* think of their children as parts of themselves, their blood, as their children's blood, their bodies as nondiscrete. Margaret Vincent "by

---

tragic dilemma of mothers whose protection of their children must take the form of violence ("Child Murder").

66. On the ambiguities and contradictions in the constructions of "natural" maternal feelings and appropriate maternal behavior, see Crawford, "Construction and Experience," esp. pp. 11–12; and Fildes, "Maternal Feelings." I have been especially helped by Mary Beth Rose, "Where Are the Mothers in Shakespeare? Options for Gender Representation in the English Renaissance," *Shakespeare Quarterly* 42.3 (1991): 291–314. Wrightson argues that infanticide was constructed as *un*natural in opposition to maternal feelings and conduct socially contructed as "natural" ("Infanticide," p. 11).

67. *A Pitilesse Mother,* sig. B-Bv.

nature should have cherisht them [her children] with her owne body, as the Pellican that pecks her owne brest to feed her young ones with her blood"; yet she kills them. In killing her children, she sheds "the blood of her owne body," "her owne deare blood bred in her owne body, cherished in her own wombe with much dearenes full forty weekes."[68] She thus inverts the image of the pelican, making the fungibility of mother-child blood a source of confusion and violence rather than self-sacrificing nurturance.[69] By contrasting Vincent's shedding of her children's blood with the pelican's donation of her own, *A Pitilesse Mother* points to the violence and self-destruction inherent in the ideal of maternal nurturance. Texts such as *A Pitilesse Mother* do not acknowledge their own contradictions; nor do they explore the implications of the contradictions they reveal *within* the ideology and practices of motherhood. The texts participate in the cultural contests regarding mothers' responsibility for their children simply by articulating these contradictions and by exploring the most extreme instances of maternal agency and authority. Despite censuring the "unnatural" agency of murderous mothers, these texts also employ various strategies to downplay the recognition that mothers might not identify with their children and might assert themselves against them.

The "House," Prodigality, and Social Suicide: Murderous Fathers—The Calverley Case

The author of *Strange and Lamentable News from Dullidg-Wells* (1678), an unusual account of a father who beats his son to death, marvels "That a Parent can be so hard-hearted to his own Child, that they from whom we received our Life, should be the promoters of our Death; *this certainly is the highest violation of the Law of Nature, and yet even of this there want not too frequent Examples.*"[70] As this writer makes clear,

---

68. Ibid., sigs. A3v, B, A4.
69. On the fungibility of bodily fluids in Renaissance constructions of the body, see Paster, *Body Embarrassed*.
70. *Strange and Lamentable News from Dullidg-Wells* (London, 1678), sig. A2, emphasis added.

child murder is a "violation of the Law of Nature," yet neither unimaginable, nor other, nor even unfamiliar. Local examples abound.

Like accounts of murderous mothers, those of murderous fathers both employ the censorious vocabulary of "unnatural" and "monstruous" and find it wanting for transgressions construed in social terms. John Taylor, for instance, in *The Unnaturall Father* (1621; fig. 4), places John Rowse's murder of his two daughters in the context of two traditions, one from the Old Testament and "our English Chronicles" focusing on male murderers, the other from local stories "fresh in memory," focusing on female murderers, such as Alice Arden of Faversham and Mistress Page of Plymouth. Taylor associates domestic murders with women and finds men who assault their family members even more shocking, for they stray out of their appropriate sphere and scale of action: "It is too manifestly known, what a number of Stepmothers and Strumpets have most inhumanly murdered their Children, and for the same have most deservedly been executed. But in the memory of man (nor scarcely in any History) it is not to be found, that a Father did ever take two Innocent Children out of their beds . . . to drown them." Taylor condemns all murder, but he also suggests a double standard: Men kill other men as part of the epic struggles recorded in "our English Chronicles." Only "stepmothers and strumpets" kill children.[71]

Despite Taylor's claim that a father's murder of his children is not to be found in human memory, the most notorious and often-represented case of child murder in early modern England centered on Walter Calverley's murder of his sons in Yorkshire in 1605. This case was so infamous that Taylor might well have known about it; it inspired multiple representations through the next century. The most immediate was a pamphlet entitled, *Two Most Unnatural and Bloodie Murthers* (1605). There are no extant dramatizations of an actual case in which

71. John Taylor, *The Unnaturall Father: Or, A Cruell Murther Committed by One John Rowse . . . upon Two of His Owne Children* (London, 1621). Reprinted in *The Old Book Collector's Miscellany*, ed. Charles Hindley, 3 vols. (London: Reeves and Turner, 1873), 2: 17. Stepmothers were widely assumed not to love their stepchildren as much as their biological offspring. See Boswell, *Kindness of Strangers*, p. 128, n. 140; and Crawford, "Construction and Experience," pp. 13, 25–26. Some pamphlets anticipate fairy tales and folk stories that displace blame for parental neglect and abuse of children onto the stepmother.

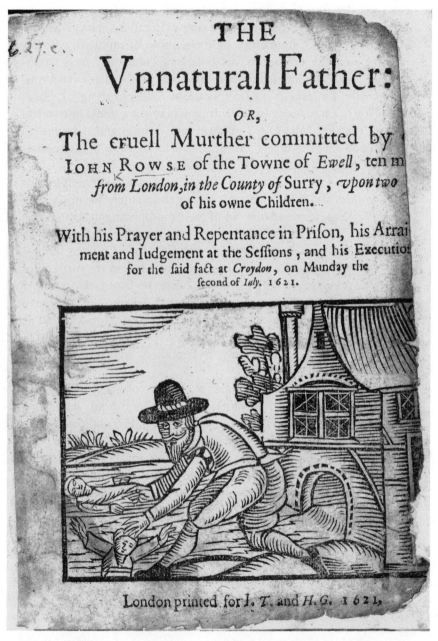

THE
Vnnaturall Father:

OR,

The cruell Murther committed by
IOHN ROWSE of the Towne of *Ewell*, ten m
from London, in the County of Surry, *vpon two*
of his owne Children.

With his Prayer and Repentance in Prifon, his Arrai
ment and Iudgement at the Seffions, and his Execution
for the faid fact at *Croydon*, on Munday the
fecond of *Iuly.* 1621.

London printed for I. T. and H. G. 1621.

Figure 4. A father drowns his daughters. Title page of *The Unnaturall Father* (1621). By permission of the British Library.

a mother murdered her child, yet the Calverley case generated *two* plays: George Wilkins's *The Miseries of Enforced Marriage* (1607) and *A York-shire Tragedy* (1608).[72] The privileged status of the drama relative to other popular materials, further heightened in the case of *A Yorkshire Tragedy* by its attribution to Shakespeare and, most recently, to Middleton, makes these dramatizations of the Calverley case more widely known and carefully studied than any of the representations of murderous mothers. But this phenomenon of cultural transmission obscures the fact that the murderous mother was a much more familiar figure in early modern popular culture, if not on the stage, than the murderous father. As Taylor's comments reveal, these plays did not alter the prevailing early modern assumption that child murder is the act of stepmothers and strumpets.'

Clustering around the Calverley case and a similar incident, the very few extant representations of murderous fathers focus on relatively privileged perpetrators, married gentlemen whose murder of their heirs is the final act in a prodigal life. The riotous living that precedes and motivates the murders is itself presented as violent and self-consuming. While pamphlets portray women as so attached to their offspring that they cannot tell the difference between their blood and their children's, pamphlets and plays portray men as so attached to their "houses," to a familial identity that includes not only offspring but ancestors, family honor, and property, that they cannot detach themselves even through assaults on the "house" since these are simultaneously assaults on themselves. Since, as I argue in Chapter 5, property could be seen as an extension of the self, to vandalize the objectifications or guarantors of

---

72. I will not discuss *The Miseries of Enforced Marriage* at any length here because it averts child murder to give the story a happy ending. Early seventeenth-century dramatizations of the Calverley case in turn inspired four later plays, none of which depicts the murder of children. Following *The Miseries of Enforced Marriage*, Aphra Behn's *The Town Fop* (1676) focuses on enforced marriage, resolving the conflicts through amicable divorce. Aaron Hill's *The Fatal Extravagance* (1720), Edward Moore's *The Gamester* (1753), and F. G. Waldron's *The Prodigal* (1794) represent prodigality as irreversible but confine its consequences to the erring individual. On these later plays, see Ernest Bernbaum, *The Drama of Sensibility: A Sketch of the History of English Sentimental Comedy and Domestic Tragedy, 1696–1780* (Cambridge: Harvard University Press, 1925), pp. 50–52, 129–32, 203–5; Laura Brown, *English Dramatic Form, 1660–1760: An Essay in Generic History* (New Haven: Yale University Press, 1981), pp. 164–65; and Catherine Belsey, *The Subject of Tragedy: Identity and Difference in Renaissance Drama* (London: Methuen, 1985), pp. 202–3, 220.

one's own social status and identity was to commit what MacDonald has called "social suicide."[73] Given the complex associations among the gentle masculine subject, his children, and his property, his murder of heirs was constructed as an extreme form of "social suicide."[74]

The two texts that offer the most detailed accounts of the Calverley case, *Two Most Unnatural and Bloodie Murthers* and *A Yorkshire Tragedy*, both appeared soon after the murders. In both texts, Walter Calverley, a young gentleman with the sizable income of seven hundred to eight hundred pounds per year, is assigned a responsible guardian after his father's death. Although a minor, Calverley betrothes himself out of love but subsequently goes to London and assents to another match proposed by his guardian. Unhappy in the arranged marriage, despite the virtue of his wife, and irked by the contradictions of his status as both gentleman and ward, independent and subordinate, Calverley grows increasingly riotous, wasting his estate, publicly insulting his wife as a strumpet and his children as bastards, and wounding the reputation of his family.[75]

Both *A Yorkshire Tragedy* and *Two Most Unnatural and Bloodie Murthers* explore the responsibility that attends a husband-father's authority. As a propertied family's eldest son, Calverley has access to and control over all the family's wealth. While primogeniture favors him it also requires him to husband these resources responsibly, using them to

73. MacDonald, *Mystical Bedlam*, pp. 128–31. In his popular polemic against suicide, *Life's Preservative against Self-Killing* (1637), John Sym describes prodigality and unthriftiness as indirect forms of self-murder.

74. When men who were heads of households committed suicide, this act also had farther reaching consequences than women's suicides because men would forfeit their estates and thus leave their wives and children beggars. See MacDonald, "Inner Side of Wisdom," p. 568.

75. All popular accounts of the Calverley case neglect to mention the family's recusancy and the toll it had taken on the estate. On Calverley's life, see the introduction to *A Yorkshire Tragedy,* ed. A. C. Cawley and Barry Gaines (Manchester: Manchester University Press, 1986), pp. 6–11; subsequent citations are located in the text and refer to this edition. The *Dictionary of National Biography* also does not mention Calverley's recusancy.

The plot of *A Pitilesse Mother* bears remarkable similarities to the plot of *Two Most Unnatural* and *A Yorkshire Tragedy:* In both stories, the married, gentle parent has three children and is frustrated in attempts to kill the youngest because it is with its wet nurse. That *A Pitilesse Mother* makes Margaret Vincent's conversion to Catholicism the motive for her murder of her children, while the accounts of Calverley's crime make no mention whatsoever of his recusancy, suggests the complicated ways in which gender and class shape representations of child murder.

care for his wife and children as well as his younger siblings.[76] Since he has the power to support or beggar his dependents, his prodigality has far-reaching consequences. As *Two Most Unnatural and Bloodie Murthers* describes this:

> He presently fell into a deepe consideration of his state, how his prodigall course of life, had wronged his brother, abused his wife, and undone his children. Then was presented before the eyes of his imagination, the wealth his father left him, and the misery hee should leave his children in.... Then sawe hee the extirpation of his family, the ruine of his antient house, which hundreds of yeeres together had bin Gentlemen of the best reputation in Yorkshire, and every one of these out of their severall objects, did create a severall distraction in him.[77]

In both *Two Most* and *A Yorkshire Tragedy,* such reflections link Calverley's prodigality, slander against his family, and murder of his children as *self*-destructive acts.[78] In the play, whose form enables a fuller exploration of Calverley's subjectivity, he expresses this as follows:

> My lands showed like a full moon about me. But now the moon's i'th' last quarter, waning, waning, and I am mad to think that moon was mine. Mine and my father's and my forefathers' generations, generations. Down

76. On primogeniture, an inheritance practice that applied largely to the gentry and above, see Houlbrooke, *English Family,* pp. 41–43, 234–38; Louis Adrian Montrose, " 'The Place of a Brother' in *As You Like It:* Social Process and Comic Form," *Shakespeare Quarterly* 32.1 (1981): 28–54; Lawrence Stone, *The Crisis of the Aristocracy, 1558–1641* (Oxford: Oxford University Press, 1965), pp. 178–83, 599–600; and Joan Thirsk, "Younger Sons in the Seventeenth Century," *History* 54 (1969): 358–77. In the various accounts of the Calverley case, primogeniture resembles infanticide in its discrimination among children, valuing some more than others and sacrificing the prospects of daughters and younger sons to the eldest son. As Tom Paine argued in 1791: "By the aristocratical law of primogenitureship, in a family of six children, five are exposed. Aristocracy has never more than *one* child. The rest are begotten to be devoured. They are thrown to the cannibal for prey, and the natural parent prepares the unnatural repast" (*The Rights of Man* [Harmondsworth: Penguin, 1984], p. 82).

77. I quote here from the edition of *Two Most Unnatural and Bloodie Murthers* that appears as appendix A to *A Yorkshire Tragedy,* ed. Cawley and Gaines, pp. 105–6; subsequent citations are located in the text and refer to this edition.

78. See, for instance, this passage in *A Yorkshire Tragedy:* "Those whom men call mad / Endanger others; but he's more than mad / That wounds himself, whose own words do proclaim / Scandals unjust to soil his better name" (2.106–10).

goes the house of us; down, down it sinks. Now is the name a beggar,
begs in me. That name, which hundreds of years has made this shire famous,
in me and my posterity runs out.
(4.70–77)

In both versions, Calverley at last realizes that his peevish prodigality
has destroyed the legacy of generations and that his ruin reaches to
include his ancestors as well as his progeny.[79]

This realization comes not in response to his suffering wife and her
entreaties for their children but when he is called to account for how
he has treated his brother, a promising divinity student jailed for one
of his own defaulted debts. In both play and pamphlet, Calverley proposes to redress the family's ruin by completing it: "I thought it the
charitablest deed I could do / To cozen beggary and knock my house
o' th' head" (*A Yorkshire Tragedy* 9.17–18). He slays his eldest two
sons against the resistance of his wife, a nurse, and a servant; then he
rides to the wet nurse's to kill his infant son. As *Two Most Unnatural
and Bloodie Murthers* describes this, Calverley, "prickt by his preposterous fate, had a desire to roote out all his owne generation: and onely
intending to murther it, was carelesse what became of himselfe" (p.
108). When first apprehended, he regrets only that he did not kill all
three heirs: "I had brought them to beggery, and am resolved I could
not have pleased God better, then by freeing them from it" (p. 109).
By killing his children, Calverley thus completes the familial murder/
suicide he had begun in his prodigality and acts, at last, as a father,
protecting his children from a fate worse than death. He construes his
murder of his heirs as his first responsible, forward-looking act: "'Tis
charity to brain you" (*A Yorkshire Tragedy* 4.102–3).[80]

79. Representations of the Calverley murders present prodigality as irreversible and
fatal. Even Aaron Hill's eighteenth-century adaptation, *The Fatal Extravagance* (1720),
in which the protagonist does not succeed in poisoning his wife and children, punishes
him for his prodigality; he commits suicide. On prodigality plays, see Richard Helgerson,
The Elizabethan Prodigals (Berkeley: University of California Press, 1976); and Marilyn
L. Williamson, *The Patriarchy of Shakespeare's Comedies* (Detroit: Wayne State University
Press, 1986), chap. 2.

80. Another seventeenth-century text constructs a gentleman's murder of his children
in very similar terms. In John Taylor's *The Unnaturall Father* (1621), the father, a fish-
monger, achieves the status of a landed gentleman and then wastes the estate he has built
up through trade. He drowns his daughters to spare them beggary. Upon apprehension,
he tells the Constable "that he did it, because he was not able to keep them, and that he

The numerous and varied representations of Walter Calverley's case thus explore the costs and contradictions of being the head of a prominent, landowning family with a history. Far from presenting property-holding, gentle males as unconstrained and autonomous, these texts reveal the particular strains of accountability to the past and the future, of being inseparable from your family and its "house." They construct subjectivity as collective and diffused, as spread across bodies and through time. The conception of a family and its estate as a "house" articulates this effectively. The house is a structure that endures yet changes, absorbing the contributions of individuals and generations, yet surviving them. This figurative structure encloses many individuals and connects them to one another and to those who precede and succeed them. It forms a collective subject out of the dead, the living, and the anticipated. Since the "house" survives any one individual or generation, it can be seen to offer a comic conception of subjectivity, dwelling on continuity rather than mortality, the communal rather than the individual. Yet the stories of child murder most often dwell on the violent, fragmenting, destructive consequences of this conception of collective identity, for both women and men, parents and children.

Dramatic and nondramatic representations of the Calverley case, then, make the husband-father-eldest son the central figure in each family member's story, if only in negative terms. In *A Yorkshire Tragedy,* the wife strategizes to preserve her dowry from her wasteful husband so that she can care for her children; she secures him a place at court, through which he might recoup his losses and support the family; finally, she wrestles with him to protect her second child from his knife thrusts, incurring serious injuries but failing to save the child. She strives to counter her husband's attacks on the family and its resources, but she has little control over the family's reputation, property, or children, all subject to her intemperate, capricious, and wasteful husband.[81]

---

was loth they should go about Town a begging: and moreover, that they were his own, and being so, that he might do what he would with them, and that they had their lives from him, and therefore he had taken their lives from them, and was contented to lose his life for them" (2:11). The pamphlet presents Rowse as acting out of a complex sense of identification with as well as ownership of his children. He asserts control over them and their futures by closing off possibilities; the murders begin in his prodigality and lead to his death. Prodigality, child murder, and suicide collapse into one.

81. Houlbrooke argues that a wife had little security against her husband's waste-fulness (*English Family,* p. 100). Presenting the wife as resourceful, yet submissive and

Although legal prosecutions and popular, ephemeral representations focus on murderous mothers, the drama privileges the story of the murderous father, and the gentle, mass-murdering father at that. In *A Yorkshire Tragedy,* this father is apprehended and sent off to execution, just like the mothers whom statutes criminalize and ephemeral texts describe. Yet in the play's last scene, his wife, seriously wounded in her unsuccessful struggle to shield her child, forgives him and sues for his life: "Dearer than all [my children] is my poor husband's life" (10.65). In accounts of murderous mothers, however complicated, even sympathetic, the bereaved husband and father never makes an equivalent claim. *The Miseries of Enforced Marriage* even manages to bring Calverley's story to a comic conclusion, redeeming his profligacy and averting violence with a windfall inheritance. Offered a new fortune and someone else to blame for his misfortunes (his guardian), the protagonist grudgingly reclaims his role as husband and father. Turning to the wife and two children he has threatened and repudiated, he announces: "You three Ile live withall."[82] Considered in the absence of plays about murderous mothers and in relation to romanticizations of the murderous father such as *The Winter's Tale,* these dramatizations of the Calverley case suggest that a father's irresponsibility and violence can be survived and forgiven, as a mother's cannot. They grant the father considerable authority over his family and its resources and hold him accountable for the actions he takes on his dependents' behalf; yet his agency—

---

loyal, none of the representations of the case reproduce Calverley's claim, in his examination before justices of the peace the day after the murder, that his wife was unfaithful and murderous: "He hathe had an intention to kill them for the whole space of two years past, and the reasons that moved him thereunto was, for that his said wife had many times theretofore uttered speeches and given signes and tokens unto him, whereby he mighte easily percieve and conjecture, that the said children were not by him begotten, and that he hath found himself to be in danger of his life sundry times by his wife" (reprinted in *A Yorkshire Tragedy,* ed. Cawley and Gaines, pp. 111–12, from Thomas Dunham Whitaker's *Loidis and Elmete* [Leeds and Wakefield, 1816], pp. 228–29; Cawley and Gaines could not find the original document). In other representations of the crime, Calverley kills the children because he thinks they are his and he acts out of responsibility toward them and not because he thinks they are illegitimate. He expresses rather than denies relation to them through murder.

None of the representations of the Calverley case include Calverley's sentencing and death, presumably because they all draw directly or indirectly on the pamphlet, which was written while Calverley was still in jail.

82. George Wilkins, *The Miseries of Enforced Marriage,* ed. Glenn H. Blayney (Oxford: Oxford University Press, 1964), line 2852.

while violent and destructive—is not as threatening as a mother's even though she has less control over the family and its resources. Like the murderous husband, the murderous father amplifies and exploits the power available to him; but he does not overturn social order or gender roles.

With its grimly generic conflict between "Wife," "Husband," and "Son," *A Yorkshire Tragedy*'s plot offers a stark sketch of *The Winter's Tale*'s first three acts. The jealous, unstable husband dismisses his wife and children as "strumpet and bastards, strumpet and bastards!" (2.103–4). Struggling with his servants and his wife for the child he wishes to kill, he screams "Give me the bastard" (5.22). His eldest and heir fears neither "vizards nor bugbears," just as Mamilius prefers stories about "sprites and goblins" (2.1.25–26). The father turns this "white boy" into his "red boy," in this case by stabbing him with his dagger (4.95; 97–98). Despite the loss of two of her children, his wife forgives him. Moving farther up social and literary hierarchies and farther away from the legal and popular arenas in which murderous mothers are the central (unforgivable) protagonists, *The Winter's Tale* translates this story of local domestic violence into a more prestigious genre, a courtly setting, and a less familiar, more magical world. It also obscures the father's agency in disposing of his children.

Old Tales, Romance, and the Throwers-out of Poor Babes

In *The Winter's Tale*, when the shepherd finds the abandoned Perdita, he assumes that he knows the story: "Though I am not bookish, yet I can read waiting-gentlewoman in the scape. This has been some stair-work, some trunk-work, some behind-door-work. They were warmer that got this than the poor thing is here" (3.3.70–74). "Reading" his discovery through the conventions of legal and popular constructions of infanticide familiar to both bookish and unbookish, the shepherd assumes that abandoning or killing children is the action of unmarried women who are most often servants. (He does elevate the story somewhat by making the mother a "waiting-gentlewoman" rather than a kitchen maid.) In his reading of the story, the shepherd reveals that a pastoral landscape and the enclosed, shameful spaces under the stairs or behind the door can come together in the person of the abandoned infant, who is simultaneously a thing dying and a thing newborn.[83]

Pamphlet accounts of child murder also conjoin these two kinds of space, of crime and of fantasy. While woodcuts accompanying pamphlets and ballads about murderous wives or husbands present them in claustrophobic, scrupulously detailed domestic settings from which there is no escape, some woodcuts depicting child murders juxtapose domestic interiors to outdoor settings. In such woodcuts, the outside is not an alternative to or escape from the domestic, but an extension of it. In the title page of *The Bloudy Mother* (1609; fig. 5), for instance, the mother and her master/lover bury one of their murdered bastards in a grave containing the bones of other victims. The scene's trees and plants contrast to the architectural details—windowpanes, floor tiles, and so forth—of the adjoining scene, in which the "unlawfull begetter of those unfortunate Babes" lies in bed "being eaten and consumed alive with Wormes and Lice." Accounts of spousal murders rarely dwell on attempts to dispose of bodies. The exceptions are vivid: Mary Aubrey dismembers her husband's body, scattering the pieces across London; John Dilworth attempts to burn his wife's body in the fireplace. In contrast, statutes defined neonatal infanticide as a crime of concealment. Seeking to hide pregnancy as well as delivery and murder, perpetrators of neonatal infanticide had to get their victims' bodies out of the house; infants' tiny corpses were relatively easy to transport and eliminate. Hence, popular representations emphasize the outside, the space for burying and abandoning.

Some pamphlets about child murder endow this landscape with a

83. My reading of *The Winter's Tale* is especially informed by Janet Adelman, *Suffocating Mothers: Fantasies of Maternal Origin in Shakespeare's Plays, "Hamlet" to "The Tempest"* (New York: Routledge, 1992), pp. 220–38; Michael D. Bristol, "In Search of the Bear: Spatiotemporal Form and the Heterogeneity of Economies in *The Winter's Tale*," *Shakespeare Quarterly* 42.2 (1991): 145–67; Peter B. Erickson, "Patriarchal Structures in *The Winter's Tale*," *PMLA* 97.5 (1982): 819–29; Carol Neely, *Broken Nuptials in Shakespeare's Plays* (New Haven: Yale University Press, 1985), chap. 5; and Gail Paster's compelling analysis of the play in *Body Embarrassed*, chap. 5, esp. pp. 260–80.

Paster and Gillian Murray Kendall ("Overkill in Shakespeare," *Shakespeare Quarterly* 43.1 [1992]: 33–50, esp. p. 43f.) acknowledge the violence threatened against Perdita, although neither addresses it in detail. In his discussion of *The Winter's Tale*, Leonard Tennenhouse acknowledges Leontes's extraordinary violence (*Power on Display: The Politics of Shakespeare's Genres* [New York: Methuen, 1986], esp. p. 178).

Figure 5. Parents bury the corpse of their illegitimate child. On the right side of the woodcut, the father suffers a "most loathsome and lamentable end" for his role in begetting and disposing of numerous infants. Title page from *The Bloudy Mother* (1609). By permission of the Houghton Library, Harvard University.

fairy-tale quality. *Natures Cruell Step-Dames* (1637), for instance, re-counts the story of Elizabeth Barnes, who makes a picnic for her eight-year-old daughter, "to intice the childe unto its slaughter, and to goe abroad with her."[84] Packing a basket with apple pie, herring pie, and raisins, "accustomed baits used by loving parents, to quiet and still their children in their unquietnesse" (sig. A2v), Barnes successfully entraps her child: "The child beholding them, did set an edge on its affections, willingly to accompany her cruell mother, in her travell towards her long home" (sig. A2v). When the child, sated from the picnic, falls asleep, her mother cuts her throat. On this pamphlet's title page (fig. 6), the mother crouches over her daughter in the foreground, stabbing her with a huge knife; in the background, a row of trees reminds viewers that this murder does not occur at home. Combining this story with other, terser accounts of women who throw their bastard children into privies or ditches, the text links these kinds of stories and the worlds in which they occur: the romance setting of "a Wood . . . in secret, and covered with darknesse" and the location more familiar from court records and pamphlets, a "[privy] vault in Rosemary Lane, by Tower Hill" (sigs. A2v, B2). As critics have long acknowledged, *The Winter's Tale* similarly combines domestic detail and the conventions of fairy tale, the familiar and the fantastic.[85]

When Perdita's story comes to its happy if outlandish conclusion, when she who was lost is found, various characters remark that the play's closing movement is "like an old tale" (5.3.117): "This news which is called true is so like an old tale, that the verity of it is in strong suspicion: has the king found his heir?" (5.2.28–30); "Like an old tale still, which will have matter to rehearse though credit be asleep and not an ear open" (ll. 62–64). This "old tale" is the story of infant abandonment whose conventions Boswell delineates: "The children are of lofty though complicated ancestry; a male figure orders the abandonment, to the regret of the mother; they are actually

---

84. *Natures Cruell Step-Dames*, sig. A2; subsequent citations are located in the text.
85. As Bristol argues: "The problem of *The Winter's Tale* is not that everything happens 'there' in *a* world of delphic oracles, tragic losses, and miraculous recoveries but that some of it happens also 'here' in *the* world of ballad-mongers, thieves, and country feasts" ("In Search of the Bear," p. 147; see also p. 163). On romance settings, see also Fredric Jameson, *The Political Unconscious: Narrative as a Socially Symbolic Act* (Ithaca: Cornell University Press, 1981), esp. pp. 110–12.

Natures
Cruell Step-Dames :
OR,
Matchlesse Monsters of the Female

Sex; *Elizabeth Barnes*, and *Anne Willis*.

Who were executed the 26. day of *April*,

1637. at Tyburne, for the unnaturall murthering of their owne Children,

Alfo, herein is contained their feverall Confeffions,
and the Courts juft proceedings againft other notorious
Malefactors, with their feverall offences
this Seffions.

Further, a Relation of the wicked Life and

impenitent Death of *Iohn Flood*, who raped
his own Childe.

Printed at London for *Francis Coules*, dwelling in
the Old-Baily. 1637.

Figure 6. In a fairy-tale wood, a mother slits her daughter's throat. Title page of *Natures Cruell Step-Dames* (1637). By permission of the Folger Shakespeare Library.

taken away and left by servants; they are found by shepherds and reared by foster parents; they subsequently rise to greatness."[86] *The Winter's Tale* is simultaneously an "old [fairy] tale" about a princess abandoned on the coast of Bohemia with identifying tokens and a cache of gold, and the unbookish, sensational story of a scape, or transgression, with its disturbing details of braining and burning, the stuff of the ballads and pamphlets that a disreputable peddler like Autolycus might sell.

Although, as the shepherd perceives, Perdita's story is intimately connected to the story of the unmarried servant woman who conceals the damning evidence of her clandestine sexuality, it is not the same story. Perdita is legitimate and a princess; her father, a king, is behind this scape.[87] The shepherd's misreading takes its place among the many mistakings around which the plot revolves. Most crucially, Leontes mistakes Hermione's kindness to Polixenes for adultery, convincing himself that it is she who mistakes: "You have mistook, my lady, / Polixenes for Leontes" (2.1.82–83). In "rebellion with himself" (1.2.354), Leontes suspects his subordinates to be "a nest of traitors" (2.3.82), revealing the extent to which household and kingdom have collapsed together. Enacting the associations I have traced in other representations of "revolted wives" (1.2.199), Leontes conflates adultery, murder, and treason and arraigns Hermione for "high treason, in committing adultery with Polixenes, . . . and conspiring with Camillo to take away the life of our sovereign lord the King, [her] royal husband" (3.2.14–17; cf. 2.1.47, 89–90).[88] He further insists that he must imprison her for his own protection: "From our free person she should be confined, / Lest that the treachery of the two fled hence / Be left her to perform" (2.1.195–97). As many critics have noticed, Leontes hysterically runs together threats to order: the "mankind witch," the traitor,

---

86. Boswell, *Kindness of Strangers*, p. 76; see also pp. 76–79, 97–98.

87. Like the shepherd, Stephen Greenblatt sees a connection between *The Winter's Tale* (and Shakespearean romance more generally) and stories of infanticidal mothers, but he does not locate that connection explicitly in violence against children. See *Shakespearean Negotiations: The Circulation of Social Energy in Renaissance England* (Berkeley: University of California Press, 1988), pp. 129–33.

88. See Chapter 1 for my discussion of the conventions shaping legal and popular representations of murderous wives. Janet Adelman argues that Leontes "finds in the culturally familiar fiction of female betrayal in marriage both an acceptable narrative for his sense of primal loss and a new adult selfhood" (*Suffocating Mothers*, p. 224).

the adulterous, murderous wife or petty traitor, the bastard child, the henpecked husband.[89]

Although the plot of *The Winter's Tale* revolves around mistakings, the characters also contest one another's readings of domestic conflict. If Leontes casts himself as the victim of a "nest of traitors," particularly of traitorous women who should, appropriately enough, be burnt at the stake, Paulina and Hermione cast themselves as a tyrant's victims. Paulina repeatedly calls Leontes a tyrant and a traitor to himself, identifying "these dangerous unsafe lunes i' the King" (2.2.30) as the source of disorder. Leontes tries to defend himself against this charge—"Let us be cleared / Of being tyrannous, since we so openly / Proceed in justice, which shall have due course" (3.2.4–6)—but Hermione dismisses even this as "rigor and not law" (3.2.114). Playing the part of tyrant and murderous husband, Leontes repeatedly threatens to execute his wife; Paulina later holds him accountable for murderous intent. Indeed, by the fifth act, Paulina so successfully converts Leontes to this interpretation of his actions that he fears that he would murder a second wife. Considered in the context of other representations of murderous wives and husbands, the play's accusatory vocabulary—"traitor!," "tyrant!"—simultaneously accrues domestic and political resonances. However exaggerated, this is the conventional vocabulary for discussing betrayal and violence between spouses, even those who are not kings and queens of Sicilia.

While it is important to identify the dynamic of accusation and counteraccusation in *The Winter's Tale*, the play is not only a contest between conventional narratives of spousal conflict. Both spouses survive the conflict, for all their suffering. When Leontes thinks Hermione plots against his life, he is wrong, as he is when he believes that he has killed her. The one irredeemable loss in the play, the sacrifice to the ultimate resolution, is the son. For this is also a story of parent-child conflict, although the levels of conflict in the play overlap so closely that they can seem indistinguishable. Despite Paulina's optimistic assertion that the newborn Perdita is "not a party to / The anger of the king nor guilty of, / If any be, the trespass of the Queen" (2.2.61–63), both Perdita and Mamilius fall victim to their parents' conflict. Leontes's identifi-

---

89. Ibid., p. 227; See also Erickson, "Patriarchal Structures," pp. 822–23; and Paster, *Body Embarrassed*, p. 271.

cation with Mamilius has even more fatal consequences for the child than his harsh refusal to see in Perdita a copy of himself will have for her. Seen by his father as a smaller version of himself and consumed by his empathy with his mother, Mamilius drops dead.

> To see his nobleness!
> Conceiving the dishonor of his mother,
> He straight declined, drooped, took it deeply,
> Fastened and fixed the shame on't in himself,
> Threw off his spirit, his appetite, his sleep,
> And downright languish'd.
> (2.3.12–17; cf. 3.2.144–45)

Taking responsibility as well as shame onto himself, Mamilius dies for *Leontes's* sins: "I have done sin: / For which the heavens, taking angry note, / Have left me issueless" (5.1.172–74).[90] Although Leontes fights with Hermione for exclusive ownership of the boy, he does not engage in detailed squabbles about how to eliminate him because Mamilius eliminates himself.

Leontes engages more directly in disposing of Perdita. The scene in which Paulina misguidedly presents Leontes with the new baby, sure that the sight of her will "soften" him, is an extraordinarily violent one, indeed angrier and more violent than most representations of child murder. Yet critics rarely dwell on the details of Leontes's proposals for disposing of Perdita, nor do they discuss Leontes's willingness to carry out these schemes himself, if need be. Even if he earns forgiveness by the fifth act, Leontes violently rejects the baby: "This brat is none of mine; /.../ Hence with it, and together with the dam / Commit them to the fire!" (2.3.93, 95–96; cf. 133–34).

In part because Leontes persuades Antigonus to "take up the bastard," we never see the father touch the baby let alone throw her on the fire or dash her brains out. As the play moves out of tragedy and into romance, it displaces blame for his angry repudiation of the baby onto those who he forces to act as the "thrower[s]-out" of the poor babe (3.3.27–28). A bear devours Antigonus and the whole crew of the ship that carried him and the baby goes down in a wreck "so that all the

---

90. See Neely on the fatal intimacy between mothers and children in Shakespearean drama (*Broken Nuptials*, pp. 172–73).

instruments which aided to expose the child were even then lost when it was found" (5.2.71–73). The play's characters hedge about the violence perpetrated against the two children and Leontes's responsibility for it. Paulina often intervenes in Leontes's self-protecting euphemisms, drawing him up short with blunt words like "killed"—"Killed? / She I killed? I did so, but thou strik'st me / Sorely to say I did" (5.1.16–18). But even when she reckons up his "poor trespasses," she counts "The casting forth to crows thy baby daughter / To be or none or little / ... / Nor is't *directly* laid to thee, the death / Of the young prince" (3.2.189; 191–92; 194–95, emphasis added).

Most of the play's characters use euphemisms for bereavement to occlude Leontes's accountability. They talk about "loss." Antigonus, for instance, refers to Perdita as "Poor thing, condemned to loss!" (2.3.191); "exposed / To loss and what may follow" (3.3.49–50). In Antigonus's dream, Hermione names her baby Perdita—she who has been lost—since she "Is counted lost for ever" (3.3.32); the oracle also explains that Leontes "shall live without an heir if that which is lost be not found" (3.2.134–36). The vocabulary of losing and finding becomes especially noticeable in the final act. Leontes explains to Perdita and Florizel that he "lost a couple" like them, and "lost" Florizel's father (5.1.132, 134). But to paraphrase Lady Bracknell, to lose one child is a misfortune, to lose two looks like carelessness. Dwelling on Leontes's "losses," the play prepares for forgiveness by sparing Leontes the direct, criminalized agency associated with murderous mothers and helping us to repress our knowledge of his crucial role in "losing" his children.

To aestheticize the very representations of child murder with which it engages, *The Winter's Tale* depends on strategies of displacement, condensation, and detachment that characterize romance.[91] The murderous parent is a king and forgiveable; he is motivated by a figment, a spider in the cup, rather than by desperate finances; he orders that his baby be abandoned, rather than killing her outright; and those to whom he delegates the task die for their part in it. Such displacements make Leontes the protagonist of the play, as a murderous mother would never be, while leading us, like so many of the play's characters, to

91. See Arthur Kirsch, *Shakespeare and the Experience of Love* (Cambridge: Cambridge University Press, 1981), esp. pp. 153, 164, 170; and Neely, *Broken Nuptials*, pp. 166–67. Kirsch argues that the strategies of romance as a form resemble those of dream-work; characters in the play identify the dream-like quality of events (3.2.82–85; 3.3.38; 4.4.461).

misrecognize what kind of a story this is, even as we sense its familiarity. *The Winter's Tale* participates in complex processes of displacement so successful that we have lost track of the play's indebtedness to those other cultural materials known to the bookish and the unbookish and to those figures on whom violence against children was displaced: unmarried mothers. As a "socially symbolic act," in Fredric Jameson's terms, the play "must reunite or harmonize heterogeneous narrative paradigms which have their own specific and contradictory ideological meaning." But in the process, historical specificity and contradiction are effaced through the "imaginary solution['s]" very success; viewers and readers are thus spared "the painful recollection of the dark underside of even the most seemingly innocent and 'life-enhancing' masterpieces of the canon."[92] In the process of turning a story of familial conflict into a fantasy of resolution, *The Winter's Tale*, like Shakespeare's other romances, excludes the mother from the action; she returns in order to forgive the father, not particularly for his role in the death of one child and the abandonment of another but for his jealous, tyrannical treatment of her.[93] By aestheticizing and forgiving domestic violence, *The Winter's Tale* shapes and articulates collective fantasies of parent-child violence without either implicating viewers in child murder or positioning them with its victims.[94] Its ability both to participate in a vast, heterogeneous cultural contestation and to distance itself has granted the play what Barbara Herrnstein Smith calls a "survival advantage" in the sibling rivalry of textual transmission and canon-formation.[95]

92. Jameson, *Political Unconscious*, pp. 144, 299, and chap. 2, passim.

93. On the elimination of mothers, see, especially, Rose, "Where Are the Mothers?" See also Neely, *Broken Nuptials;* and Phyllis Rackin, *Stages of History: Shakespeare's English Chronicles* (Ithaca: Cornell University Press, 1990), p. 187.

94. In the terms of Gail Kern Paster's provocative argument that "the romance plot is not a story of lost children—a story privileging the parental perspective—but a story of lost *parents* ... seen from the perspective of the child," these detachments enable the viewer to repress identification with the victim of violence, the threatened, abandoned child (*Body Embarrassed*, p. 274).

95. Barbara Herrnstein Smith, "Contingencies of Value," in *Canons*, ed. Robert von Hallberg (Chicago: University of Chicago Press, 1984), pp. 5–39, esp. p. 31. The pamphlets and ballads about infanticide have also "endured" or "survived" in that they are still extant. But such materials are less accessible, less widely circulated and discussed. Paradoxically, you need to be a relatively privileged research scholar, with access to libraries and grants, to work with these once popular materials.

On the "dangers" of "aestheticizing culture" and the importance of redrawing a dis-

Early modern discourse about child murder was more diverse than either legal attempts to confine infanticide to poor, unmarried women or *The Winter's Tale* would have us believe. I do not seek here to map a terrain of negligible, bizarre statutes, ballads, and pamphlets from which *The Winter's Tale* triumphantly emerges. Nor do I think that, even if we know about these other texts, we can hear the voices of infanticidal mothers in *The Winter's Tale*. To hear those voices, we must turn to other kinds of texts entirely.[96] Instead, I suggest that Shakespearean romance depended on the fascination with parental violence then pervading the culture while erasing the evidence of its own conditions of possibility.[97] We continue to collude in this process of associating child murder with mothers while valuing plays in which elite, murderous fathers, whose violence can be forgiven, are the protagonists. If asked about instances of infanticide in Shakespeare, most specialists will remember Lady Macbeth's imagery rather than Leontes's act.

In focusing not only on retrieving neglected discourses once widely circulated—finding what has been lost—but also on the difference that privileging some texts and abandoning others has made in our understanding of the past, I wish to emphasize how the "literary" has been constituted against texts more obviously and messily engaged in social process. Early modern contests about child murder point to the "perplexingly relative" value not only of children's lives but of texts.[98] The stories that remain most familiar from these contests are those most divorced from explicit reference to material conditions, those at the

---

tinction between text and context, see Gabrielle M. Spiegel, "History, Historicism, and the Social Logic of the Text in the Middle Ages," *Speculum* 65.1 (1990): 59–86. I do *not* want to join in redrawing the boundaries which it is precisely my goal to problematize. But in attending to how the vast array of representations of child murder have been digested, refined, and aestheticized in the processes of transmission, I am concerned with the differing prestige of various textual "kinds." For other interventions in the canon debates, see Wendell V. Harris, "Canonicity," *PMLA* 106.1 (1991): 110–21; and John Guillory, "Canonical and Non-Canonical: A Critique of the Current Debate," *ELH* 54.3 (1987): 483–527.

96. James Holstun challenges the assumption that "all cultural conflicts, all exercises of power and resistance necessarily register themselves inside canonical cultural artifacts" ("Ranting at the New Historicism," *English Literary Renaissance* [1989]: 189–225, esp. p. 198).

97. I am thus interested, in Stephen Greenblatt's phrase, in how the "traces of social circulation" have been "effaced" in *The Winter's Tale* (*Shakespearean Negotiations*, p. 5).

98. In his discussion of infanticide, Wrightson refers to the "perplexingly relativ[e]" value of infant life ("Infanticide," p. 10).

privileged, elite end of social and literary hierarchies. Just as Perdita was not simply lost but abandoned to die, the popular and legal texts about infanticide underpinning *The Winter's Tale* have not been lost or forgotten but repudiated as bastards; even their traces in the play have been ignored.

V. WITCHCRAFT AND THE THREAT OF THE FAMILIAR

Accounts of domestic crime destabilize distinctions between powerful and powerless, victimizer and victim, oppressor and oppressed.[1] Attempting to account for conflict erupting within the household, these texts discover the laborious, even violent, processes by which domestic power is achieved and maintained; they explore the contests for authority that threaten order at every turn. Like petty traitors or infanticidal mothers, witches are culturally positioned both as victims of their social and economic conditions and as victimizing others, in this case those more socially and economically empowered than they.[2] In contrast

---

1. In researching this chapter, I found the appendixes to Wallace Notestein's *A History of Witchcraft in England from 1558–1718* (New York: Russell and Russell, 1965), and his detailed discussion of cases and texts throughout, invaluable. I am also particularly indebted to Keith Thomas, *Religion and the Decline of Magic* (New York: Scribners, 1971), esp. chaps. 14–18. Excerpts from many pamphlets can be found in *Witchcraft in England, 1558–1618*, ed. Barbara Rosen (1969; reprint, Amherst: University of Massachusetts Press, 1991).

2. The vast majority of accused witches were women. On the number of women executed for witchcraft in Tudor and Stuart England, see Christina Larner, who places the number at under five hundred (*Witchcraft and Religion: The Politics of Popular Belief*, ed. Alan Macfarlane [Oxford: Basil Blackwell, 1984], p. 72); and E. William Monter,

to accounts of petty treason or infanticide, however, representations of witchcraft scrutinize contests for authority between households, as well as within them. According to historians of English witchcraft, the conflict often began when a poor, elderly, unmarried woman demanded charitable assistance and was denied; those who denied her, fearing her bitterness and vengefulness, ameliorated their panic and guilt by turning the tables: They accused her of bewitching them. Thus the accuser and the accused each perceived him or her self as the injured party.[3] The

---

who estimates less than one thousand ("The Pedestal and the Stake: Courtly Love and Witchcraft," in *Becoming Visible: Women in European History,* ed. Renate Bridenthal and Claudia Koonz [Boston: Houghton Mifflin, 1977], pp. 119–36, esp. p. 130). See also Alan Macfarlane, *Witchcraft in Tudor and Stuart England: A Regional and Comparative Study* (London: Routledge, 1970), pp. 59–60.

On the significance of the fact that at least 80 percent of the accused were women, see, especially, Alan Anderson and Raymond Gordon, "Witchcraft and the Status of Women—The Case of England," *British Journal of Sociology* 29 (1978): 171–84; Clarke Garrett, "Women and Witches: Patterns of Analysis," *Signs* 3.2 (1977): 461–70, and the responses to him by Claudia Honegger and Nelly Moia in *Signs* 4.4 (1979): 792–804; Marianne Hester, *Lewd Women and Wicked Witches: A Study of the Dynamics of Male Domination* (New York: Routledge, 1992), chaps. 6–8; Christina Larner, *Witchcraft and Religion,* ed. Macfarlane, chap. 3; Monter, "Pedestal and the Stake," pp. 132–33; and Karen Newman, *Fashioning Femininity and English Renaissance Drama* (Chicago: University of Chicago Press, 1991), pp. 55–58. Unlike most historians of witchcraft, Carol F. Karlsen makes gender her central category of analysis (*The Devil in the Shape of a Woman: Witchcraft in Colonial New England* [New York: W. W. Norton, 1987], esp. chap. 5).

3. Scholars have argued that accusations of witchcraft signaled a breakdown of communal values and justified refusals of poor relief. "It was those who offended against the ideals of a cooperative society by refusing to help their neighbours who found themselves bewitched" (Alan Macfarlane, "Witchcraft in Tudor and Stuart Essex," in *Crime in England, 1550–1800,* ed. J. S. Cockburn [Princeton: Princeton University Press, 1977], pp. 72–89, esp. p. 85). By traditional standards, "it tended to be the witch who was morally in the right and the victim who was in the wrong" (Thomas, *Religion,* p. 553). A witchcraft accusation thus enabled the accusers to displace responsibility for their own failures of charitability and their misfortunes onto others, particularly those poorer and less socially powerful than themselves (Macfarlane, *Witchcraft,* chap. 15, and "Witchcraft in Tudor and Stuart Essex," esp. pp. 83–85). As David Warren Sabean clarifies, "it is not that weak marginal people are the witches but only that in a contest in which magic plays a role, the powerful win" (*Power in the Blood: Popular Culture and Village Discourse in Early Modern Germany* [Cambridge: Cambridge University Press, 1984], p. 109). See also G. R. Quaife, *Godly Zeal and Furious Rage: The Witch in Early Modern Europe* (New York: St. Martin's Press, 1987), chaps. 11 and 12; Macfarlane, *Witchcraft,* esp. chaps. 6 and 12 (Macfarlane later refutes this argument in *The Origins of English Individualism: The Family, Property, and Social Transition* [New York: Cambridge University Press, 1978], pp. 1–2); and Thomas, *Religion,* pp. 552–60 and chap. 17. This cycle, as Thomas argues, reveals "how the relatively secure might be haunted by their ill-treatment of the poor" (p. 558).

offenses the witch suffers and the danger she offers are inextricably connected; one seventeenth-century law clerk comments that it is "dangerous . . . for any man to live neere this people, to give them any occasion of offence."[4]

Belief in the occult fueled fears that these loiterers at the household's and community's margins might find devious ways to express their anger and redress their grievances. Even Sir Reginald Scot, one of the earliest and best-known skeptics about witchcraft, links witchcraft practices to poison, which was associated with women's covert violence, criminality, and domestic treachery. Arguing that Exodus 22:18 ("Thou shalt not suffer a 'witch' to live.") refers to poisoners rather than sorcerers, Scot insists on the association of women and poison: "As women in all ages have been counted most apt to conceive witchcraft . . . so also it appeareth, that they have been the first inventers, and the greatest practisers of poisoning, and more naturallie addicted and given thereunto than men." Scot thus casts poison as a form of female power in which he can believe; in his view, poison, by empowering the weak, inverts social and domestic hierarchies in disturbing ways:

> Trulie this poisoning art called *Veneficium,* of all others is most abhominable; as whereby murthers maie be committed, where no suspicion maie be gathered, nor anie resistance can be made; the strong cannot avoid the weake, the wise cannot prevent the foolish, the godlie cannot be preserved from the hands of the wicked; *children maie hereby kill their parents, the servant the maister, the wife hir husband,* so privilie, so inevitablie, and so incurablie, that of all other it hath been thought the most odious kind of murther.[5]

For Scot, the only plausible, scripturally prohibited, legally actionable witchcraft is a form of petty treason. Even as he challenges and ridicules the belief in magic, Scot justifies the belief in and fear of insubordinate dependents, of the weak who treacherously overpower the strong.

4. Thomas Potts, *The Wonderfull Discoverie of Witches in the Countie of Lancaster* (London, 1613), sig. E2v.

5. Reginald Scot, *The Discoverie of Witchcraft,* first published in 1584 (London: Centaur, 1964), pp. 112–13, p. 113, emphasis added; in *The Adultresses Funerall Day* (London, 1635), discussed in Chapter 1, Henry Goodcole also links poison, witchcraft, and petty treason. On the connection of witchcraft to poison, see also Macfarlane, *Witchcraft,* p. 16; and Sabean, *Power in the Blood,* p. 110.

Despite his skepticism, Scot participates in the pervasive early modern association of witchcraft with domesticity: Witches undermine domestic order, hinder domestic and agricultural production (particularly "women's work"), and baffle sexuality and reproduction. Although they were rarely live-in servants, women vulnerable to suspicion and prosecution lived hand-to-mouth by performing various tasks for hire, begging, selling brooms, or gathering firewood; like servants, then, they knew their victims' routines well enough to disrupt them. Like servants, too, their familiarity with their "superiors' " bodily needs and vulnerabilities—even bodily wastes—was feared to empower them. Forced to depend on scraps for subsistence, they turned refuse into weapons, using hair and nail clippings and soiled clothing in their spells. In actual prosecutions suspected witches were rarely related by blood to their victims and accusers, but they were sometimes accused of afflicting and killing their marital relations, especially their husbands, by means of witchcraft.[6] As Christina Larner argues, "In situations of domestic stress and tension in which men resort to violence, women use witchcraft."[7] Even in cases in which accuser and accused were not related, witchcraft accusations and prosecutions made tensions among family members and between neighbors visible. Popular representations of witchcraft

6. For accounts of women who bewitch their husbands to death, or try to, see *The Examination and Confession of Certain Wytches at Chensford* (1556), reprinted in *Witch Hunting and Witch Trials: The Indictments for Witchcraft from the Records of 1373 Assizes Held for the Home Circuit A.D. 1559–1736*, ed. C. L'Estrange Ewen (London: Kegan Paul, 1929); *The Lawes against Witches and Conjuration* (London, 1645); and *A True Relation of the Araignment of Eighteene Witches. That Were Tried, Convicted, and Condemned, at a Sessions Holden at St. Edmunds-bury* (London, 1645). Only those witches who were also guilty of petty treason were burnt at the stake. See also Macfarlane, *Witchcraft*, p. 169; Notestein, *History of Witchcraft*, p. 182; and Alan R. Young, "Elizabeth Lowys: Witch and Social Victim, 1564," *History Today* 22 (1972): 879–85. Deborah Willis focuses on how representations of witchcraft dwell on women's roles as the mothers or caretakers of small children and as domestic workers; Willis also stresses that friction *between* women fuelled witchcraft accusations and prosecutions. I am grateful to Willis for sharing with me part of her unpublished manuscript, *Notorious Defamations: Gender, Cultural Practice, and the Rise of Witch-Hunting in Early Modern England*. Willis's arguments will be available in abbreviated form in her "Shakespeare and the English Witch-Hunts: Enclosing the Maternal Body," in *Enclosure Acts: Sexuality, Property, and Culture in Early Modern England*, ed. Richard Burt and John Michael Archer (Ithaca: Cornell University Press, forthcoming). See also Karlsen, *Devil in the Shape*, esp. pp. 134–47.

7. Christina Larner, *Enemies of God: The Witch-hunt in Scotland* (London: Chatto and Windus, 1981), p. 96; Thomas, *Religion*, p. 561.

thus enable us to look at the anxieties generated within families and the roles witchcraft accusations played in displacing and negotiating those tensions.

Inside the household or hovering at its margins, witches were known and unknown, familiar and dangerous. In this they conjoined the characteristics of domestic "outsiders within"—dependents feared to be insubordinate—and scapegoated cultural others (such as Jews, Catholics, Moors). Positioned simultaneously as "internal and external enemies," as Carlo Ginzburg suggests, witches were threats and scapegoats who resided *inside* the community.[8] In addition to being themselves dangerous familiars, witches were thought to act as mothers to a demonic brood of "familiars" or "imps" (see figs. 7 and 8). In contrast to Continental witchcraft lore, English belief emphasized the relationship between the witch and her "familiars," usually described as small, domestic animals such as "kitlyns," weasels, puppies, and toads. As Michael MacDonald points out, the afflicted may have taken some comfort in attributing anxiety and illness to "familiar agents and comprehensible forces."[9] Yet the very familiarity of witches and their imps—their apparent innocuousness—also made them especially disquieting. How could one distinguish a needy neighbor from a demonic threat? How could one know whom to trust?

In the late sixteenth and seventeenth centuries, the law attempted to make just such distinctions. Like petty treason and infanticide, witchcraft generated new legislation in Tudor and early Stuart England,

8. Carlo Ginzburg, "The Witches' Sabbat: Popular Cult or Inquisitorial Stereotype?" in *Understanding Popular Culture: Europe from the Middle Ages to the Nineteenth Century,* ed. Steven L. Kaplan (Berlin: Mouton, 1984), pp. 39–51, esp. p. 43. On familiars, and their uniqueness to English witch belief, also see Clive Holmes, "Popular Culture? Witches, Magistrates, and Divines in Early Modern England," in *Understanding Popular Culture,* ed. Kaplan, pp. 85–111, esp. pp. 97–99; Michael MacDonald, *Mystical Bedlam: Madness, Anxiety, and Healing in Seventeenth-Century England* (Cambridge: Cambridge University Press, 1981), pp. 203–4; Gail Kern Paster, *The Body Embarrassed: Drama and the Disciplines of Shame in Early Modern England* (Ithaca: Cornell University Press, 1993), chap. 5, esp. pp. 256–60; and Thomas, *Religion,* pp. 445–46. Notestein points out that Jacobean legislation made keeping a familiar a felony (*History of Witchcraft,* pp. 104, 189, 202–3). The searches for witches' marks represent the "Englishing" of Continental witch belief—the mark, a sign of the witch's pact with the devil, becomes a teat by which she suckles her familiar. Familiars (a cat and a dog, respectively) are actually characters in two plays, *The Witch* and *The Witch of Edmonton.*

9. MacDonald, *Mystical Bedlam,* p. 210.

Figure 7. A witch feeds her familiars. From *A Rehearsall Both Straung and True, of Hainous and Horrible Actes Committed By Elizabeth Stile* (1579). By permission of the British Library.

which was influenced by and contributed to other legal and social efforts to criminalize poverty and women.[10] This legislation engendered a surge in prosecutions. As Alan Macfarlane argues: "The trial of witches was second only to the trial of thieves. It was not a peripheral or marginal crime, but of central importance. There were few years when indict-

10. The blurred distinctions between cunning-people and midwives might have exposed women healers to prosecution (MacDonald, ibid., pp. 177–78, 190, 212–13). In *Not of Woman Born: Representations of Caesarean Birth in Medieval and Renaissance Culture* (Ithaca: Cornell University Press, 1991), Renate Blumenfeld-Kosinski argues that the *Malleus Maleficarum* distinguishes between good and bad midwives and associates only the latter with witchcraft. See her assessment of the effect of witch-hunts on women in medicine (pp. 105–17). For the argument that distinctions could be drawn between cunning-women and midwives, see Monica Green, "Women's Medical Practice and Health Care in Medieval Europe," *Signs* 14.2 (1989): 434–73, esp. pp. 451–52.

On the criminalization of women, see Allison P. Coudert, "The Myth of the Improved Status of Protestant Women: The Case of the Witchcraze," in *The Politics of Gender in Early Modern Europe*, ed. Jean R. Brink, Coudert, and Maryanne C. Horowitz (Kirksville: Northeast Missouri State University Press, 1989), pp. 61–89; Brian Easlea, *Witch-Hunting, Magic, and the New Philosophy: An Introduction to Debates of the Scientific Revolution, 1450–1750* (Sussex: Harvester Press, 1980), pp. 7–8, 17–18, 30, 33–34; Larner, *Witchcraft and Religion*, ed. Macfarlane, pp. 60–63; and Quaife, *Godly Zeal,* chaps. 6 and 7.

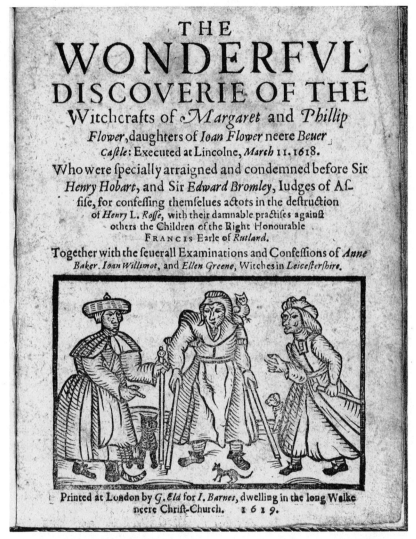

THE
WONDERFVL
DISCOVERIE OF THE
Witchcrafts of *Margaret* and *Phillip*
Flower, daughters of *Ioan Flower* neere *Beuer*
Caſtle: Executed at Lincolne, *March* 11. 1618.

Who were ſpecially arraigned and condemned before Sir
Henry Hobart, and Sir *Edward Bromley*, Iudges of Aſ-
ſiſe, for confeſſing themſelues actots in the deſtruction
of *Henry* L. *Roſſe*, with their damnable practiſes againſt
others the Children of the Right Honourable
FRANCIS Earle of *Rutland*.

Together with the ſeuerall Examinations and Confeſſions of *Anne*
Baker, *Ioan Willimot*, and *Ellen Greene*, Witches in *Leiceſterſhire*.

Printed at London by *G. Eld* for *I. Barnes*, dwelling in the long Walke
neere Chriſt-Church. 1 6 1 9.

Figure 8. Witches and their familiars. Title page of *The Wonderful Discoverie of the Witchcrafts of Margaret and Phillip Flower* (1619). By permission of the Henry E. Huntington Library and Art Gallery, San Marino, California.

ments did not occur."[11] Yet by the late sixteenth century, skeptics questioned the existence of witches and the justifications for prosecuting them. Throughout the seventeenth century, preachers and divines, lawyers and other legal personnel, physicians, and scholars engaged in lively debates over witches, the sources and manifestations of their power, and how their witchcraft should be discovered, proved, and proceeded against.[12]

The texts in the controversy combine medical, legal, and theological analyses while attending to popular belief, without which the witchcraft phenomenon could not have occurred. Many historians agree that, in England, the phenomenon of witch persecution was neither "a spontaneous expression from below" nor a "lawyer-led campaign from above."[13] According to Clive Holmes, the formal prosecution of witches resulted, instead, from "a complex series of transactions between various elite and popular elements," producing what Ginzburg describes as a cultural "compromise formation" combining elements from above and below.[14] At the height of the prosecutions, popular and elite belief overlapped in certain ways; in addition, there were differences of opinion among the elite. Historians variously argue that the elite worked to transform popular opinion; that the elite manipulated "popular credulity about witchcraft" which "provided the governing elite with a means to reshape public attitudes toward poor and marginal members of the village community"; that popular belief resisted elite pressures

11. Macfarlane, "Witchcraft in Tudor and Stuart Essex," p. 75.

12. Many texts about the processes of discovering and proving witchcraft define and protect certain professions. Matthew Hopkins (*The Discovery of Witches* [London, 1647]) and John Stearne (*A Confirmation and Discovery of Witchcraft* [London, 1648]) defend witch finding as itself a profession. In *A Briefe Discourse of a Disease Called the Suffocation of the Mother* (London, 1603), Edward Jorden argues that the investigation of cases of possession is the province of physicians. Accounts of witch trials by legal personnel emphasize that it is the job of magistrates, justices of the peace, and other legal personnel to ferret out and prosecute witchcraft (see, for instance, *The Lawes Against Witches*; Potts, *Wonderfull Discoverie*; *The Most Strange and Admirable Discoverie of the Three Witches of Warboys* [London, 1593]; and [W.W.], *A True and Just Recorde, of the Information, Examination and Confession of All the Witches, Taken at S. Oses in the Countie of Essex*, [London, 1582]). Divines present witchcraft as heresy and/or satanic intervention, as a crime against God and the church, and thus as most properly within their own prerogative.

13. Larner, *Witchcraft and Religion*, ed. Macfarlane, p. 21, see also pp. 32, 74–76; and Thomas, *Religion*, p. 460, see also pp. 499, 583.

14. Holmes, "Popular Culture?" p. 87; Ginzburg, *Ecstasies: Deciphering the Witches' Sabbath*, trans. Raymond Rosenthal (New York: Pantheon, 1991), pp. 11, 296–314, see also "Witches' Sabbat," p. 40.

and retreated into its own "anti-culture," leaving doubt as to whether "changes in reputable literate belief necessarily communicated themselves to the poor and the illiterate by a process of seeping-down."[15] What is important here is that at the height of witch prosecutions in England, popular and elite cultures were not discrete and that each influenced and was shaped by the other. Witchcraft discourses reside at an intersection of the two; for instance, some "popular" pamphlets were written by legal personnel.[16] Furthermore, in the figure of the witch, different social classes found a source of threat they could collectively believe in and work to eliminate.[17]

15. Holmes, "Popular Culture?" pp. 92–105; MacDonald, *Mystical Bedlam,* p. 208; and E. P. Thompson, "Anthropology and the Discipline of Historical Context," *Midland History* 1.3 (1972): 41–55, esp. p. 54.

16. Justice Fenner commissioned *The Most Strange and Admirable Discoverie of the Three Witches of Warboys* (1593), which was based on notes kept on the case from the start; Brian Darcy, justice of the peace, may well have written *A True and Just Recorde at . . . S. Oses* (1582); Thomas Potts, a London lawyer acting as clerk in the court at Lancaster, describes how the justices commissioned him to prepare a transcript of the trials there, then reviewed his work, which was published as *The Wonderfull Discoverie of Witches in the Countie of Lancaster* (1613); Matthew Hopkins, the notorious witch finder, wrote his own, self-justifying, text, *The Discovery of Witches;* Edward Fairfax's *A Discourse of Witchcraft as It Was Acted in the Family of Mr. Edward Fairfax* (1621) and Mary Moore's *Wonderfull News from the North. Or, A True Relation of the Sad and Grievous Torments, Inflicted upon the Bodies of Three Children of Mr. George Muschamp . . . by Witchcraft* (London, 1650), which I treat at some length at the end of this chapter, were written by the parents of possessed children. In contrast to this representative but not exhaustive sample, Henry Goodcole, minister of Newgate, is one of the few authors of pamphlets about spousal or child murder about whom we have any biographical information. On the authorship of pamphlets, see Holmes, "Popular Culture?" pp. 93, 108, n. 30; Macfarlane, *Witchcraft,* p. 85; and Notestein, *History of Witchcraft,* passim, esp. the appendixes.

17. On the statutes prohibiting witchcraft and their focus on *maleficium* or harmful *actions,* see Holmes, "Popular Culture?" pp. 87; Larner, *Witchcraft and Religion,* ed. Macfarlane, pp. 19, 24; Macfarlane, *Witchcraft,* chap. 2; Notestein, *History of Witchcraft,* chap. 1 and pp. 101–6; and Thomas, *Religion,* pp. 442–43. In the 1604 statute: "Greater stress was laid on the punishment of intention to use witchcraft as well as its actual use: intending to hurt or destroy people or property was punishable 'although the same be not effected and done' " (Macfarlane, *Witchcraft,* p. 15). Legal and literary constructions of treason also emphasized intention: see Steven Mullaney, *The Place of the Stage: License, Play, and Power in Renaissance England* (Chicago: University of Chicago Press, 1988), chap. 5.

The high point for prosecutions was Elizabeth's reign, especially the 1580s and 1590s; thereafter, prosecutions died away long before the repeal of the witchcraft act in 1736. See Larner, *Witchcraft and Religion,* ed. Macfarlane, p. 18; Macfarlane, "Witchcraft in Tudor and Stuart Essex," pp. 74, 79, and *Witchcraft,* pp. 28, 57, and chap. 16; Notestein, whose book, *History of Witchcraft,* is structured around the rise and fall of prosecutions; Barbara J. Shapiro, *Probability and Certainty in Seventeenth-Century England: A Study of*

Most texts in this heterogeneous controversy dwell on whether witches were agents who could be held accountable for their *maleficium*. Only those texts that justify the prosecution of suspected witches construct them as agents. Those texts that defend women against prosecution also deny them agency as the price of that protection. Linking the drama to these theoretical discussions of witches' agency, I focus on the conditions under which witchcraft discourses constructed women as agents, although I make some reference to the agencies historical women may have found through witchcraft beliefs and practices.

Subject-Extensions and Bodily Permeability

In early modern England, witches were thought to make images of their victims out of wax or clay, which they would then prick with pins or thorns (to cause pain or localized illness) or burn and bury (to cause consumption and death). In a crime that produced little material evidence, these images offered incriminating "proof" of guilt.[18] According to beliefs that pervaded popular and elite culture, witches made these images to resemble and represent a particular victim: "like unto the shape of the person whom they meane to kill"; "of the proportion of a childe which she was intended to work her mischief against."[19] These images also bore the names of the intended victims. In one text, Elizabeth Style confesses that she and her confederate baptized wax pictures

---

the Relationships Between Natural Science, Religion, History, Law, and Literature (Princeton: Princeton University Press, 1983), chap. 6; and Thomas, *Religion*, pp. 451–52.

18. Richard Bernard, *A Guide to Grand-Jury Men, Divided into Two Bookes* (London, 1627); and *Lawes against Witches*; see also Notestein, *History of Witchcraft*, pp. 109–10. Discovering the image was also thought by some to reverse the witch's spell (see Stearne, *Confirmation and Discovery*, sigs. H2–H2v). Good witches who discover and reverse the spells of bad witches often show reflections of the bewitcher to the bewitched (see, for instance, *The Witch of Wapping. Or An Exact and Perfect Relation, of the Life and Devilish Practises of Joan Peterson* [London, 1652], in *Reprints of English Books, 1475–1700*, ed. J. A. Foster [Ingram, Penn., 1939–1940], pp. 3–4; and Alexander Roberts, *A Treatise of Witchcraft* [London, 1616]). See also Macfarlane, *Witchcraft*, pp. 122, 125; and Thomas, *Religion*, pp. 548–49.

19. Potts, *Wonderfull Discoverie*, sig. B3v; Stearne, *Confirmation and Discovery*, sigs. H2–H2v.

in the names of those they wished to torment.[20] The correspondence that the witch intended thus mattered more than any visible resemblance.

According to Karen Newman, accounts of witches' participation in processes of representation construct them as makers of meaning and as capable of displaced violence by this means. Newman emphasizes "the etymological force of the word [*maleficium*], its root in the verb *facio,* to make, construct, fashion, frame, build, erect, produce, compose. The fashioning of such images . . . suggests the power and danger of mimesis, of likeness."[21] The widespread belief in witches' use of images endowed their "craftiness" with extraordinary power, as Newman here articulates. For instance, the account of Johane Harrison's "witch-*crafts,* and most damnable practises" appended to *The Most Cruell and Bloody Murther* (1606), describes Harrison's trunk of paraphernalia, which included a parchment anatomizing the body, with the heart in full color. She confesses "that she had power (by the helpe of that parchment, man & womans bones, and man and womans haire) to inflict [pain] in any joynt, synnow, or place of the body, by only but pricking the point of a needle in that place of the parchme[n]t, where in his or her body she would have them tortured." When she wanted to kill "she gave a pricke in the middle of ye parchment, where she had placed the heart."[22] Although some texts present witches as engaged in a demonic form of domesticity and cottage industry, that is, producing these images and then roasting or burying them in inversions of the housewifely tasks of cooking and gardening, texts such as the one just quoted depict witches as learned and skilled.[23]

20. Joseph Glanvill, *Saducismus Triumphatus: Or, Full and Plain Evidence Concerning Witches and Apparitions* (London, 1681), sigs. Kk5–Kk5v. On naming the images, see also James I, *Daemonologie* (1597), in *Minor Prose Works of King James VI & I,* ed. James Craigie (Edinburgh: Scottish Text Society, 1982), p. 31.

21. Newman, *Fashioning Femininity,* p. 66.

22. *The Most Cruell and Bloody Murther Committed by an Innkeepers Wife, Called Annis Dell . . . with the Severall Witchcrafts, and Most Damnable Practises of One Johane Harrison and Her Daughter* (London, 1606), sig. C3. See also *A Rehearsall Both Straung and True, of Hainous and Horrible Actes Committed by Elizabeth Stile, Alias Rockingham* (London, 1579), in *Reprints of English Books,* ed. Foster, pp. 8–9.

23. Other discussions of witches' use of images include *The Divels Delusions or a Faithfull Relation of John Palmer and Elizabeth Knott Two Notorious Witches* (St. Albans, 1649), in *Reprints of English Books,* ed. Foster, p. 6; E.G., *A Prodigious and Tragicall History of the Arraignment, Tryall, Confession, and Condemnation of Six Witches at Maidstone* (London, 1652), reprinted in *A Collection of Rare and Curious Tracts* (London: John

Texts also emphasize the vulnerability of victims—however healthy, virtuous, and socially and economically secure—through their material representations. The correspondence between image and original is so close that a person's "copy" can harm him or her. Just as *The Winter's Tale* depicts Leontes's horrified, violent response to Paulina's suggestion that Perdita is a *copy* of him, discourses about witches' image-magic suggest that copies of the self could be perceived as deeply threatening.[24] The distinction between the real and the represented, the self and the image, thus blurs to the point of collapse. That collapsed distinction makes visible anxieties about bodily vulnerability and permeability, about access to the body and life by means of material objects.

Although Newman argues that "witches threatened hegemonic patriarchal structures precisely not through their bodies but through their representational powers: as cultural producers," their work as cultural producers was closely connected to their power over the bodies of their victims.[25] That power was, in turn, associated with the witches' own bodies, which were similarly understood as complexly connected to and invested in objects as well as closely identified with the bodies of their victims. Witches' representational powers, so central to the cultural constructions of the threat they offered, were not understood as sep-

---

Russell Smith, 1838), p. 8; James I, *Daemonologie*, pp. 31–32; Potts, *Wonderfull Discoverie*, sig. B3v and passim; and documents surrounding the Overbury scandal—at the trial, lead pictures of a copulating man and woman were produced as evidence that Lady Frances, countess of Essex, had used witchcraft to procure the love of the earl of Somerset (*True and Historical Relation of the Poysoning of Sir Thomas Overbury... Collected out of the Papers of Sir Francis Bacon, the Kings Attorney-General* [London, 1651]). Reginald Scot relates an incident of fraud, in which one woman who accused another was caught planting the image of a heart for which she was looking (*Discoverie of Witchcraft*, pp. 220–21). See Thomas, *Religion*, pp. 513–14.

24. The connection between making and manipulating images and treason draws on a deep unease about the accessibility of the monarch's image. On Elizabeth I's regulation of royal portraiture, see David Scott Kastan, "Proud Majesty Made a Subject: Shakespeare and the Spectacle of Rule," *Shakespeare Quarterly* 37.4 (1986): 459–75, esp. p. 462. Newman discusses "the potency and fear surrounding monarchical representation and its potential use in political and social rebellion" (*Fashioning Femininity*, p. 66). On the role of images in accusations of treasonous witchcraft, see Stuart Clark, "King James's *Daemonologie*: Witchcraft and Kingship," in *The Damned Art: Essays in the Literature of Witchcraft*, ed. Sydney Anglo (London: Routledge and Kegan Paul, 1977), pp. 156–81, esp. pp. 158–59, 164; see also Notestein, *History of Witchcraft*, pp. 24–28, 52–53, 93–96, 276–77. In Thomas Dekker's *The Whore of Babylon*, a conjuror prepares a wax image of Titania as one of the treasonous plots to overthrow her; he plans both to stick pins in the heart, and to bury it (2.2.206–214).

25. Newman, *Fashioning Femininity*, p. 69.

arable from their bodies. Nor was witchcraft, although spiritual and supernatural, divorced from the life of the body in the material world. Representation, in this case, was about the production of concrete images; it was about the manipulation of the material world. If representation and the body were intimately linked, so were witches and their victims.

Bodily excretions and excrescences, household objects, and worn items of clothing were considered so much parts of the self that witchcraft belief construed them as avenues of entry, fragile thresholds of vulnerability. Since the subject was infused and invested in these "objects," witches could gain access to their victims by means of apparently inanimate, insignificant, discarded castoffs. *The Wonderful Discoverie of the Witchcrafts of Margaret and Phillip Flower* (1619), for instance, describes the charge against Anne Baker for burning a child's hair and nail parings and thereby causing its illness and death. In *Newes from Scotland* (1591), Agnis Tompson claims that if she had gotten any piece of linen "which the king [James I] had worne and fouled" she would have been able to bewitch him to death in terrible agony.[26] As these examples reveal, the permeable boundaries around the subject in early modern England extended to include objects (property, bodily products and parts) that might be considered subject-extensions.[27]

26. *The Wonderful Discoverie of the Witchcrafts of Margaret and Phillip Flower, Daughters of Joan Flower* (London, 1619), in *Collection of Rare and Curious Tracts*, p. 15; *Newes from Scotland, Declaring the Damnable Life and Death of Doctor Fian, a Notable Sorcerer, Who Was Burned at Edenbrough in January Last* (London, 1591), sig. B4v. In such instances, disloyal servants could play an important role in providing the possessions that would endanger their masters. For instance, *Newes from Scotland* describes how the loyalty of the attendant of James's chamber prevented this scheme. Also, when the earl of Rutland fired Margaret Flowers as a domestic servant, she used his son's worn glove, obtained by means of her position, to bewitch the son and heir to death: "As that glove did rot and wast, so did the liver of the said Lord rot and wast" (*Wonderful Discoverie . . . Flower,* p. 16).

Discussions of legal procedures against witches include locks of hair among the limited kinds of physical evidence that might be found in suspects' houses. See Bernard, *Guide,* and *Lawes against Witches,* which is clearly indebted to it. See also Thomas: "One could harm a man by manipulating his hair, his fingernail parings, his sweat or his excrement, all of which contained his vital spirits" (*Religion,* p. 438).

27. Natalie Z. Davis argues that in sixteenth-century France, "the boundary around the conceptual self and the bodily self was not always firm and closed" ("Boundaries and the Sense of Self in Sixteenth-Century France," in *Reconstructing Individualism: Autonomy, Individuality, and the Self in Western Thought,* ed. Thomas C. Heller, Morton Sosna, and David E. Wellbery [Stanford: Stanford University Press, 1986], pp. 53–63, esp. p. 55). As Davis and other scholars argue, in early modern Europe, as here and now, subjectivities

In addition to appropriating and manipulating these subject-extensions, witches could dictate their victims' behavior, depriving them of agency, or facilitate demonic possession. Witches were thus understood as persons separate from or outside of their victims, yet simultaneously inside of them. Like our conception of the virus, alien but inside, hostile but included, the construction of the witch attempted to describe a threat perceived as not precisely locatable, a consequence of the unfixed boundary between self and other. This conception of witches as invading and undermining their victims' bodies corresponds to the cultural positioning of witches as inside (well-known members of the community and near neighbors) and outside (perceived enemies and sources of threat). The fear of intimacy crucial to representations of spousal and master-servant conflict here extends outside the household and beyond the skin.

Even those medical discourses that proposed "natural," physiological causes for the physical symptoms of bewitchment and possession reminded readers of the permeability and vulnerability of the human body. Physician Edward Jorden describes human bodies as "subject to be hurt and offended" by numerous external causes of disease and vulnerable to "the perturbations of the minde": "For seeing we are not maisters of our own affections, wee are like battered Citties without walles, or shippes tossed in the Sea, exposed to all maner of assaults and daungers, even to the overthrow of our owne bodies."[28] This conception of the

---

were inter-subjectivities; persons defined themselves and were culturally positioned in relation to others. Macfarlane's argument that "a central and basic feature of English social structure has for long been the stress on the rights and privileges of the individual as against the wider group or the State" does not apply to women or servants, or indeed to anyone other than male property owners (*Origins of English Individualism,* p. 5).

28. Jorden, *Briefe Discourse,* sigs. Gv, G2v. On the fragility of both mind and body, and the sympathy between the two, see MacDonald, *Mystical Bedlam,* pp. 178–98; Ronald C. Sawyer, " 'Strangely handled in all her lyms': Witchcraft and Healing in Jacobean England," *Journal of Social History* 22.3 (1989): 461–85, esp. pp. 468–69; and Julie Solomon, "Mortality as Matter of Mind: Towards a Politics of Problems in *All's Well That Ends Well*," *English Literary Renaissance* 23 (Winter 1993): 134–69. On the connection between bewitchment and illness, see MacDonald, *Mystical Bedlam,* pp. 198–217; Macfarlane, *Witchcraft,* chap. 13; and Sawyer, " 'Strangely handled'." See also discussions of bewitchment as a cause of sterility in Nicholas Fontanus, *The Womans Doctour* (London, 1652), sigs. K2v–K3; and Jacob Rueff, *The Expert Midwife* (London, 1637), sigs. Aa2v–Aa3, Bb4v, Dd8. On the policing of bodily boundaries, see also Mary Douglas, *Purity and Danger: An Analysis of Concepts of Pollution and Taboo* (New York: Frederick

body as assailable and beyond control also contributed to an understanding of disease as a kind of possession: MacDonald finds that those who were ill "suffered from plucking sensations or convulsions that made them look as if they were manipulated by invisible creatures"; and according to Ronald Sawyer, "Patients talked about being suddenly struck by something from the outside and about odd sensations of things (most commonly mice) running up and down their bodies."[29] Even skeptics like Jorden argued that witches could exploit this sense of bodily uncontrol, undermining their victims' health simply by causing fear and anxiety, whether or not they actually had the power to cause disease.

Paradoxically, in witchcraft discourses the only representations of the body as closed or sealed occur in accounts of possession. Again and again, these texts describe how the possessed person cannot open her mouth to speak, eat, or drink. Concerned bystanders often force quills between the possessed person's clenched teeth in order to feed her or him. In *A Tryal of Witches, at the Assizes Held at Bury St. Edmonds* (1682), for instance, a possessed child's mouth is sealed shut, "insomuch, that they could not open her Mouth to give her breath, to preserve her Life without the help of a Tap which they were enforced to use." In *The Most Wonderfull and True Storie, of a Certaine Witch Named Alse Gooderidge* (1597), after a possessed boy accuses Satan of being the father of lies, "Foorthwith his mouth was cloased up, and hys teeth set fast in his head, insomuch that hee laboured to have opened them with his owne hands, but he could not."[30] In such texts, the

---

A. Praeger, 1966). On the historically particular determination of bodily boundaries, see Barbara Duden, "History beneath the Skin," *Michigan Quarterly Review* 30 (Winter 1991): 174–90; Phyllis Mack, *Visionary Women: Ecstatic Prophecy in Seventeenth-Century England* (Berkeley: University of California Press, 1992), esp. p. 85; and Paster, *Body Embarrassed*, passim.

29. MacDonald, *Mystical Bedlam*, p. 209; Sawyer, " 'Strangely handled'," p. 469.

30. *A Tryal of Witches, at the Assizes Held at Bury St. Edmonds . . . 1664. Before Sir Matthew Hale, Kt.* (London, 1682), reprinted in *Collection of Rare and Curious Tracts*, p. 10; *The Most Wonderfull and True Storie, of a Certaine Witch Named Alse Gooderidge* (London, 1597), sig. C4. For accounts of cases of possession in which the mouth became the site of struggle, see *The Most Strange and Admirable Discoverie of the Three Witches of Warboys;* Mary Moore, *Wonderfull News from the North;* and G.B., *A Most Wicked Worke of a Wretched Witch Wrought . . . on . . . Richard Burt* (London, 1592). In his argument that most supposed cases of possession are misdiagnosed cases of a disease called "suffocation of the mother," Edward Jorden claims that the primary symptoms of this disease

bodily boundary around the subject is closed only because the subject must share that locked body with the devil. When the body is understood as the arena of struggle between the subject and the devil, the entrances are locked and barred to exclude intruders. This sealed boundary isolates rather than protects the possessed victim.

Witchcraft was informed by, and in turn heightened, widespread anxieties about the body's assailable, indefensible openings. According to popular belief, as codified and censured by Reginald Scot, witches can "thrust into the mind or conscience of man, what it shall please them." Simultaneously attacking body and mind, outer and inner, witches could harm from a distance, not only by means of images but by means of their "furious eies" and "angrie lookes" or their contaminating breath: "They belch up a certeine breath, wherewith they bewitch whomsoever they list."[31]

The popular belief that witches could hurt their victims without touching them articulated concerns about domestic as well as bodily boundaries. One could not flee the witch, or lock her out, or use material means to refix and seal that boundary between self and other. George Gifford challenges, but reports, the popular belief that "their spirits cannot bee taken heede of, nor kept out with doores and wals as theeves and murtherers [can], but come in when they bee sent, and doe so many harmes." William Dragge, writing about those diseases caused by witchcraft, explains that when witches are disguised as animals, "they lie lurking in holes . . . seeking our ruine and mischief, while we sleep securely, little distrusting anything when we lie down."[32] According to these beliefs, potential victims are safe neither in their own skins nor in their own homes.

Even when they think they are alone, they may be accompanied by a malicious enemy, assiduously working to do them harm. *The Witches of Northamptonshire* (1612) narrates how Mistress Belcher is afflicted. "For being alone in her house, she was sodainely taken with such a griping,

---

are "*difficulty* of breathing" and "privation of *voyce and speech*" (*Briefe Discourse,* sig. E3v). On the mouth as a gendered site of struggle, see also Caroline Walker Bynum, *Holy Feast and Holy Fast: The Religious Significance of Food to Medieval Women* (Berkeley: University of California Press, 1987); and Sabean, *Power in the Blood,* chap. 3.

31. Scot, *Discoverie of Witchcraft,* pp. 162, 236, 399, 237.

32. George Gifford, *A Dialogue Concerning Witches and Witchcraftes* (London, 1593), sig. H3; William Dragge, *Daimonomageia: A Small Treatise of Sicknesses and Diseases from Witchcraft, and Supernatural Causes* (London, 1665), sig. Cv.

and gnawing in her body, that she cried out." Although she is alone, she thinks she sees her tormentor before her. Her brother, determined to assist his sister, approaches the witch's house but is mysteriously hindered. Despite the fact that he cannot approach the suspected witch's house, she has access to him wherever he goes. "The Impe of this Damme, and both Impes of the Devill, beeing glad that they were both out of his reach, shewed presently that they had longer armes then he, for he felt within short time after his comming home that hee was not out of their reach." Like his sister, he is wracked with pain although he is safely home. In addition to working through their imps, witches themselves might use invisibility to do harm and yet to appear innocent. Temperance Lloyd, for instance, confessed "that she can go unto any place invisible, and yet her Body shall be lying in her Bed."[33]

In addition to the more obviously magical means of imps and invisibility, witches were thought to invade the home through the exchange of objects.

> Sometimes they make natural Remedies to produce preternatural Effects; as by giving the party somewhat to eat, but that that is eaten hath no power to raise such strange Symptoms, but rather gives power to the Witch, by giving any to, or receiving any thing from the party that is to be bewitched; and until then, some Witches have confessed that they could not have their minds, or power to bewitch.[34]

The belief that social exchange with a potential witch might empower her to cause harm could thus function to justify shunning one's neighbors, particularly the poor, old women among them. It rationalized the ostracism of "potential" witches, thereby exacerbating the social and economic conditions that fostered witchcraft prosecutions.[35]

A witch might even use her own body to harm a victim, thus making it the image that she then manipulates. In *A True and Impartial Relation of the Informations against Three Witches* (1682), Anthony Jones testifies that he saw Susanna Edwards "gripe and twinkle her Hands upon her

---

33. *The Witches of Northamptonshire* (London, 1612), sig. B3; *A True and Impartial Relation of the Informations against Three Witches, viz. Temperance Lloyd, Mary Trembles, and Susanna Edwards* (London, 1682), sig. F3.

34. Dragge, *Daimonomageia*, sig. Cv.

35. On the dangers of exchange and the wariness about gifts, see Macfarlane, "Witchcraft in Tudor and Stuart Essex," pp. 85–86, and *Witchcraft*, p. 105.

188 / DANGEROUS FAMILIARS

own Body, in an unusual manner: whereupon this Informant did say unto her, Thou Devil, thou art now tormenting some person or other." [36] It was later discovered that at this same time, Grace Barnes was plagued with prickings and stabbings in her heart. Although a relationship, even an identification, is assumed between the witch's body and that of her victim, the witch does not cause herself pain. She is like a carrier of a disease who infects others while herself remaining healthy.

The witch could be controlled or punished by means of this blurred boundary between herself and her victims. One popular way to confirm bewitchment and to provide relief from it was to scratch the witch and draw her blood. Just as witches were thought to bewitch by means of willingly surrendered blood—that with which they rewarded their imps—their spells were reversed by means of forcibly extracted blood. Obviously, this belief legitimated physical retaliation for a grievance. Since letting blood from the witch was thought to cure her victim, this practice also confirms a complex identification between the witch's body and that of her victim. [37]

Another means of access to and power over a witch was through the objects or persons she had herself bewitched. In *Daimonomageia*, Dragge advises the afflicted to "Punish the thing bewitched . . . burning the Excrements of one bewitched, hath made her [the suspected witch's] *Anus* sore; . . . stopping up Bottles of that Drink that hath been bewitched, hath made the Witch able neither to urine or deject, until they were opened." [38] Just as witches used their victims' bodily extensions and outflowings to harm them, their victims could use those same bodily outgrowths, which could be clipped off or collected and put in a "witch-bottle," to cause the witch pain, to interrupt her power, to get her

36. *A True and Impartial Relation of the Informations against Three Witches*, sig. F.
37. On witch-scratching, see Dragge, *Daimonomageia*, sig. Bv; H. F., *A True and Exact Relation, of the Severall Informations, Examinations, and Confessions of the Late Witches Arraigned and Executed in the County of Essex* (London, 1645), reprinted in *Collection of Rare and Curious Tracts;* and George Gifford, *A Discourse of the Subtill Practises of Devilles by Witches and Sorcerers. By Which Men Are and Have Bin Greatly Deluded* (London, 1587). See also Holmes, "Popular Culture?" p. 96. On bloodletting as a cure, see MacDonald, *Mystical Bedlam*, pp. 191–92. On informal practices of counter-witchcraft, and how these depend on an identification between the witch and her own property, see Macfarlane, *Witchcraft*, esp. chap. 7; Notestein, *History of Witchcraft*, pp. 20–22, 29, 258–60; and Thomas, *Religion*, pp. 530–31, 548–51. *The Witch of Edmonton* dramatizes the practice of thatch-burning.
38. Dragge, *Daimonomageia*, sig. C3.

under control.[39] This was because bodily effluvia were conceived of as extensions of the subjectivities of both witch and victim; each antagonist inhabited these seemingly inanimate scraps.

Many learned writers argued that popular counterstrategies against witchcraft further confound the distinction between witches and their victims. In *A Discourse of the Subtill Practises of Devilles by Witches* (1587), Gifford argues that the recourse to such counterstrategies as charms, scratching suspects, and consulting white witches implicates the superstitious: "For when as they ascribe power unto such things to drive out devils, what are they but witches?"[40] As John Gaule says some sixty years later, "If these (or the like) be signs, to try and know a Witch by; certainly it can be no other Witch but the user of them."[41] According to learned commentators such as Gifford and Gaule, popular strategies for counteracting witchcraft, which allow the victim to seize some agency, simply collapse the distinction between witches and victims.[42]

Just as their victims felt that witches recognized and exploited their bodies' vulnerable entry points, suspected witches' bodies might betray them, first to the devil's temptations and later to discovery, apprehension, and prosecution. The *female* body's particular maleability suited women to be the devil's "*passive* and *pliable vehicles.*" As Henry More

39. On witch-bottles, which are still found in excavations, see Thomas, *Religion*, pp. 543–44.

40. Gifford, *A Discourse of the Subtill Practises*, sig. H3.

41. John Gaule, *Select Cases of Conscience Touching Witches and Witchcraft* (London, 1646), sig. E3. For a positive view of the value of consulting white witches and trusting their testimony, see Bernard, *Guide*.

42. For the recourse of the bewitched to "white witches" and cunning-people in order to be unwitched, see also *A Rehearsall Both Straung and True*, pp. 2–3; Roberts, *Treatise of Witchcraft; Tryal of Witches, at the Assizes Held at Bury St. Edmonds;* and William Perkins, who, in *A Discourse of the Damned Art of Witchcraft* (London, 1608), argues that even good witches deserve the death penalty (sigs. L7v–L8 and passim). Although Perkins takes the most extreme view, all of these writers disapprove of "unwitching" practices as collapsing the distinction between witches and victims. Jorden argues that while white witches' cures can have a placebo effect (*Briefe Discourse*, sigs. G4v–H), they have no "real" efficacy. See also Marijke Gijswijt-Hofstra, "The European Witchcraft Debate and the Dutch Variant," *Social History* 15.2 (1990): 181–94, esp. pp. 185, 189; Larner, *Witchcraft and Religion*, ed. Macfarlane, chap. 4; Macfarlane, *Witchcraft*, chap. 8; and Thomas, *Religion*, chap. 8.

Several historians argue that hostility toward white witchcraft was an elite idea that never really gained popular acceptance (Holmes, "Popular Culture?" pp. 102–3; and Thomas, *Religion*, p. 449). In addition, the elite themselves employed cunning-folk (Holmes, "Popular Culture?" p. 103) and physicians used the techniques of white magic (MacDonald, *Mystical Bedlam*, pp. 177–78, 190, 210–13).

explains: "The Divell gets into their body, and by his subtile substance, more operative and searching than any fire or putrefying liquour, melts the yielding *Compages* of the body to such a consistency, and so much of it . . . as is fitt for his purpose, and makes it plyable to his imagination: and then it is as easy for him to work it into what *Shape* he pleaseth, as it is to work the Aire into such forms and figures as he ordinarily doth."[43] Witchcraft belief grants witches extraordinary capacities for transcending bodily limitation—they can assume different shapes, become invisible, or fly—yet such belief attributes these capacities to traditionally feminine moral and physical weakness. As Eve's gender exposed her to Satan's temptations, so women's especially defenseless, fluid, penetrable, and manipulable "natures" made them vulnerable to demonic seduction.

Although the judicial process in England did not rely on torture as did witch prosecutions in Scotland and on the Continent, witches' own bodies constituted a primary source of evidence against them. Their guilt and their choice of supernatural bonds over social ones was assumed to be mapped onto and manifested in their bodies.[44] Those who sought evidence through their examinations of suspects' bodies thus emphasized how these bodies differed from those of normal, innocent people. The inquiry into the suspected bodies provided one means for redrawing a distinction between the witches and their neighbors and family members, between the devil and "us," between the dangerous and the familiar.

One strategy used in both prosecutions of witches and scholarly

43. Glanvill, *Saducismus Triumphatus*, sig. G5; Henry More, *An Antidote to Atheisme* (London, 1653), sig. K7v. On the fluidity and maleability of the female body, see Mack, *Visionary Women*, chap. 1.

44. Although torture was not used in England, as it was on the Continent, suspects were mistreated and this clearly played a role in extracting confessions from them. Perkins endorses torture in some cases (*Discourse of the Damned Art*); Robert Filmer challenges him on this, insisting on *caution* in proceeding against witches (*An Advertisement to the Jury-men of England, Touching Witches* [London, 1653]). On the "indirect pressures" to which suspects were subjected, see Macfarlane's and Notestein's chapters on the practices of Matthew Hopkins (Macfarlane, *Witchcraft*, chap. 9; Notestein, *History of Witchcraft*, chap. 8).

On torture and testimony, see Page du Bois, *Torture and Truth* (New York: Routledge, 1991); Elizabeth Hanson, "Torture and Truth in Renaissance England," *Representations* 34 (1991): 53–84; John H. Langbein, *Torture and the Law of Proof: Europe and England in the Ancien Régime* (Chicago: University of Chicago Press, 1977); and Paster, *Body Embarrassed*, p. 254.

debates about witchcraft involved simultaneously associating witches with the feminine and dissociating them from it. Various writers struggled to explain why the majority of witches were women by drawing on constructions of women as curious, impressionable, vengeful, and loquacious; yet they also distinguished witches from other women. For instance, witches could not cry: "Their hearts are so hardened, that not so much as their eyes are able to shead teares, threaten or torture them as you please: God not permitting them as may bee thought to dissemble their obstinacy in so horrible a crime; No not the women, though that sex bee ready to shead teares upon every light occasion."[45] The skeptical Reginald Scot challenged the assumed connection between virtuous femininity and tears: "But God knoweth, many an honest matrone cannot sometimes in the heavines of her heart shed tears; the which oftentimes are more readie and common with craftie queanes and strumpets, than with sober women."[46] Yet the claim that witches could not cry continued to be influential, so much so that those who wrote about accused witches who *did* appear to cry presented them as "fakers." Edmond Bower, for instance, claims that Anne Bodenham made "an artificiall noyse, that one would have thought she wept" but did not *really* cry.[47]

The primary evidence offered by suspects' bodies came in the form of witches' or devil's marks, which were supposed to provide evidence that witches suckled their familiars, or Satan himself, on supernumerary teats. These marks were discovered in searches by "juries of matrons," that is local women, often neighbors of the suspect, in some cases related to the victims/accusers.[48] These juries, which had to report their findings

---

45. *The Witches of Northamptonshire,* sig. C2v. In endorsing the water ordeal, James connects the refusal of the water to "receive [witches] in her bosom" and the inability of witches to shed tears (*Daemonologie,* p. 56).

46. Scot, *Discoverie of Witchcraft,* p. 46.

47. Edmond Bower, *Doctor Lamb Revived, or, Witchcraft Condemn'd in Anne Bodenham a Servant of His* (London, 1653), sig. F2.

48. In *The Witches of Northamptonshire,* local women search a suspect on their own initiative (sig. Dv). In *The Tryal of Witches . . . at Bury St. Edmonds,* the jury of matrons includes women involved in the case. Juries of matrons were hustled up on the premises in most cases; the jury that searches Elizabeth Sawyer, for instance, includes two "grave Matrons, brought in by the Officer out of the streete, passing there by chance" (Henry Goodcole, *The Wonderfull Discoverie of Elizabeth Sawyer a Witch, Late of Edmonton* [London, 1621], sig. B3). On the searching of witches, see James C. Oldham, "On Pleading the Belly: A History of the Jury of Matrons," *Criminal Justice History* 6 (1985): 1–64,

on oath before the judge, consistently refused to "recognize" the bodily marks they found as in anyway familiar, similar to the flaws on their own bodies. In H.F.'s *A True and Exact Relation, of the Severall Informations... of the Late Witches,* two women who search the accused recognize yet deny the similarity between what they find and hemorrhoids: "These Informants found that the said Mary had bigges or teates in her secret parts, not like Emerods, nor in those places where women use to be troubled with them." In this text, the accused woman is baffled by the "evidence" discovered on her own body; the informants' testimony estranges her from her body, which she has never herself scrutinized so closely and suspiciously: "She saith she knows not unlesse she were born with them; but she never knew she had any such untill this time, they were found in those parts upon the said search."[49] In terms of her own experience of her body, the search creates rather than finds "proofs."

In the same text, another informant, reporting on the search of another accused woman, testifies that the teats she finds "were not like Pyles, for this Informant knows well what they are, having been troubled with them her self." Yet another informant, a midwife, testifies that she finds marks on suspects unlike any other marks she has seen on women's bodies. Finally, "Marian Hocket had no such Bigges, but was found in the same parts not like other honest women." In this final instance, it becomes clear that the point is not just to find "bigges," marks, or teats, but to find evidence that the suspects are "not like other honest women." Even if a woman's body was unmarked, she was suspected of cutting off her marks, of asserting control over what her body looked like and could reveal.[50] Yet, as some skeptics insisted, "Very few people in the

---

esp. pp. 8–10, 16; and Paster's especially helpful discussion in *Body Embarrassed,* chap. 5, esp. pp. 244–60.

Ralph Gardiner describes how the process depended on women's shame and on fraud (*England's Grievance Discovered* [London, 1655], sig. P2v). Hopkins (*Discovery of Witches*) defends searching; Gaule challenges Hopkins (*Select Cases,* sig. B3v). Bernard advises justices of the peace that searchers should take their task seriously, should search the suspect more than once, and should be sworn (*Guide,* sigs. K12–K12v).

49. H.F., *A True and Exact Relation,* pp. 15–16.

50. Ibid., pp. 22, 24. In *Most Wonderfull... Gooderidge,* one woman is suspected of cutting her mark off (sig. B3); another curses those who search her: "Whilest they stripped her, she cursed the daie of her birth, making great outcries, and using bitter speeches

World are without privie Marks upon their bodies, as Moles or stains, even such as Witchmongers call *The Devils privie Marks*... and many an honest man or woman have such excrescences growing upon their bodies, as these Witchmongers do call, *The Devils Biggs*."[51] Since, according to Thomas Ady, disease and age, rather than immorality or guilt, cause such marks, they cannot be used to fix the distinction between good and bad, victims and witches, us and them.

Accused witches were thus held to an exacting yet inarticulable standard. John Stearne, assistant to Matthew Hopkins, the notorious witch-finder, attempted to distinguish between natural and supernatural bodily irregularities, but concluded that the distinctions that matter most are unspeakable: "I could further explain more at large, if it were fitting: for, *All things* (as the proverb is) *ought not to be spoken at all times,* much lesse printed."[52] Just as Stearne refuses to delineate explicitly the standard by which accused women were judged while yet advocating that they be stripped and searched, the judicial procedures that scrutinized accused women's bodies for "proofs" rifled and displayed those bodies while yet insisting on propriety. *The Most Strange and Admirable Discoverie of the Three Witches of Warboys* describes how a jailor and his wife examine Alice Samuel's body *after her execution,* and find a lump that confirms the verdict: "which both he and his wife perceiving, at the first sight thereof meant not to disclose, because it was adioyning to so secret a place, which was not decent to be seene: yet in the ende, not willing to conceale so straunge a matter, and decently covering that privie place a little above which it grewe, they made open shewe thereof unto divers that stood by."[53] The jailor and his wife manage to satisfy their sense of bodily decorum and propriety, especially regarding the female body, while yet making an "open shewe" to "divers that stood by."[54]

---

against all that offered to accuse her" (sig. C). Stearne (*Confirmation and Discovery*) also discusses suspicions that suspected women pull their marks off or "make them away."

51. Thomas Ady, *A Candle in the Dark: Or, A Treatise Concerning the Nature of Witches and Witchcraft* (London, 1656), sig. R4.

52. Stearne, *Confirmation and Discovery*, sig. G3v.

53. *The Most Strange and Admirable Discoverie of the Three Witches of Warboys*, sigs. O3v–O4.

54. In *Most Wonderfull... Gooderidge,* searchers find two marks on Elizabeth Wright (under her arm and on her shoulder); they then put her clothes back on, leaving the place where she is marked bare "that it might be seen both of Sir Humfrey, maister Graisley, and divers others of good worth, as indeede it was" (sig. B3). I discuss the

Thus, witches and their victims (or accusers and *their* victims) were all understood as vulnerable through their bodies, not because pain could be inflicted on them directly but because the body provided a means by which the subject could be apprehended, manipulated, invaded, possessed, or discovered. Witchcraft belief observed no fixed distinction between body and spirit. Nor, in the material realm, did it observe a clear distinction between animate and inanimate matter, between the bodily self and objects. The subject extended to encompass outgrowths exceeding the skin: hair, nails, urine, feces. In addition, witchcraft discourses scrutinized a vexingly complex, shifting relation between bewitchers and bewitched. As in other accounts of domestic crime, the violence of witches' *maleficium* and of the processes of accusation and prosecution served to negotiate a disturbingly intimate relation, to violate an indistinct boundary in order to redraw it. In village quarrels and assize trials; in learned debates among jurists, theologians, and physicians; and in the "ridiculous fictions" sold by balladmongers—that is, in legal practice with life-and-death consequences for women as well as in a diverse range of representations with less direct material consequences—contests over these boundaries used the figure of the witch to focus inquiry into a complex constellation of fears. Paradoxically, for the witch to serve this purpose, agency and power had to be attributed to poor, old women.

Witchcraft and Agency

At the height of witchcraft accusations and prosecutions, popular and elite belief conjoined to construct witches as agents and to hold them accountable for their actions. In contrast, those who held a skeptical view of witches and witchcraft, and thus sought to protect women from persecution, insisted that the accused were victims of false charges or delusion. They assumed that women, especially the old, poor, quarrelsome women most often accused of witchcraft, could not be powerful enough to harm. Those writers with the most conventional views of

---

proprieties shaping the display of the female body in representations of women's executions in " 'Gentlemen, I have one thing more to say': Women on Scaffolds in England, 1563–1680," *Modern Philology,* forthcoming.

witchcraft granted witches and thereby women the most transgressive power.

The sternest view of witches, as maliciously powerful and accountable for their actions, informed the accusations, the legal statutes that enabled prosecution, the decisions of legal personnel, and the justifications of legal prosecution which included King James's own *Daemonologie* (1597) and extended to Joseph Glanvill's *Saducismus Triumphatus* (1681). The most extreme belief in witches' agency insists that their voluntary league with the devil—"The yeelding of consent upon covenant"—matters more than their actions' destructiveness. William Perkins, for instance, who argues for the death penalty for all witches, defines a witch as "a Magician, who either by open or secret league, *wittingly* and *willingly, consenteth* to use the aide and assistance of the Devill, in the working of wonders."[55] In such definitions, as well as in the legal statutes that increasingly dwelt on the covenant with the devil and refused a distinction between good and bad witches, the focus rests on the suspect's consent, rather than on the resulting acts, good or bad. Since no supernatural work can be that of a "natural" man "it is the mans consent, contract and covenant alone" that prove him (or her) a witch "not the act it selfe."[56]

As witchcraft prosecutions proceeded and as dissenting voices began to be raised and published, those who insisted on witches' agency and accountability expressly refused the skeptical claims that witches were, instead, powerless victims. Writers such as Henry More and Joseph Glanvill insist that witches are not doting, melancholy old women; instead, they insist that witches are powerful and dangerous. According to such writers, witches appear feeble and foolish simply as part of the devil's clever plan to keep his influence and methods secret and his agents *incognito.*[57]

55. Perkins, *Discourse of the Damned Art,* sigs. L5v, L4, emphases added.
56. John Cotta, *The Triall of Witch-craft* (London, 1616), sig. Q3. James I argues that children cannot be held responsible as witches because they are not capable of reason or of informed consent (*Daemonologie,* p. 54).
57. Counterfeiting is the only imaginable form of agency in discussions of possession. While cases of possession proclaim the vulnerability, penetrability, and uncontrol of the body, Jorden (*Briefe Discourse*) counters this by arguing that those who claim to be possessed are, instead, prodigies of bodily control, entirely responsible for their bodies' unusual symptoms. Like him, Samuel Harsnett locates agency in imposture; see *A Discovery of the Fraudulent Practises of John Darrel* (London, 1599).
Regarding possession, see Stephen Greenblatt, *Shakespearean Negotiations: The Cir-*

These writers locate the source of witches' consent, of their willingness to conspire with the devil, in their *anger*. We have seen how accounts of petty treason dwell on the anger and frustration of subordinates, or their sense of grievance without recourse to legitimate means of redress. In contrast, anger is curiously absent from most accounts of parents killing their children. Anger reappears as central in accounts of witchcraft.[58] Learned defenders of witchcraft belief claim that witches are vulnerable to Satan's overtures when they are angry; that anger stems as much from an explosive combination of irritability and powerlessness assumed common among women as from particular injuries. Alexander Roberts, for instance, argues that women are especially prone to anger: "This sex, when it conceiveth wrath or hatred against any, is unplacable, possessed with unsatiable desire of revenge, and transported with appetite to right (as they thinke) the wrongs offered unto them." When women are given authority, they abuse it: "Where they can command thay are more fierce in their rule, and revengefull in setting such on work whom they can command."[59] They can thus be counted on to succumb to the temptation of power and to misuse it once they have it.

As John Stearne points out, poverty exacerbates both the sense of grievance and the inability to redress it: "They would have their wants satisfied and their desires fulfilled, be it by what means it possible can be, (as I may say) right or wrong." "And when their power herein answereth not their will," the devil intervenes to offer them the means to attain their desires.[60] Writers such as Roberts and Stearne thus use

culation of Social Energy in Renaissance England (Berkeley: University of California Press, 1988), chap. 4; Karlsen, *Devil in the Shape,* chap. 7; Notestein, *History of Witchcraft,* pp. 137–45, and chap. 4; Michael MacDonald's edition of and introduction to the documents regarding the Mary Glover case, *Witchcraft and Hysteria in Elizabethan London: Edward Jorden and the Mary Glover Case* (London: Tavistock/Routledge, 1991); and Thomas, *Religion,* pp. 477–92.

58. While discourses about witchcraft present women's anger as wholly villainous and destructive, men's anger was allied with heroism in a variety of contexts in Renaissance England. See Gordon Braden, *Renaissance Tragedy and the Senecan Tradition: Anger's Privilege* (New Haven: Yale University Press, 1985). Karlsen also argues that witches were likely to be angry women, especially those who publicly articulated their anger (*Devil in the Shape,* pp. 127–30).

59. Roberts, *Treatise of Witchcraft,* sig. G2; Stearne, *Confirmation and Discovery,* sig. Cv.

60. Stearne, *Confirmation and Discovery,* sig. B2; Roberts, *Treatise of Witchcraft,* sig.

the illogic of witchcraft accusations—the attribution of supernatural power to the socially marginalized and powerless—to explain why these particular individuals are liable to turn rage into strength.[61] In witchcraft, angry, powerless women find an alternative to their own limited physical, social, and economic power.[62] In *The Famous History of the Lancashire Witches* (n.d.), for instance, a witch whom the mayor of Lancashire had previously ordered to be whipped bewitches him so that he strips himself naked and runs through the streets lashing himself bloody.[63] This is an example of witchcraft as the revenge of the powerless, the black counterpart of the meek inheriting the earth.

Witches themselves, in their confessions, often credit their ill will with the power to accomplish malice. For instance, in a deposition taken in Suffolk in 1645, Susanna Stegold insists on her anger's power to kill her husband through wishes rather than acts: "After her husband beinge a bad husband she wished he might dept from her meaneinge

---

G2. Stearne's depiction of why women are particularly prone to witchcraft closely parallels Roberts (who comes first).

61. Those assigned or recognized as having destructive agency are persistently constructed as women, of lower class than their accusers, old, and unmarried—in short, as socially marginalized. Although there were exceptions to all of these categorizations, this was the usual profile. On the conventional portrait of the witch, see Larner, *Witchcraft and Religion*, ed. Macfarlane, pp. 72–73; Macfarlane, "Witchcraft in Tudor and Stuart Essex," pp. 79–80, and *Witchcraft*, pp. 110–12, 155; and Thomas, *Religion*, chap. 16.

For pamphlet accounts of male witches, see *A True Discourse. Declaring the Damnable Life and Death of One Stubbe Peeter, a Most Wicked Sorcerer* (London, 1590); *Newes from Scotland*; *The Most Strange and Admirable Discoverie of the Three Witches of Warboys*; Potts, *Wonderfull Discoverie*; *A True Relation of the Araignment of Eighteene Witches at St. Edmundsbury*; *Divels Delusions*; and *The Tryall and Examination of Mrs. Joan Peterson . . . for Her Supposed Witchcraft* (London, 1652). For pamphlet accounts of married witches, see *The Most Strange and Admirable Discoverie of the Three Witches of Warboys*; Potts, *Wonderfull Discoverie*; Roberts, *Treatise of Witchcraft*; and Bower, *Doctor Lamb Revived*. Goodcole's *The Wonderfull Discoverie of Elizabeth Sawyer A Witch* describes her as married although the play based on this pamphlet, *The Witch of Edmonton*, excludes all reference to Sawyer's husband. See also Macfarlane, *Witchcraft*, p. 164; and Notestein, *History of Witchcraft*, pp. 114–15. For discussions of prosperous witches, see Potts's account of Alice Nutter (sigs. O3–O3v) and James I's *Daemonologie* (pp. 22, 24); see also Notestein, *History of Witchcraft*, pp. 98, 116. Many young women who were daughters of older suspected witches were also prosecuted for witchcraft. See *The Examination and Confession of Certain Wytches at Chensford*; Potts, *Wonderfull Discoverie*; and *The Wonderful Discoverie . . . Flower*.

62. Potts claims that there are two kinds of people who practice witchcraft: those who are poor and seek wealth and those who, although they might be wealthy, seek revenge (*Wonderfull Discoverie*). Many texts present these as the alternatives.

63. *The Famous History of the Lancashire Witches* (London, n.d.), pp. 7–8.

as she sd that he shold die and psently after he died mad . . . but beinge asked whither she bewitched him to dead or noe, [she] sd she wished ill wishes to him and what so ever she wished came to pas."[64] Although many historians have assumed that witches were executed "for an offence which we now know they could not have committed," Susanna Stegold's confidence in the power of her ill wishes suggests that it may not be accurate to describe all witches as falsely accused.[65] While some suspects denied accusations or were coerced and manipulated into confessions, some also believed themselves to be the agents of an anger that blew apart their socially constructed subject-positions as dependent, subordinate, and submissive, an anger that upset social order by overturning its distributions of power.[66]

If anger was the source of witches' power, and sometimes feared as a kind of agency in itself, speech was the primary means of expressing that anger, of provoking the devil, and of enacting ill will. For witches, speech was effective, that is, destructive, action. "Where men might use knives, women used words," as Christina Larner argues.[67] Countless pamphlets describe how an accused witch, after some slight, refusal, or injury, "went away murmerring and grumbling"; or, "went away, muttering and mumbling to her self."[68] When a misfortune followed, those who had spurned the suspect and at whom she grumbled attributed their bad luck to her words.

The "border between tongue-lashing and witchcraft" was perceived to be narrow;[69] further, the common association of women and words enabled an association of witchcraft with both. According to Alexander Roberts, the majority of witches were women because, among other reasons, "they are of a slippery tongue, and full of words."[70] This loquacity leads them to enlist their family members and "inward ac-

---

64. *Witch Hunting and Witch Trials*, ed. Ewen, p. 298.

65. Alan Macfarlane, "A Tudor Anthropologist: George Gifford's *Discourse* and *Dialogue*," in *The Damned Art*, ed. Anglo, pp. 140–55, esp. p. 145.

66. On the power attributed to ill will and the notion that all deaths are murders, see Macfarlane, *Witchcraft*, p. 203.

67. Larner, *Witchcraft and Religion*, ed. Macfarlane, p. 86.

68. *A Full and True Relation of the Tryal, Condemnation, and Execution of Ann Foster* (London, 1674), sig. A2v; H.F., *True and Exact Relation*, p. 6.

69. Macfarlane, *Witchcraft*, p. 159.

70. Roberts, *Treatise of Witchcraft*, sig. G2.

quaintance" and thus disperse "the poyson" of witchcraft. Many writers describe how the devil first approached witches when they were cursing.[71] The criminalization of women often focused on their speech. Lynda Boose points out: "The punishments meted out to women are much more frequently targeted at suppressing women's speech than they are at controlling their sexual transgressions"; those women whose tongues were "under [their] own control rather than under the rule of a man" were especially vulnerable to punishment.[72] As depicted in accounts of witchcraft, volubility both predisposed women to witchcraft and became the tool of their violence and transgression once Satan empowered them as avengers.

Speaking was so closely allied to witches' transgressive agency that accounts of the apprehension and prosecution of witches represent their disorderliness and malice by means of their nonstop, aggressive speech. In *The Wonderfull Discoverie of Witches in the Countie of Lancaster* (1613), a thorough account of multiple trials in 1612, Thomas Potts describes how Anne Whittle, one of the accused, talks compulsively: "Her lippes ever chattering and walking [*sic*]: but no man knew what." Further, Elizabeth Device cannot contain or govern herself: "Even at the Barre, when shee came to receive her Triall (where the least sparke of Grace or modestie would have procured favour, or moved pitie) she was not able to containe her self within the limits of any order or government: but exclaiming, in very outragious manner crying out against her owne children, and such as came to prosecute Indictments & Evidence . . . against her." Device increases her ranting in order to prevent her nine-year-old daughter from testifying against her. "Her Mother, according to her accustomed manner, outragiously cursing, cryed out against the child in such fearefull manner, as all the Court did not a little wonder at her, and so amazed the child, as with weeping teares shee cryed unto my Lord the Judge, and told him, she was not able to speake in the presence of her Mother." With some astonishment at Device's indomitability, Potts reports that "No intreatie . . . could put her to silence, thinking by this her outragious cursing and threatning of the child, to

71. See, for instance, the dramatic and pamphlet accounts of Elizabeth Sawyer, the witch of Edmonton.

72. Lynda E. Boose, "Scolding Brides and Bridling Scolds: Taming the Woman's Unruly Member," *Shakespeare Quarterly* 42.2 (1991): 179–213, esp. p. 184.

inforce her to denie that which she had formerly confessed against her Mother."[73] At last, courtroom personnel remove Elizabeth Device and set her daughter up on a table to give her evidence. As presented by Potts, the mother's interruptions of and competition with the judicial procedures of examining witnesses and collecting evidence prove the threat she poses; she must be excluded from the trial and from the social order, both of which she disrupts.

In locating Elizabeth Device's disorderliness in her unbridled speech, Thomas Potts's text connects the witch with scolds and shrews and the legal and popular efforts to control such women and their speech. As David Underdown explains: "The scold who cursed a more fortunate neighbor and the witch who cast a spell were both rebelling against their assigned places in the social and gender hierarchies."[74] Thinking of witchcraft in relation to scolding points not only to the demonization of women's speech but also to witchcraft as an avenue of transgressive agency, as something women did as well as something done to them.[75] Yet, as Catherine Belsey makes clear, if "witches were women who broke silence and found an unauthorized voice," they also "paid a high price for the privilege of being heard."[76]

Of course, speech was not constructed as transgressive only for

73. Potts, *Wonderfull Discoverie*, sigs. D2, F2–F2v, F4v–G.

74. David Underdown, *Revel, Riot, and Rebellion: Popular Politics and Culture in England, 1603–1660* (Oxford: Oxford University Press, 1985), p. 40. See also Susan Dwyer Amussen, *An Ordered Society: Gender and Class in Early Modern England* (Oxford: Basil Blackwell, 1988), pp. 122–23; Holmes, "Popular Culture?" pp. 104–5; and Mack, *Visionary Women*, chap. 3.

75. On the gendering of transgressive speech, as well as evidence that women verbally asserted themselves nonetheless, see Catherine Belsey, *The Subject of Tragedy: Identity and Difference in Renaissance Drama* (London: Methuen, 1985), pp. 184–91; Boose, "Scolding Brides"; Patricia Higgins, "The Reactions of Women, with Special Reference to Petitioners," in *Politics, Religion, and the English Civil War*, ed. Brian Manning (London: Edward Arnold, 1973), pp. 179–222; Mack, *Visionary Women*, esp. chaps. 1, 2, and 3; Keith Thomas, "Women and the Civil War Sects," *Past and Present* 13 (1958): 42–62; and David Underdown, "The Taming of the Scold: The Enforcement of Patriarchal Authority in Early Modern England," in *Order and Disorder in Early Modern England*, ed. Anthony Fletcher and John Stevenson (Cambridge: Cambridge University Press, 1985), pp. 116–36. On the complex connections among gender, witchcraft, anger, and transgressive speech in colonial America, see Jane Kamensky, "Words, Witches, and Women Trouble: Witchcraft, Disorderly Speech, and Gender Boundaries in Puritan New England," *Essex Institute Historical Collections* 128.4 (1992): 286–307.

76. Belsey, *Subject of Tragedy*, p. 191. For a discussion of the conditions under which women's speech on scaffolds was recorded and the culturally available scripts for women's executions, see my " 'Gentlemen, I have one thing more to say'," forthcoming.

women. While women were punished as witches and scolds, men were also punished for sedition, libel, and slander. Their punishments could be extraordinarily vicious. Those convicted of sedition might be whipped, set in a pillory, and mutilated, for example, their ears cut off, their nostrils slit, and their faces branded with a double "S" for "sower of sedition." (These disfigurements were carried out in public on two separate occasions, one for each side of the face). This ordeal could be followed by life imprisonment.[77] For publishing his voluminous anti-theatrical tract, *Histriomastix,* William Prynne was not only disfigured (his ears severed) but he was silenced: His book was burned publicly, and, in his imprisonment, he was "to be restrained from writing, neither to have pen, ink, nor paper." These punishments transformed the producers of transgressive speech into texts in which their faults could be read: the mutilated face as well as, in Prynne's case, a paper worn on his head announcing "an infamous libel against both their majesties, state and government."[78] Unlike witches, offenders such as Prynne were not executed; there was not a widespread stereotype of "the slanderer" or "the libeler" as there was of the witch or the scold; neighbors were not licensed to punish these offenses on their own through shaming rituals; and the numbers of those tried and/or convicted of criminal speech cannot compete with the numbers of those prosecuted and convicted for witchcraft. Nevertheless, notorious cases of libel like Prynne's reveal the power and threat imputed to transgressive speech in early modern England and the brutal attempts to control it, whether it issued from literate, educated men or from illiterate, impoverished women.

Just as Prynne's book constituted the evidence against him, witches' speech provided the primary means of condemning them. Henry Goodcole's account of Elizabeth Sawyer's examination emphasizes that her tongue was both the instrument by which she injured others and the means by which she was herself exposed and defeated: "That tongue

77. For an example of this punishment, see the proceedings against Dr. Alexander Leighton for libel in 1630, and against William Prynne in 1632–1633, in *Cobbett's Complete Collection of State Trials,* ed. Thomas B. Howell (London: Bagshaw, 1809), vol. 3. On Prynne's trial and punishment, see Leah S. Marcus, *The Politics of Mirth: Jonson, Herrick, Milton, Marvell, and the Defense of Old Holiday Pastimes* (Chicago: University of Chicago Press, 1986), p. 169 and chap. 6 passim.

78. *State Trials,* ed. Howell, vol. 3, cols. 580 and 576.

which by cursing, swearing, blaspheming, and imprecating, as afterward she confessed, was the occasioning cause, of the Divils accesse unto her, even at that time, and to claime her thereby as his owne, by it discovered her lying, swearing, and blaspheming; as also evident proofes produced against her, to stop her mouth with Truths authority." Her false swearing and oaths condemn her in the eyes of the judge and jury: "Thus God did wonderfully overtake her in her owne wickednesse, to make her tongue to be the meanes of her owne destruction, which had destroyed many before."[79]

In his assertion that Elizabeth Sawyer's tongue betrayed her, Goodcole engages in the contemporary controversy regarding the veracity and admissibility of witches' confessions. Some contemporary writers argue that the accused's own account of her actions can and must be believed: "The voluntarie confession and examination of a Witch, doth exceede all other evidence." Such writers argue, despite Scot and his followers, that there is no reason to doubt people's accounts of themselves and their own actions; subjects can distinguish between "those things which are only in imagination, and those which are reall and indeede."[80] Many writers stress that witches have nothing to gain in incriminating themselves, and that they maintain their confessions even at the moment of death, that privileged point of truth speaking.[81]

Yet even those who defend the judicial use of confessions address

79. Goodcole, *The Wonderfull Discoverie of Elizabeth Sawyer A Witch*, sigs. A4v–B; sig. B.

80. Potts, *Wonderfull Discoverie*, sig. E2; Cotta, *Triall of Witch-craft*, sig. M2v. The usual rules governing evidence were suspended in cases of witchcraft. For instance, the spouses and children of the accused were allowed to testify against him or her. See Larner, *Witchcraft and Religion*, ed. Macfarlane, pp. 44–58; Macfarlane, *Witchcraft*, pp. 17–20, 170; Notestein, *History of Witchcraft*, pp. 44–45, 108–14; and Shapiro, *Probability*, chap. 6. Ady, *Candle in the Dark*; Bernard, *Guide*; Filmer, *Advertisement*; Gifford, *Dialogue*; and Perkins, *Discourse of the Damned Art* all advocate caution in making a case against a witch. Thus, even those who believed in witchcraft became increasingly uncertain of how to *prove* it in a court of law. As a result, Cotta argues in 1616 that "many cases justly necessarily and unavoidably stand perpetually inscrutable undecided and never determined, as certaine proofes and evidences of the limitation and annihilation of mans knowledge in many things of this life" (sig. Dv). Many legal theorists particularly worried that the disregard for usual procedures of investigation and standards of evidence in witchcraft trials would undermine due process in the legal system as a whole. By 1646, for instance, Gaule argues that it is more threatening to order to routinely execute the innocent on mere suspicions than it is for witches to exist (*Select Cases*, sigs. CII–CIIV).

81. *The Triall of Maist. Dorrel, or A Collection of Defences against Allegations Not Yet Suffered to Receive Convenient Answere* (London, 1599), sig. F3.

the various reasons for suspecting an imprisoned, old woman's statements. John Gaule, for instance, in his *Select Cases of Conscience Touching Witches and Witchcraft* (1646), argues that a witch's

> owne mouth can speake her owne guilt best, and may not amisse be taken for a right discovery of her own conscience. Nor doth her Sexe any whit invalid her own testimonie against her self. Nevertheless it would be wel considered whether she was forced to it, terrified, allured, or otherwise deluded. And withall, if in her owne mind and perfect senses; If not out of some Melancholy humour or discontentment working to say anything through tediousnesse of life.[82]

Such arguments, paradoxically, grant a witch's speech credibility and authority only that she may condemn herself.

Even those such as Gaule, who endorsed witches' confessions, conceded that witches might be either coerced or deluded.[83] The debate surrounding the value of witches' confessions addressed the confused, indistinct relation between what people believed witches could do and the powers that they could be *proved* to possess in a court of law. The concern with confessions extended beyond the courtroom and into popular culture, since many confessions were published as part of pamphlet accounts of witches' crimes and punishments. Some writers, such as Goodcole, justify the publication of witches' confessions as a means to counter "ridiculous fictions" and "most base and false ballets"; others worry that confessions "tend more to the satisfaction of curiositie than of use, and therefore are not without some danger published."[84]

Thus, constructions of witches as agents, who intentionally cause harm through their curses, and as speaking subjects, who autonomously and transparently confess the truth of their intention and action, present their agencies of speech, action, and will as destructive, as manifest in malice and violence. There was, however, another perspective available within the discourses ascribing power and agency to witches. Largely

---

82. Gaule, *Select Cases,* sig. I12v.

83. See *A True and Just Recorde . . . S. Oses* for the role of Judge Darcy in extracting confessions. In his *Discovery of Witches,* Hopkins responds to charges that he coerced confessions. On scholarly debates surrounding the reliability of witches' confessions, see Ginzburg, *Ecstasies,* esp. pp. 9–10, 13; and Thomas, *Religion,* pp. 516–19.

84. Goodcole, *The Wonderfull Discoverie of Elizabeth Sawyer A Witch,* sig. A3v; Cotta, *Triall of Witch-craft,* sig. L4.

outside of courtrooms, the belief in "white" witches demonstrates that witches' power was not construed as wholly negative or destructive.[85] Although some theorists argued that white witches should be executed even if they acted benevolently because they got their power in occult, non-Christian ways, members of all social classes in urban and rural areas believed in and depended on white witches' constructive, healing, protective powers.

Those who defined themselves as healers and prognosticators—as white witches—stood at an empowering but dangerous conjunction of medicine, the occult, and popular belief. Many of those accused of "black," felonious witchcraft had spent long, prosperous careers as cunning-people. One cunning-man, Marsh, "hath so long gratified the Country people with his Conjurations, that time and ignorance stiles him a good *Witch,* or a white *Witch.*" Joan Peterson, the notorious "witch of Wapping," is referred to as a "practitioner in Physick": "Now this *Joan Peterson,* it should seem, was both [a good and bad witch]; for as it was clearly proved, that she had done much mischief, so there were divers that came to witnesse that she had cured them of several diseases." Eighty-year-old Anne Bodenham, "adicted to Popery," a gossip, reading teacher, and storyteller, successfully supported herself as a cunning-woman. Earning respect as well as maintenance, she was "alwayes called... Mris. *Boddenham.*"[86] In each of these cases, the local community depended on, valued, and supported the white witch as a healer and general problem-solver, an agent who could effect positive change. Interestingly, these examples of persistent belief in witches as benevolent agents come from the second half of the seventeenth century, when learned belief in witches' agency was declining. The fates of these cunning-people, however, who were ultimately convicted of black witchcraft, and the context of these reports of their powers, in narratives

85. The drama is densely populated with cunning-women and white witches who function as agents of transformation: see Medea in Greene's *Alphonsus, the King of Aragon;* Lyly's *Mother Bombie* and Dipsas in *Endymion;* Heywood's *Wise Woman of Hogsdon;* and Maudlin in Jonson's *Sad Shepherd,* among others. These are all minor characters to whom agency and power are yet attributed. On Maudlin, see Marcus, *Politics of Mirth,* p. 137; on *The Wise Woman of Hogsdon,* see Jean E. Howard, "Scripts and/versus Playhouses: Ideological Production and the Renaissance Public Stage," *Renaissance Drama,* n.s. 20 (1989): 31–49, esp. pp. 40–47.

86. *Divels Delusions,* p. 3; *Tryall and Examination... Joan Peterson* (London, 1652), reprinted in *Reprints of English Books,* ed. Foster, p. 9; *Witch of Wapping,* pp. 2–3; Bower, *Doctor Lamb Revived,* sig. E2.

of their prosecutions, reveal how positive constructions of witches' agency could readily overturn, leaving cunning-people vulnerable to accusation and prosecution. To be perceived as a liminal, supernaturally empowered agent was to be perceived as suspect and to risk persecution.

Agency was so widely attributed to witches, and was so crucial to legal prosecutions, that its defenders had to explain how the supernaturally empowered could be caught, imprisoned, and tried. As Scot cynically asserts, "If [witches] were so subtill, as witchmongers make them to be," they would persuade the devil to "inrich" and "enoble" them and to grant them "all worldlie felicitie and pleasure." Yet, as Scot argues, witches were most often among the impoverished, ignoble, and miserable. Furthermore, Scot inquires, if witches are so dangerous that they must be executed, why do they allow themselves to be captured?

> When with all their familiars, their ointments, &c.: whereby they ride invisiblie, nor with all their charmes, they can neither conveie themselves from the hands of such as laie wait for them; nor can get out of prison, that otherwise can go in and out at a mouse hole; nor finallie can save themselves from the gallowes, that can transubstantiate their owne and others bodies into flies, or fleas, &c.: who seeth not, that either they lie, or are beelied in their miracles?[87]

Various explanations were proposed in response to such skepticism. *A Rehearsall Both Straung and True, of Hainous and Horrible Actes Committed by Elizabeth Stile* (1579), for instance, represents Mother Stile as insisting on her own agency—if she did not *choose* to enter jail, they would never be able to capture her: "Further she saieth, that if she had bin so disposed, fower or five, or more of the best men in Windsor, should not have brought her to the Gaile, but that she came of her owne accorde."[88] In his *Daemonologie,* James I is even more ingenious, claiming that being apprehended and detained by a private person will not impede witches' power.

---

87. Scot, *Discoverie of Witchcraft,* pp. 63, 396.
88. *A Rehearsall Both Straung and True,* p. 12; see also *Tryall and Examination . . . Joan Peterson,* pp. 4–5.

But if on the other parte, their apprehending and detention be by the lawfull Magistrate, upon the just respectes of their guiltinesse in that craft, their power is then no greater than before than ever they medled with their master. For where God beginnes justlie to strike by his lawfull Lieu-tennentes, it is not in the Devilles power to defraude or bereave him of the office, or effect of his powerfull and revenging Scepter.[89]

James here uses the paradox of witches' power essential to the legal construction of witchcraft as a crime—witches are supernaturally empowered but can be defeated through the judicial system—to confirm the divine sanction of government.[90] Juxtaposing a witch's confession from a pamphlet with James's learned, kingly defense of prosecutions shows how popular and learned belief could work together to fuel and justify witchcraft prosecution.

The confluence of popular and elite belief that enabled the upsurge of prosecutions began to split apart as belief in witches as powerful agents began to lose prestige and credibility. Some skeptics believed in God and the devil, but not in witches; others believed in the possibility of witchcraft, but doubted that witchcraft charges could be proved in court. Although skeptics of various orientations began to raise doubts relatively early, these doubts only gradually took hold to inform legal practice any more than sporadically. Popular belief in witches probably survived; but suspicions and accusations ceased to manifest themselves in formal legal accusations.[91]

The interpretation that finally gained prominence among the learned elite (clerics, physicians, and legal personnel) was that witches were, at worst, vessels and instruments, at best, falsely accused. According to

89. James I, *Daemonologie,* p. 35.

90. See Clark, "King James's *Daemonologie,*" p. 166. See also Thomas Heywood and Richard Brome, *The Late Lancashire Witches,* ed. Laird H. Barber (New York: Garland, 1979): "Witches apprehended under / hands of lawfull authority, doe loose their power; / And all their spels are instantly dissolv'd" (ll. 2631–33).

91. On the persistence of popular belief after the trials ceased and the statutes were repealed, see Gijswijt-Hofstra, "European Witchcraft," pp. 183–85; Annabel Gregory, "Witchcraft, Politics and 'Good Neighbourhood' in Early Seventeenth-Century Rye," *Past and Present* 133 (November 1991): 31–66; MacDonald, *Mystical Bedlam,* pp. 208, 216–17; Macfarlane, *Witchcraft,* p. 88; Notestein, *History of Witchcraft,* pp. 330–33; Sawyer, " 'Strangely handled'," p. 467; and Thomas, *Religion,* pp. 453–54, 581. On the growth of skepticism among the elite and the splitting apart of popular and elite beliefs, see Thomas, *Religion,* chap. 18.

scholars such as Stuart Clark, skepticism relied on a learned tendency to insist that "the real agent of *maleficium,* true or illusory, was the Devil."[92] Those writers who opposed the brutality and illogic of witch prosecutions could build on the learned reluctance to attribute agency to witches, insisting that witches could not be held accountable for actions they did not themselves have the power to perform. According to Thomas Ady, "The Grand Errour of these latter Ages is ascribing power to Witches."[93]

Those who worked to counter the persecution of witches and to deflate confidence in their power emphasized what unlikely candidates old women made as the devil's chosen instruments: "What an unapt instrument is a toothles, old, impotent, and unweldie woman to flie in the aier? Truelie, the divell little needs such instruments to bring his purposes to passe." Furthermore, witches could not possibly command the devil, as they claimed to do: "Can ye lesse give power unto the greater, shall a silly old creature scarse able to bite a crust insu[n]der, give authority & power to ye prince of darkness?"[94] Thus, according to John Gaule, the construction of witches as agents and commanders is a nonsensical delusion: "Though they seeme Ladies and Mistresses of their Arts & acts; yet are they indeed but Satans meer slaves and Vassals. Commanding openly that power, as if they were superiour to him: and yet secretly invoking it, as inferiour."[95] According to this view, poor, old women are what they seem: powerless.

Scot addresses the fact that many witches confessed their own agency by claiming that they came to believe in other people's fear of them: "These miserable wretches are so odious unto all their neighbors, and so feared, as few dare offend them, or denie them anie thing they aske:

---

92. Clark, "King James's *Daemonologie,*" p. 170; see also Anderson and Gordon, "Witchcraft and the Status of Women," p. 175. On the complex, contradictory relation between agency and accountability in learned treatises on witchcraft, see Easlea, *Witch-Hunting,* pp. 7–32; on the difference between clerical belief, which understood the devil as the agent and witches as instruments, and lay belief, which attributed "great power and independence to the forces of evil," see MacDonald, *Mystical Bedlam,* p. 175. Thomas defines the belief in witchcraft "as the attribution of misfortune to occult human agency" (*Religion,* p. 436).

93. Ady, *Candle in the Dark,* sig. A3.

94. Scot, *Discoverie of Witchcraft,* p. 34; Gifford, *Discourse of Subtill Practises,* sig. F4v; see also Scot, ibid., pp. 37–38, 397.

95. Gaule, *Select Cases,* sig. G3v.

whereby they take upon them; yea, and sometimes thinke, that they can doo such things as are beyond the abilitie of humane nature."[96] Scot insists that witches cannot be held accountable for actions they could not possibly have accomplished, no matter what they themselves believe: "There can be no sinne without consent, nor injurie committed without a mind to doo wrong. Yet the lawe saith further, that A purpose reteined in mind, dooth nothing to the privat or publike hurt of anie man; and much more that an impossible purpose is unpunishable. . . . A sound mind willeth nothing but that which is possible."[97] Scot claims that a deluded person is not capable of informed consent and thus cannot be held accountable; that intention without action is not illegal; and that no one can will or consent to an action that it is not possible to perform. He zeroes in on the relationship between agency and accountability that befuddles others; he insists that the two cannot be separated. Even if witches claim to have willed the impossible, this proves only that they are deluded or have been coerced.

> The poore old witch is commonlie unlearned, unwarned, and unprovided of counsell and freendship, void of judgement and discretion to moderate hir life and communication, hir kind and gender more weake and fraile than the masculine, and much more subject to melancholie; hir bringing up and companie so base, that nothing is to be looked for in hir speciallie of these extraordinarie qualities; hir age also is commonlie such, as maketh her decrepite, which is a disease that mooveth them to these follies.[98]

Scot delineates the many reasons why witches were more likely to be victims than villains; yet he accepts all the hierarchies (of gender, class, age, and economics) that subject old women, finding these constraints insurmountable and wholly determining. Scot's compassionate portrayal of the accused as "daunted with authoritie, circumvented with guile, constrained by force, compelled by feare, induced by error, and deceived by ignorance" challenges the logic and ethics of witchcraft prosecutions, reminding legal and moral authorities that they were more likely to abuse their own power over such women than to be their

96. Scot, *Discoverie of Witchcraft*, pp. 29–30.
97. Ibid., p. 64.
98. Ibid., p. 53; see also pp. 52–54 and Gifford, *Dialogue*, sig. K2v.

victims.[99] But Scot's grammatical positioning of witches as the objects of verbs (daunted, constrained, compelled, deceived) precludes the possibility that they might be agents. Even when they so imagine themselves, they are "deceived by ignorance." When witches confess, they are not asserting themselves but instead are succumbing to confusion and intimidation; the devil or their interrogators speak in those confessions; they do not. The skeptical tradition constructs witches as either "active deceivers" or as victims of "passive delusion"; it acknowledges them agents only when it impugns them as charlatans.[100]

Skeptics take to its furthest extreme the insistence that witches are the devil's instruments. Asserting the illogic of killing witches in an attempt to get rid of the devil, Gifford defends witches by removing power from them: "The witch doth not provoke forward the Devill, but the Devill bearing swaye in the heart setteth hir on." They are "instruments" and "the very vassals and bondslaves of the devil: they have no power to do, or to authorize him to do anything."[101] The devil lets them seem to have power so that the "guilt, the hatred, of all those Mischiefs & Malignities" will be displaced onto them.[102] As the seventeenth century progressed, skepticism began to gain influence among the elite and witchcraft ceased to be constructed as a crime that could be proved and prosecuted until, in 1736, the statutes against witchcraft were repealed. This process spared women's lives. It did so, however, by denying them agency and emphasizing their evident powerlessness and their embeddedness in a social and material world in which they are "toothles, old, impotent, and unweldie." The notion that old women might be able to cause disease and death through their ill will became laughable. As the social order denied such women influence and au-

99. Scot, *Discoverie of Witchcraft*, p. 64.

100. These terms come from Webster, *The Displaying of Supposed Witchcraft* (London, 1677), chap. 2. To dismiss witches' confessions completely is to position one's self with the skeptics who denied witches any agency. Examining the beliefs *of* rather than *about* witches and attempting to imagine witches as subjects as well as victims, Ginzburg looks to their confessions as evidence not of what they did but of what their myths were, that is, what they believed (*Ecstasies*, pp. 3, 9–10, and passim).

101. Gifford, *Discourse of Subtill Practises*, sigs. F4v, G.

102. Gaule, *Select Cases*, sig. G4. On the end of witch prosecutions, see also John Putnam Demos, *Entertaining Satan: Witchcraft and the Culture of Early New England* (New York: Oxford University Press, 1982), pp. 387–400; and MacDonald, *Witchcraft and Hysteria*, pp. xlvii–lv.

thority, the legal process and learned, skeptical discourses denied their capacities for supernatural power.

Drama, Eros, and Witches' Agency

In the early seventeenth century, the drama influenced and reflected the widespread interest in witchcraft. Located at an intersection of elite and popular culture, learned and folk belief, the drama participates in the controversy over witches' agency. A relatively large number of Stuart plays include witches, most notably: William Shakespeare's *Macbeth* (1606); John Marston's *Sophonisba* (1607); Ben Jonson's *The Masque of Queens* (1609); Samuel Rowley, Thomas Dekker, and John Ford's *The Witch of Edmonton* (1621); Thomas Middleton's *The Witch* (1619–1627); and Thomas Heywood and Richard Brome's *The Late Lancashire Witches* (1634).[103] The plays all arrived on the stage after witch prosecutions peaked (1580s and 1590s) but as the controversy over witches' accountability was intensifying. Some draw on learned demonology and Continental witch lore (*Sophonisba, The Witch, The Masque of Queens*); some draw on popular belief and recent prosecutions (*The Witch of Edmonton* and *The Late Lancashire Witches*); some combine these elements (*Macbeth*).

Witches appear on the stage far more frequently than other criminal women. As we have seen, very few dramatizations survive of early modern women's domestic crimes. Even the witchcraft plays are as likely to be wholly fanciful (*The Witch, The Masque of Queens*) as they are to be based on recent, local cases (*The Witch of Edmonton* and *The Late Lancashire Witches*). Furthermore, the witch is the protagonist of the main plot in only one of these plays (*The Late Lancashire Witches*).

These entertainments debuted in very different venues before distinctly different audiences: *The Masque of Queens* was a court masque, which was performed at Whitehall and incorporated members of the court, including the queen, among its players; *Macbeth* was performed both at the Globe and before King James I; *Sophonisba* was performed

103. I cite *Sophonisba, The Witch,* and *The Witch of Edmonton* from the Revels edition of *Three Jacobean Witchcraft Plays: "Sophonisba," "The Witch," and "The Witch of Edmonton,"* ed. Peter Corbin and Douglas Sedge (Manchester: Manchester University Press, 1986). Citations from the plays are located in the text and refer to this edition.

in a private theater (the second Blackfriars) by a boy company (the children of the Queen's Revels); *The Witch* was performed by the King's Men at Blackfriars (1609–1616); *The Witch of Edmonton* was performed at court by the Prince's Men (December 29, 1621) as well as previously at the Cock-Pit and at the private Phoenix theater; *The Late Lancashire Witches* was performed at the Globe.[104] *The Witch of Edmonton* and *The Late Lancashire Witches* also explicitly connect themselves to other forms of popular culture; they dramatize cases of which there are also ballad and pamphlet accounts and they incorporate such popular festivities as a morris dance, a skimmington (or shaming ritual), and popular practices of counterwitchcraft.

While the drama sometimes presents witchcraft as trivial and amusing and at other times as deeply threatening, the dramatic options closely correspond to the previously identified positions in the controversy over witches' agency. The plays that grant witches the most power also confine them to the subplot and/or eliminate them from the play's conclusion and reordered community by executing them or, more generously and less realistically, by allowing them to vanish. *The Late Lancashire Witches,* the one play that weaves witches throughout the action and locations, making them protagonists, also trivializes them and their *maleficium.* To achieve a central location on the stage or to survive the conclusion, witches must be associated with the carnivalesque, as agents of festive, temporary, reversible disorder.

Standing outside nature and the law and at the margins of dramatic representation, the witch reveals one set of particularly extreme, paradoxical conditions under which women could be construed as powerful in early modern English culture. As Phyllis Rackin asserts: "Excluded from Shakespeare's stage and denied by the logic of patriarchal discourse, incomprehensible within the categories of patriarchal thought,

---

104. For information on the conditions of performance for all these plays, see Anthony Harris, *Night's Black Agents: Witchcraft and Magic in Seventeenth-Century English Drama* (Manchester: Manchester University Press, 1980); on *The Witch of Edmonton,* see Anthony Dawson, "Witchcraft/Bigamy: Cultural Conflict in *The Witch of Edmonton,*" *Renaissance Drama,* n.s. 20 (1989): 77–98, esp. p. 64; on *The Witch,* see Anne Lancashire, "*The Witch:* Stage Flop or Political Mistake?" in '*Accompaninge the Players': Essays Celebrating Thomas Middleton, 1580–1980,* ed. Kenneth Friedenreich (New York: AMS, 1983), pp. 161–81, esp. p. 161; on *The Late Lancashire Witches,* see Herbert Berry, "The Globe Bewitched and *El Hombre Fiel,*" in *Shakespeare's Playhouses* (New York: AMS, 1987), pp. 121–48.

the inconceivable reality of female authority and the intolerable fact of female power could be rationalized only in terms of the supernatural."[105] This positioning of women as egregious and demonic makes transgression the condition under which women can be constituted as powerful and produces the overwhelming sopecter of the unlawful, unnatural woman. As Catherine Belsey points out: "The demonization of women who subvert the meaning of femininity is contradictory in its implications. It places them beyond meaning, beyond the limits of what is intelligible. At the same time it endows them with a (supernatural) power which it is precisely the project of patriarchy to deny."[106] In the particular case of witches, the drama represents this supernatural power as taking various forms and having various effects, but it remains outside of law, nature, and social order and does not (permanently) reorder or recenter the plays' distributions of cultural power.

Many dramatizations of witches as powerful, dangerous agents associate their agency with female sexual desire, thus demonizing it, too. In Marston's *Sophonisba*, for instance, Sophonisba's sexual desire is displaced onto the witch, thus enabling Sophonisba to move toward her heroic apotheosis, that is, her suicide. Early in the play, Sophonisba eagerly awaits the consummation of her marriage and scoffs at her maid's distaste for the body, especially the female body (1.2). But as the play progresses and Sophonisba's desire is repeatedly thwarted, she comes to interpret her erotic/romantic choice of her bridegroom, Massinissa, as tragic and disastrous. As Sophonisba freezes into a symbol of chaste virtue destined for death, Erictho, the enchantress, absorbs her desire and agency, outwitting the villainous Syphax to get what she wants: sex. When Syphax asks Erictho to make Sophonisba love him through magic, Erictho instead dupes Syphax into thinking she herself is Sophonisba; she is thus able to enjoy him sexually. She describes her "thirsty womb" (4.1.8) as motivating this duplicity:

> We, in the pride and height of covetous lust,
> Have wished with woman's greediness to fill

105. Phyllis Rackin, *Stages of History: Shakespeare's English Chronicles* (Ithaca: Cornell University Press, 1990), p. 194.

106. Belsey, *Subject of Tragedy*, p. 185. Also see Phyllis Mack on the relationship between witches and prophets: "Woman might speak in public only insofar as she was out of the law" ("Women as Prophets during the Civil War," *Feminist Studies* 8.1 [1982]: 19–45, esp. p. 28; and *Visionary Women*, passim).

Our longing arms with Syphax' well-strung limbs.
And dost thou think, if philters or hell's charms
Could have enforced thy use, we would have damned
Brain-sleights? No, no. Now we are full
Of our dear wishes. Thy proud heat well wasted
Hath made our limbs grow young.
(5.1.13–20)

Having demonized and displaced female sexual desire onto the enchantress in order to make room for Sophonisba's heroic suicide, the
play allows the enchantress to disappear, sated. In *The Witch*, Hecate
is similarly characterized by her roving, voracious sexual desire, which
she satisfies with her son and with Almachildes, whom she enjoys as
an incubus (1.2.196–98);[107] her son even proposes her cat as a potential
sexual partner for her. In both of these plays, the witches use the disguise
of another woman's body in order to attain their desires. Witchcraft
enables them to outwit the age and ugliness that are assumed to disqualify them from sexual congress.

Popular pamphlet accounts of English witchcraft also reveal a prevalent association of witchcraft with sexualities constructed as evil and
unnatural because of their association with the devil; with animals; and
with postmenopausal women, whose desire was assumed to be bound-
less, unsatisfiable through socially acceptable means, and destructive
because it could not be (pro)creative.[108] Some women accused as
witches were known for "living very lewdly" or for having illegitimate
children.[109] In many other cases, the connection of witchcraft with

107. In *A True and Just Recorde . . . S. Oses,* a suspected witch is also accused of having
sex with her son.

108. Many popular accounts of witchcraft reveal profound unease about the sexuality
of postmenopausal women, an unease relieved through cruel humor. In *The Most Strange
and Admirable Discoverie of the Three Witches of Warboys,* for instance, a convicted witch,
Mother Samuel, pleads her belly, that is, attempts to defer her execution by claiming to
be pregnant, despite her advanced age (fourscore). The response of those present, as
presented in the pamphlet, is riotous mirth; her claim to be pregnant "set all the company
on a great laughing" (sig. O2v). (On another older woman who pleaded the belly, see
the ballads about Mary Compton, aged between fifty and seventy, *The Pepys Ballads,* ed.
Hyder E. Rollins, 8 vols. [Cambridge: Harvard University Press, 1929–1932], vol. 7,
ballads 428–31.) The circumscription of female sexuality within the reproductive is
revealed in the documents regarding the Essex divorce trial, which describe Lady Frances
Howard's eagerness to consummate her marriage as her desire "to be made a mother"
(*State Trials,* ed. Howell, vol. 2, col. 786).

109. *The Apprehension and Confession of Three Notorious Witches. Arreigned and by Justice
Condemned and Executed at Chelmes-forde* (London, 1589).

sexuality had nothing to do with the suspect's observed or suspected conduct with other human beings. Instead, it was located at a disturbing, titillating point of contact between the natural and the supernatural, the human and the demonic, in a boundary-crossing congress that, as the seventeenth century progressed, was increasingly understood and described as sexual. Elizabeth Weed, for instance, describes sexual services on demand as one of the perks of her Faustus-like compact with the devil: "The office of the man-like Spirit was to lye with her carnally, when and as often as she desired, and ... hee did lye with her in that manner very often."[110] In such instances, the interplay between female agency and eroticism works to discredit both.

When they confess to attentions received from "man-like" spirits, accused witches delineate their fantasies of ideal sexual partners. In *A True and Exact Relation*, Elizabeth Clarke testifies that for six or seven years, the devil would "appeare to her three or foure times in a weeke at her bed side, and goe to b-d to her, and l-e with her halfe a night together in the shape of a proper Gentleman, with a laced band, having the whole proportion of a man, and would say to her, *Besse I must l-e with you*, and shee did never deny him." Far from placing sexual fantasies of congress with the devil outside society and nature, such confessions show how categories of gender and class shape sexual fantasy; Elizabeth Clarke's scandalous incubus is depicted as "a proper Gentleman." Clarke's confession also powerfully conveys her loneliness, poverty, and craving for emotional and financial support. She confesses that imps like "little kitlyn"[s] come to her in bed, suckle her, and promise not to hurt her but to "helpe her to an Husband, who should maintaine her ever after."[111] The desire constructed by Elizabeth Clarke's trial as demonic and damning sounds amazingly homely: the desire for a proper Gentleman to have sex with, and for sympathy, food, protection, and maintenance. While the drama presents Erictho's or Hecate's sexual "greediness" as fantastic or funny and does not punish it, judicial proceedings both criminalize women's desire *and* represent it as more familiar than demonic. Plays, pamphlets, and proceedings *all* associate witches' power with the satisfaction of female sexual desire, which

110. *The Witches of Huntingdon, Their Examinations and Confessions* (London, 1646), sig. A3v.

111. H.F., *True and Exact Relation*, pp. 2, 6.

requires outwitting men through disguise or circumventing them entirely with the devil.

In addition to enabling women to feed their "thirsty wombs," witchcraft was also thought to enable witches to interfere in the sexual lives of others. Playing on conceptions of sexual desire as invading from without, the drama explores the role of such malicious outsiders in instilling, removing, or manipulating eros, which was already understood as invasive.[112] This interference focuses on men. Whether they seek the witch's assistance or are the victims of her spells, magic works to frustrate and humiliate them and to support women's integrity and self-determination. Many witch plays focus on the coercion of sexual choice—rape and enforced marriage; but while physical, financial, and parental pressures act to constrain women, witches do not. When male characters turn to witches as a means to secure women's love, the witches consistently refuse to provide this service. They can interfere with intercourse but cannot control love, which is depicted as too deeply rooted in the subject's consciousness to be tampered with. As this works out in the plots, witches can manipulate male characters' sexual responses but cannot interfere in female characters' feelings, desires, or wills.

In *Sophonisba,* for instance, the plot focuses on attempts to force Sophonisba to abandon her love for Massinissa and to marry Syphax for political reasons. After his threats to rape Sophonisba fail to woo her, Syphax appeals to the enchantress, Erictho. Before she deceives him for the purposes of her own pleasure, Erictho explains that while she can get Sophonisba into his bed, "Love is the highest rebel to our art" (4.1.170). The plots of *The Witch* also revolve around enforcement. We first meet the witches when Almachildes approaches them to get love charms that will make wenches sexually cooperative (indeed, sexual initiators) (1.1.90–95). Further, when Sebastian solicits Hecate to interfere in his betrothed's enforced marriage, she explains that she can prevent consummation and cause strife, but she cannot dissolve the marriage.

112. On the classical and humanist traditions of conceiving eros as invading the subject mysteriously and uncontrollably from without, and as allied with magic in its ability to penetrate the boundaries of the self, see Ioan P. Couliano, *Eros and Magic in the Renaissance,* trans. Margaret Cook (Chicago: University of Chicago Press, 1987), chaps. 4 and 6; and John J. Winkler, *The Constraints of Desire: The Anthropology of Sex and Gender in Ancient Greece* (New York: Routledge, 1990), chap. 3. Both Couliano and Winkler describe how practitioners of erotic spells sought to make themselves less vulnerable to erotic and magical bonds while exploiting the vulnerabilities of others.

> We cannot disjoin wedlock.
> 'Tis of heaven's fastening. Well may we raise jars,
> Jealousies, strifes and heart-burning disagreements,
> Like a thick scurf o'er life...
>   ...but the work itself
> Our power cannot disjoint.
> (1.2.172–77)

The Witch does, however, dramatize the powers most typically attributed to the witch: She can provoke desire or inhibit performance by causing impotency. The latter provides a great deal of mirth in the play. In preventing sexual performance, witches most often targeted the male body, revealing its humiliating and unconcealable vulnerability. *The Late Lancashire Witches* dramatizes how, through means as simple as tying a knot, in this case in a codpiece point, witches could cause impotency.[113] This impotency, too, is treated as comic.

In these comic treatments of (female) witches' ability to undermine their (male) victims' sexual performance, the penis plays the role of a subject-extension; it is part of the body, yet it reacts and moves involuntarily; it can be manipulated by outside forces as if it were a puppet. As James I explained in regard to the earl of Essex's purported impotency, attributed to witchcraft and in relation only to his wife: "If the Devil hath any power, it is over the flesh, rather over the filthiest and most sinful part thereof, whereunto original sin is soldered"; "If the power of witchcraft may reach to our life, much more to a member, not so governed by the fancy, wherein the Devil hath his principal operation."[114] In the drama, the particular vulnerability of this ungovernable member is staged as the vulnerability of male victims to female erotic agents, who use magic to fulfill or protect female volition and desire and to thwart, defeat, or ignore male desire. Given the anxiety surrounding both impotency and female sexual assertiveness, this interplay between supernaturally empowered female erotic agents and embarrassingly embodied male victims provides another manifestation

---

113. On magical means of causing impotency and barrenness, such as tying knots, see Angus McLaren, *Reproductive Rituals: The Perception of Fertility in England from the Sixteenth Century to the Nineteenth Century* (London: Methuen, 1984), pp. 39–43; and Stuart Clark, "Inversion, Misrule, and the Meaning of Witchcraft," *Past and Present* 87 (1980): 98–127, esp. p. 120, and "King James's *Daemonologie*," p. 176.

114. *State Trials*, ed. Howell, vol. 2, col. 801.

of a gendered economy of power: For women to be constituted as powerful, men must be constituted as weak. Women's puissance is therefore represented in terms of male sexual impotency, and it is allied nervously to the comic and to the charivari schema of women on top and men on the bottom.

The humor also relates to a reluctance in the drama to take very seriously witches and their power. As the witchcraft prosecutions of the late sixteenth and early seventeenth centuries demonstrate, late Tudor/early Stuart culture took witchcraft seriously enough to make it a criminal, capital offense. Yet, with the notable exception of *The Witch of Edmonton,* the stage overwhelmingly portrays witchcraft as trivial and humorous. Even in *The Witch of Edmonton,* when Mother Sawyer's neighbors first complain to Sir Arthur Clarington and a justice, seeking to justify their persecution of her, Sir Arthur says: "Nay, if she be a witch, and the harms she does end in such sports, she may 'scape burning" (4.1.63–64). By allying witchcraft with the festive rather than the criminal, the drama, which entered the witchcraft controversy relatively late, participated in the cultural process that gradually marginalized and discredited belief in witchcraft. These plays suggest that being a witch was not inevitably fatal or damning; together with the work of skeptics such as Scot and Gifford, they might ultimately have helped to spare women's lives.

In most plays about witchcraft, the witch or witches survive the play's conclusion. In *Sophonisba,* as we have seen, Erictho disappears, sated and unscathed. In *The Witch,* we last see the witches concocting a charm to help the duchess eliminate Almachildes and festively dancing off. They are acting villainously, yet they get away with it. Indeed, all of the female characters in the play (the duchess, Francisca, and Florida) are allowed to survive their transgressions, although these have included murder plots and sexual license. In *Macbeth,* after the witches show Macbeth the apparitions that slyly predict the play's final movement, they dance an "antic round" and vanish. The witches who escape punishment do not seem human; nor do the plays suggest how a local, human community's failures contribute either to women's decisions to practice witchcraft or their vulnerability to suspicion. Their escapes do not translate into compassion for or defenses of accused women.

The drama sometimes invests witches with supernatural power, often allied with eros, which allows them to survive the play's closure by vanishing yet excludes them from the world of social relations. The drama seldom depicts the story of the woman who dwells in and responds to the social community, who is granted agency, but whose agency is construed negatively and punished. Written and performed while the actual suspects were still in prison and the case was being investigated, *The Late Lancashire Witches* defers the witches' punishment, telling the story only to the time of their apprehension. In contrast, *The Masque of Queens* displays the hags as bound captives. *The Witch of Edmonton,* the only play to enact the standard plot shaping most witchcraft accusations and prosecutions, ends with the execution of the witch.

The Witch of Edmonton, unlike any of the other plays, vividly depicts the relation of witchcraft belief to social conflict and explores why this particular character chooses witchcraft in response to her social situation. Mother Sawyer complains that her neighbors treat her maliciously because she is poor, old, powerless, and ugly. She argues that her neighbors' accusations and suspicions make her a witch.

> Some call me witch,
> And, being ignorant of myself, they go
> About to teach me how to be one . . .
>
> .   .   .
>
> This they enforce upon me, and in part
> Make me to credit it.
> (2.1.8–10, 14–15)

If she is to be considered infamous, she wants power, specifically the power to get revenge and redress grievances: "'Tis all one / To be a witch as to be counted one" (2.1.118–19). Mother Sawyer articulates her experience of enforcement in the context of the play's other enforcements: Win must marry Frank because she is pregnant by her master; Old Thorney must convince Frank to marry to save their estate; Frank submits to the "enforced" and bigamous marriage to avoid paternal disapproval and to insure his inheritance. The play also emphasizes Elizabeth Sawyer's isolation and vulnerability by silently erasing the husband that she mentions in Henry Goodcole's pamphlet about the case.

Creating a voice for Mother Sawyer, the play allows her to describe a process of subject-formation that involves both enforcement and agency, the two central concerns of witchcraft plays: Powerlessness, poverty, and the imputation of witchcraft are forced on her, yet she also chooses to seize whatever power she can through the outlaw status by which she is constituted. Scholars often quote this passage because, in it, the witch, generally constructed as either villain or victim, positions herself as both. To the end, Mother Sawyer refuses to accept all the blame; she questions the decorums of acceptable and unacceptable power in her culture, which promote many metamorphoses and enchantments more destructive than hers: "A witch? Who is not?" (4.1.103).[115]

Although the play grants Mother Sawyer a platform from which to speak and the power to redress her grievances, it ultimately eliminates her from the play's community. Nor does it grant her the prestige of tragic heroism. Even Mother Sawyer, the most complexly, vividly characterized of the stage's witches, is not a female Dr. Faustus, dominating the main plot and commanding the audience's attention. Instead, the play that bears her name confines her to the subplot; she appears in four of the play's thirteen scenes while Frank Thorney appears in seven. If Frank Thorney—a spineless, yet murderous, bigamist—has a rival as the play's protagonist, it is not Mother Sawyer, but her familiar, Dog. Dog, like Frank, appears in seven scenes. More important, Dog connects the play's multiple plots. In the main plot, he inspires Frank Thorney to kill one of his two wives; helps him to carry out the scheme; and then rejoices, "shrugging as it were for joy," when Frank is discovered. In the subplot in which we meet Dog, he acts as Mother Sawyer's familiar, rescuing her from lonely bitterness, acting as her ally and protector, and enabling her to avenge her grievances. When she longs to *be* a witch since she is *called* one but does not know where to begin, Dog instructs her. In the end, however, he abandons her to apprehension and execution. In the comic subplot, Dog befriends young Cuddy Banks, plays pranks, and dances in the morris. Of the three characters with whom Dog associates, only Cuddy Banks survives.

As the only character who figures in each of the three plots, Dog

115. Dawson points to the uniqueness of this oft-quoted passage: "None of the other witch plays of the period display the witch in the process of turning to witchcraft" ("Witchcraft/Bigamy," p. 80).

links three conventional, apparently distinct story lines: that of domestic violence, here enforced marriage, bigamy, and a man's murder of his wife; that of witchcraft, here an old, impoverished woman's search for revenge against her more privileged, uncharitable, suspicious neighbors; and, finally, the plot of festive inversion, here a young man's playful disregard for his father's values, which manifests itself in pranks, games, and love charms with no permanent or destructive consequences. This last plot contrasts both the main plot, in which young people obey their parents with tragic consequences, and the other subplot, in which the witch's disorderliness and reliance on a familiar to secure her desires end in murder and her own death. Dog demonstrates that witchcraft is simultaneously about domestic *and* communal relations when he intervenes in Mother Sawyer's vexed relations with her neighbors and in Frank's marriage, when he visits Frank's bedside or suckles Mother Sawyer, and when he ventures into the local community to dance in the morris or bedevil villagers. Acting as Mother Sawyer's demonic lover/infant as well as her avenger, Cuddy's loyal pet, and a prankster, Dog passes easily between the supernatural and the social, the consoling and the destructive. Although Dog stands out as an unlikely dramatic character, he is, in fact, only an especially vivid manifestation of the early modern preoccupation with "familiar" threats and threatening "familiars." The interplay of the three plots, through Dog's agency, demonstrates that what links stories of murderous conflict between spouses, popular festivity, and witchcraft is the disruptive agency of the dangerous familiar.

Written collaboratively by playwrights who "span the spectrum of popular to élite drama," *The Witch of Edmonton* participated in the movement of the Prince's men "from the popular end of the market, when they had performed mainly in the provinces, to their period at the Phoenix, which was a fashionable indoor theatre catering for a richer and more theatrically experienced audience."[116] It did so by upholding law and order and by fostering what Kathleen McLuskie calls the "modulation of superstition into comedy."[117] The transformation to comedy

---

116. Kathleen McLuskie, *Renaissance Dramatists* (Atlantic Highlands, N.J.: Humanities Press, 1989), chap. 3, esp. p. 72.

117. Ibid., p. 72. On *The Witch of Edmonton,* see Viviana Comensoli, "Witchcraft and Domestic Tragedy in *The Witch of Edmonton,*" in *Politics of Gender,* ed. Brink, Coudert, and Horowitz, pp. 43–59; Dawson, who explores how the play works through "anxiety

is complete in *The Late Lancashire Witches* (1634). Like *The Witch of Edmonton,* this play is based on an actual case, but it unambiguously presents the *maleficium* of the witches, who were at that time in jail, as comic. As Mrs. Generous announces: "This night wee'l celebrate to sport:/'Tis all for mirth, we mean no hurt."[118] In this play, the witches are able to move from the subplot into the main plot only because they are made ludicrous and dismissed as threats. The head witch is also married (to one Squire Generous) and prosperous. The play's ability to dramatize witchcraft as comic rather than tragic depends in part on changing attitudes toward witches as agents.

Stuart Clark suggests that the flippant treatment of witches and witch-craft in much of the drama stems from the dependence of witchcraft belief on inversion and misrule, which are also associated with the comic.[119] In *The Late Lancashire Witches,* for instance, the witches' pranks overturn gender and class hierarchies: They disrupt the sport of the "gentle" huntsmen; they turn the Seely household upside down, so that servants direct their masters and children chastise their parents; and they make a bridegroom impotent on his wedding night, leading his wife to beat him and prompting the community's censure in the form of a skimmington. In addition, after several gentlemen tease a bastard about his illegitimacy, the witches stage a dumb show that reveals that the gentlemen were all fathered by servants or tradesmen— a tutor, a tailor, a groom—and only the bastard has a "gentle" father. Because, unlike Mother Sawyer, they do not mean harm or vigorously turn authority figures' standards of judgment against them, these witches' playful inversions are short-lived and easily reversed; they effect neither permanent change nor reassessment.[120] Even Mr. Generous,

---

about social change" ("Witchcraft/Bigamy," p. 78); McLuskie, *Renaissance Dramatists,* pp. 63–73; Jonathan Dollimore, *Radical Tragedy: Religion, Ideology, and Power in the Drama of Shakespeare and His Contemporaries* (Sussex: Harvester, 1984), pp. 176–77; Paster's provocative discussion in *Body Embarrassed,* chap. 5, esp. pp. 251–60; and Peter Stallybrass, "*Macbeth* and Witchcraft," in *Focus on Macbeth,* ed. John Russell Brown (London: Routledge, 1982), pp. 189–209, esp. p. 206. Of the play's critics, Dawson has made the most concerted effort to explore the plot interrelations. Although he does not develop this insight, Dawson also points out that Dog is at the play's "theatrical center" (p. 84, see also p. 88).

118. Thomas Heywood and Richard Brome, *The Late Lancashire Witches,* ed. Barber, ll. 2080–81; subsequent citations are located in the text.

119. Clark, "King James's *Daemonologie,*" pp. 163–64; see also his "Inversion."

120. "In the theatre, as in carnival, sexual inversion temporarily turns the world upside

stunned to realize that he has harbored a witch "under mine own roofe, mine own bed, my bosome," briskly orders his wife out of bed and hands her over to the authorities (l. 2451). The immediate restoration of order eclipses her uncertain fate, a fate the playwrights present as irrelevant to the comic closure; in the epilogue, they cautiously decline to anticipate judgment on the accused. Although popular accounts of actual crimes, even those written before trial and execution, usually place great emphasis on the expected restoration of order through pun- ishment, in *The Late Lancashire Witches* it does not really seem to matter what becomes of the witches once they have been apprehended. In contrast to Mother Sawyer, who haunts and compromises a comic conclusion, the Lancashire witches seem as easily dissolved as their spells. The play grants them little power to effect change or threaten order, while simultaneously holding them accountable for their actions.

Seeing the comic treatment in *The Late Lancashire Witches* as a matter of chronology, Anthony Harris argues that it reveals a post-Jacobean decline in the fear of witchcraft. Yet Harris also points out that the accusations against the witches are presented as credible; the play is *not* skeptical, nor is it sympathetic: "Although Mother Sawyer performs deeds of far greater lasting harm—causing insanity and death—she is presented much more sympathetically than are the witches in the [later] play, even though their activities are comparatively harmless."[121] In *The Late Lancashire Witches,* as Anthony Dawson points out, "the witches' power is hardly taken seriously—they constitute only a contained dan- ger."[122] Marshalling considerable primary evidence, Herbert Berry ar- gues that *The Late Lancashire Witches* is "the case for the prosecution written and performed while the defendants were unsentenced"; thus the "evidence" against the accused women is both sufficient to lead to their conviction in Lancashire and such that its enactment on a London stage with little alteration could constitute a comic entertainment.[123] Written in the midst of a criminal investigation and riddled with con- tradictions, the play makes visible the processes of change: the charges

down, but only to reinforce, not subvert, the traditional order" (Underdown, *Revel, Riot, and Rebellion,* p. 38).

121. Harris, *Night's Black Agents,* p. 178.
122. Dawson, "Witchcraft/Bigamy," p. 86.
123. Berry, "The Globe Bewitched," p. 131.

are credible but the offenses are pranks; the witches are trivialized yet are still legally accountable. The play stands at the intersection of the popular and elite cultures then struggling to separate themselves.

Humor accompanied and facilitated the skepticism by which elite culture distinguished itself from popular belief in witches. E. P. Thompson argues that when "the polite culture abandoned magic, this marked a dissociation, not only of sensibility, but between the polite and vulgar cultures," which, regarding witchcraft belief, could not previously have been distinguished as such.[124] By 1681, for instance, Joseph Glanvill can claim that witty skepticism about witchcraft has become the mark of the elite: "Those that know any thing of the world, know, that most of the looser *Gentry,* and the small pretenders to *Philosophy* and *Wit,* are generally deriders of the *belief of Witches,* and *Apparitions.*"[125] While including a varied audience in its in-jokes, *The Late Lancashire Witches* may have helped an urban elite define itself through its ability to laugh at what the vulgar might find threatening. In this play, according to McLuskie, "the problems of rural hierarchy, and the disruption occasioned by witchcraft accusations" can be safely and amusingly "reproduced for the entertainment of an urban audience."[126] The urban audience can laugh, in part, because the social conflicts addressed through belief in and accusations against witches were not really their problems.

Although the trend toward dismissing witchcraft accusations and viewing witches' offenses as pranks can be seen as positive for women, the fates of the accused women in the Lancashire case show that skepticism about witchcraft was a mixed blessing in terms of legal practice, as well as at the level of representation. Several of the accused died of gaol fever waiting for Charles I to investigate and dismiss the charges against them; although the king concluded that the charges were a hoax and those who survived were not convicted or punished, there is evidence that they were never released.[127]

124. Thompson, "Anthropology," p. 54; see also Larner, *Witchcraft and Religion,* ed. Macfarlane, p. 18.

125. Glanvill, *Saducismus Triumphatus,* sig. F3.

126. McLuskie, *Renaissance Dramatists,* p. 83. On the comedy of *The Late Lancashire Witches,* see Harris, *Night's Black Agents,* pp. 176–79; and McLuskie, ibid., pp. 73–85. On inversion, see Clark, "Inversion," and "King James's *Daemonologie,*" pp. 174–75; Dawson, "Witchcraft/Bigamy," p. 87; and Stallybrass, "*Macbeth* and Witchcraft."

127. On Charles I's review of the evidence, and the relation between the play and

Macbeth, "Malice Domestic," and the Threat of the Familiar

In presenting witchcraft as comically turning the world upside down, the drama frequently locates witches in a space apart, a female-dominated world placed both outside of the household and at the margins of dramatic representation. Although *The Late Lancashire Witches* and *The Witch of Edmonton* present witches as participants in other characters' communities and social relations, they also marginalize them. *The Late Lancashire Witches* makes the witches the creators of a temporary festive space of inversion. *The Witch of Edmonton* locates Mother Sawyer in the subplot and on the community's margins; it is her familiar, Dog, not Mother Sawyer herself, who travels freely among the play's locations and communities. More fanciful plays keep the witches separate, in a world that the other characters visit but that safely contains them. In *Sophonisba*, for instance, Erictho lives amidst the ruins of a temple; majesty and reverence now are juxtaposed with decay, disregard, and filth.

> Where statues and Jove's acts were vively limned,
> Boys with black coals draw the veiled parts of nature
> And lecherous actions of imagined lust;
> Where tombs and beauteous urns of well-dead men
> Stood in assured rest, the shepherd now
> Unloads his belly; corruption most abhorred
> Mingling itself with their renowned ashes.
> Ourself quakes at it.
> There once a charnel-house, now a vast cave,
>
> . . .
>   There, that's my cell.
>
> (4.1.153–61, 167)

Erictho's description of her cell allies her with debased bodiliness and with those locations marked out for its accommodation: the privy, the brothel, the charnel house.[128] Here, the "parts of nature" and their

---

the actual prosecution, see Berry, "The Globe Bewitched," and Notestein, *History of Witchcraft*, chap. 7.

128. See Mullaney, *The Place of the Stage,* chap. 1, on the significance of such marginal locations.

"lecherous actions," which should be "veiled," are instead crudely drawn; feces despoil the ashes of those once renowned. This description associates those made disreputable by age, class, and gender—boys, shepherds, the witch; it also juxtaposes the evidences of mortality—graffiti, bodily waste, ruins, ashes—with the witch's transcendence of mortality and history. For Erictho is also allied with the sacred. Her cell is at the center of human, bodily life yet also at its margins, as the privy is essential to the household and its members yet located outside. Furthermore, although Erictho is segregated from the political struggles and battles of the play's central action, Syphax must come to her when force and authority fail him.

Similarly, in *The Witch*, Hecate lives in "this damned place" (1.2.110). It is a place apart that the other characters visit; it is populated with familiars and cluttered with such gruesome ingredients for spells as dead babies. Alarmed at Hecate and where she lives, Sebastian hopes "That I may never need this hag again" (1.2.180). He needs her, as the play does, but only temporarily; the play does not lead us to think about any of the characters consulting her again. Once she has served her purpose, she disappears. Since Hecate and Erictho never enter the realm of law and order, where the other characters live, they can survive the plays' conclusions. They do not have to be excluded or eliminated because they were never integrated into the plays' communities.

In *Macbeth*, the witches, "embodied agents of storm and disorder," appear in "an open place" and on a "heath"; they never enter the world of the other characters, who must come to them.[129] Yet, in *Macbeth*, unlike *The Witch* or *Sophonisba*, the boundary between the world of the witches and the world of the other characters is indistinct. Peter Stallybrass sees the witches as ambiguously positioned as Scottish village witches and as inhabitants of another world.[130] Similarly, Lady Macbeth stands between witches who occupy a separate, supernatural world and witches as members of the community, family, and household. Although *Macbeth* locates its witches in a space apart—at the margins that are also a locus of power separate from and in competition with the

129. The first phrase is from Janet Adelman, " 'Born of Woman': Fantasies of Maternal Power in *Macbeth*," in *Cannibals, Witches, and Divorce: Estranging the Renaissance,* ed. Marjorie Garber (Baltimore: Johns Hopkins University Press, 1987), pp. 90–121, esp. p. 96.

130. Stallybrass, "*Macbeth* and Witchcraft," p. 195.

throne—the play also offers, in the figure of Lady Macbeth, the drama's most vivid manifestation of the witch as a dangerous familiar and her witchcraft as "malice domestic," as an invasion of the household and its daily life.

In her invocation of "murdering minions," her desire for unsexing, her association with inverted maternity and nurturance (dashing out the brains of a suckling infant; pouring her spirits in Macbeth's ear like poison), and her reliance on covert tactics (drugging the grooms and proposing an assault on the sleeping Duncan), Lady Macbeth is allied both to the witches and to the female criminals of earlier chapters.[131] In her brilliant analysis of the play, Janet Adelman emphasizes its construction of female power as a familiar as much as supernatural threat.

> The often noted alliance between Lady Macbeth and the witches constructs malignant female power both in the cosmos and in the family; it in effect adds the whole weight of the spiritual order to the condemnation of Lady Macbeth's insurrection. But despite the superior cosmic status of the witches, Lady Macbeth seems to me finally the more frightening figure. For Shakespeare's witches are an odd mixture of the terrifying and the near comic.[132]

According to Adelman, *Macbeth,* like most other witchcraft plays, ultimately dwells on the threat that comes from within the household (here from the violent wife); the witches disappear in a puff of smoke.[133]

---

131. On the association of Lady Macbeth and the witches, see Adelman, " 'Born of Woman'," pp. 96–97; Dympna Callaghan, "Wicked Women in *Macbeth:* A Study of Power, Ideology, and the Production of Motherhood," in *Reconsidering the Renaissance,* ed. Mario de Cesare (Binghamton: MRTS Press, 1992), pp. 355–69; Marcus, *Puzzling Shakespeare: Local Reading and Its Discontents* (Berkeley: University of California Press, 1988), pp. 104–5; Newman, *Fashioning Feminity,* chap. 4; and Stallybrass, "*Macbeth* and Witchcraft," pp. 196–97. On the symbolic cancellations of female power and disorderliness, see these critics, as well as Jonathan Goldberg, "Speculations: *Macbeth* and Source," in *Shakespeare Reproduced: The Text in History and Ideology,* ed. Jean E. Howard and Marion F. O'Connor (New York: Methuen, 1987), pp. 242–64. On witches as disorderly women, see Boose, "Scolding Brides," pp. 184–85, 195–96, and passim; Dawson, "Witchcraft/Bigamy," pp. 85–86; and Underdown, *Revel, Riot, and Rebellion,* p. 254.

132. Adelman, " 'Born of Woman'," pp. 98–99.

133. On the trivialization of the witches, their representation as "pranksters," see Adelman (ibid., p. 99); and Harry Berger, Jr., "Text against Performance in Shakespeare: The Example of *Macbeth,*" in *The Power of Forms in the English Renaissance,* ed. Stephen

Macbeth demonstrates how witches can be used to focus an inquiry into human agency without themselves being represented as agents. Throughout the play, the witches' prophesies and Macbeth's choices commingle, making Macbeth's agency and accountability the central question. He first responds to the witches' predictions by disclaiming responsibility: "If chance will have me king, why, chance may crown me / Without my stir."[134] Thereafter, he consistently refuses responsibility: "Thou canst not say, I did it" (3.4.50). Although the witches predict rather than act, in inspiring ambition they become catalysts to violence. For Macbeth, as for the protagonists/perpetrators of domestic violence, ambitious desire immediately slides into violence. Macbeth receives his first preferment through the dishonor and execution of another; he consistently sees others' lives as obstacles to his goals—"I had else been perfect" (3.4.21). But ambition does not simply "slide" into murder for Macbeth; Lady Macbeth forges the connection. "Art thou afeard / To be the same in thine own act and valor, / As thou art in desire?" (1.7.40–42). *Macbeth* uses female characters—the witches and Lady Macbeth—to instill ambition, translate that ambition into violent action, and thus cast doubt on ambition and agency as associated with violence.

Despite the fog machines and dry ice that many performances use to distinguish the play's open spaces as frightening and mysterious, *Macbeth* stages a series of domestic conflicts. As an assault on king, kinsman, and guest, Macbeth's murder of Duncan is a domestic crime—"malice domestic" (3.2.28)—that conflates the domestic and political and betrays loyalties at all levels. Lady Macbeth's first response to the "official" report of Duncan's murder is "What! in our house?" (2.3.90); her staged indignation dwells on the violation of domesticity. Even in the midst of the murder, Lady Macbeth heartens her husband in housewifely terms: Clean up the blood and put on your nightgown. In her madness, she is obsessed with the inability to get clean.

Throughout, the play parallels the cosmic and political disorder that

Greenblatt (Norman, Okla.: Pilgrim Books, 1982), pp. 49–79, esp. p. 67. This is similar to the comic treatment of witches and witchcraft in the rest of the drama.

134. William Shakespeare, *Macbeth,* in *The Complete Works of Shakespeare,* ed. David Bevington, 4th ed. (New York: Harper Collins, 1992), 1.3.145–46; subsequent citations are located in the text.

Macbeth precipitates by murdering Duncan with domestic disruption: troubled sleep and chaotic meals. Since Macbeth has murdered sleep, his curse is that he "shall sleep no more!" (2.2.39); Lady Macbeth walks in her sleep (5.1). Like the murder of sleep, the banquet that Banquo interrupts becomes a central image of disorder in the play. Macbeth imagines distress in terms of beds and tables: "We will eat our meal in fear and sleep / In the affliction of these terrible dreams / That shake us nightly" (3.2.19–21). Similarly, when one of the lords imagines restored order after Macbeth is dethroned and Malcolm crowned, he envisions it in the concrete domestic terms of bed and board.

> we may again
> Give to our tables meat, sleep to our nights,
> Free from our feasts and banquets bloody knives,
> Do faithful homage, and receive free honors
> All which we pine for now.
> (3.6.33–37)

Just as accounts of petty treason dwell on the violation of the central sites of domestic life—the bed and the table—these visions of disorder and restored order focus on sleeping and eating.

Even Macbeth's attempts to conceal the murders he commits or commissions associate him with domestic crime and its perpetrators. He attempts to displace responsibility onto those even more intimate with the victims than he: first Duncan's grooms; then his sons, Malcolm and Donalbain, whom he accuses of "cruel parricide" (3.1.33); and, finally, Fleance. Macbeth manipulates the familiar fear of murderous dependents to disguise his own intimate betrayal of kinsman, king, and guest.

If the murder of Duncan is the play's central domestic crime and the source of its subsequent disruptions, the assault on MacDuff's castle and the murder of all his pretty ones is its most explicit assault on the family. In the only scene in which we see a mother and child, the only glimpse of "orderly" domestic life, violence shockingly intrudes and we must watch it happen. While the invasion is brutal, the disruption has already begun before the armed men arrive. The play attributes the murder of Lady MacDuff and her children not only to Macbeth's orders but to MacDuff's abandonment of his family. As Lady MacDuff argues, in resentment and anger:

> Wisdom? To leave his wife, to leave his babes,
> His mansion, and his titles in a place
> From whence himself does fly? He loves us not,
> He wants the natural touch.
> (4.2.6–9)

Malcolm also questions MacDuff's decision (4.3). The domestic crime here resides in the betrayal from within as much as the invasion from without.

We have seen how structural inversion shapes accounts of petty treason as well as dramatizations of witchcraft, allying both with comic form and popular festivity. Following this structure, *Macbeth's* preternaturally aggressive women require inadequate, impotent men who abandon their sons through death or flight.[135] Within this structure, closure can come only through reversion to traditional gender hierarchies and conceptions of domestic order. In *Macbeth,* this takes the form of the elimination of the play's female characters, natural and supernatural. If witches circumvent men by having sex with the devil, in this play the male hero circumvents women by being "not of woman born." The play also dissociates him from the feminine and the familial in distinctly violent ways: He is "untimely *ript*" from his mother's womb; his wife and children are slaughtered.

Critics have demonstrated the cosmic and political significance of domestic and familial disorder in the play and in other representations of witchcraft. Clark argues that "if familial and political duties were analogous, if the state was based ultimately on the actions of heads of households, then . . . the condition of a society dominated by women must have been seen as one of fundamental contrariety."[136] Similarly, Stallybrass points out that "if the state and family were founded together, witchcraft founded the antistate together with the antifamily."[137]

---

135. Consider Duncan, Banquo, and MacDuff; see Adelman, " 'Born of Woman'," p. 108.

136. Clark, "King James's *Daemonologie*," p. 176.

137. Stallybrass, "*Macbeth* and Witchcraft," p. 203. On the Macbeths as an "unholy," inverted family see Adelman, " 'Born of Woman' "; Clark, "Inversion," pp. 125–26;

As Adelman suggests, in *Macbeth,* the antifamily is *the* family. There is no alternative. Disorder begins at home and stems from the members of the household, not from the bearded women on the heath. When increasing skepticism about witchcraft and demonology made it less possible to displace blame for such conflict onto witches, the family was left to reflect on itself. As Stephen Greenblatt argues in reference to *King Lear,* the lost strategy of displacing blame onto supernatural agents forces the unsettling scrutiny of family members' responsibility for disorder: "Is it a relief to understand that the evil was not visited upon the characters by demonic agents but released from the structure of the family and the state by Lear himself?"[138]

Adelman's and Greenblatt's interpretations of *Macbeth* and *King Lear* as tragedies that explore the possibility of demonic agency as a source of domestic disorder but, finally, locate the threat in the familiar, point to the void left when skepticism disqualified demonic possession and bewitchment as explanations for anger, violence, and conflict. Returning to nondramatic representations of witchcraft, we can explore the strategies and resources for coping with tensions that families, especially stepfamilies, lost to skepticism. In the early modern period, stepfamilies were the "antifamilies" found everywhere; constituted through marriage as much as through blood, these families, like the weird sisters, cast doubt on the conception of the family as "natural." Each of the following three texts simultaneously tells two stories: the narrative of familial conflict that generates the accusation and the accusatory narrative that displaces blame for that conflict onto the witch. Each of these texts prioritizes the two stories differently: one presents the story of bewitchment as an imposture and the story of family conflict as "true" and as motivating the deception; another simultaneously and unselfconsciously tells the two competing stories and leaves the reader uncertain which to privilege; another presents the story of familial conflict as the lie, which is fabricated or exaggerated to disguise bewitchment presented as "actual."

In *A Discovery of the Fraudulent Practises of John Darrel* (1599), Samuel

---

Goldberg, "Speculations," p. 259; Newman, *Fashioning Femininity,* chap. 4; and Stallybrass, "*Macbeth* and Witchcraft."

138. Greenblatt, *Shakespearean Negotiations,* p. 122.

Harsnett, as part of his program of exposing demonic possession as an imposture and exorcists as charlatans, asserts that one young woman feigned possession as a strategy for securing kinder treatment from her verbally and physically abusive stepfather. When Katherine Wright began "swelling" and having visions, "her sayd father in law made much of her: ... she finding this alteration in her said fathers usage towardes her, thereupon grew to bee indifferently well ... yet she did still pretende to bee troubled with her former kinde of fancies and apparitions, and in her fits of swelling, did voluntarily make her selfe to seeme worse then indeede she was." She kept this up for thirteen to fourteen years, "partly because shee was by that occasion much made of, and for that shee feared, that if she had shewed her selfe to have beene perfectly well for any long season, her father in lawe would have fallen to his former hard usage of her." In Harsnett's account, Katherine Wright solicits better treatment by counterfeiting affliction; she asserts her agency by pretending to be a victim. Although Harsnett treats Katherine fairly sympathetically, reserving most of his censure for the exorcist, John Darrel, he also allies her strategy with imposture and fraudulence. For him, the story of the conflict between the stepfather and the stepdaughter is unambiguously the "true" one.[139]

In *Wonderfull News from the North. Or, A True Relation of the Sad and Grievous Torments, Inflicted upon the Bodies of Three Children of Mr. George Muschamp ... by Witchcraft* (1650), the author, mother of the possessed children, produces a fragmented, contradictory text that defends the children's claims of bewitchment yet simultaneously reveals an alternative story of conflict between spouses and between stepparents and stepchildren. In her attempts to refute the second narrative, the author makes it available to us. The author, Mary Moore, accuses one Dorothy Swinow of attempting to make her miscarry; of bewitching her children, especially her daughter Margaret; and of bewitching to death her infant,

139. Harsnett, *A Discovery of the Fraudulent Practises of John Darrel,* sig. Qqv. MacDonald argues that possession often occurred in very pious families as a way for adolescents to rebel "against the tyranny of domestic theocracy" (*Mystical Bedlam,* p. 202). Thomas similarly claims that in such environments possession could enable the expression of forbidden impulses or provide a means of attracting adults' attention (*Religion,* pp. 480–81). See also Sabean, *Power in the Blood.* On possession, counterfeiting, exorcism, and Harsnett, see Greenblatt, *Shakespearean Negotiations,* chap. 4.

Sibilla. Moore is motivated to write because she has difficulty persuading others, including her husband, to believe her and to instigate a formal prosecution.

In the course of the text, it becomes clear that the author's inconsistencies are produced, in part, by her multiple positions as the mother of what we now rather optimistically call a "blended" family. The title identifies the bewitched children as those of Mr. George Muschamp, and the author as one Mrs. Moore, who signs the preface to the courteous reader, referring to God's "preservation of Me and my Children."[140] Scholars disagree about the authorship of *Wonderfull News*. Elaine Hobby lists the pamphlet as a male-authored work falsely attributed to a woman; I find no internal evidence for this claim. Other scholars follow the text's own preface in attributing authorship to Mary Moore. These scholars also recognize that the author has a close relationship to the story she tells, although they do not unravel the complex evidence the text offers regarding Moore's identity. Hilda L. Smith and Susan Cardinale remark that "Moore's own child is named as a victim"; Wallace Notestein identifies Mrs. Moore as "a friend" of the bewitched Muschamp children's mother."[141] I think, however, that the text reveals that Mrs. Moore and the mother of the Muschamp children are one and the same; at the time she writes, Mrs. Moore is married to Edward Moore, but has children by George Muschamp. In their house live her children by her first marriage (the Muschamps), Moore's children from his first marriage, and some cousins. In the course of the story, Mrs. Moore also bears and loses a child (Sybilla Moore) who she fears has been bewitched in the womb.

The confusion of names, paternities, and allegiances in the household contributes to the difficulty of identifying the narrator and her relation to and investment in the story she tells. She often refers to herself in the third person, as "the mother" of the afflicted. Although Moore recounts her frustration that the justices will not pay attention or move against Swinow, she places the defenses of her conduct in her daughter's

---

140. Moore, *Wonderfull News from the North,* sig. A2.
141. Elaine Hobby, *Virtue of Necessity: English Women's Writing, 1649–88* (Ann Arbor: University of Michigan Press, 1989), pp. 240, 250; Hilda L. Smith and Susan Cardinale, *Women and the Literature of the Seventeenth Century: An Annotated Bibliography Based on Wing's "Short-Title Catalogue"* (New York: Greenwood Press, 1990), pp. 86–87; Notestein, *History of Witchcraft,* p. 363.

mouth. At one point, for instance, Moore presents the bewitched girl's perspective, which slides into her own:

> No Justice abroad, no Peace at home, what should become of her mother? for that Godlesse thiefe *Dorothy Swinow,* by the instigation of the Divell, had hardned the heart of both Judges and Justices against her, and now at this instant (sayd she) is using meanes to harden her husbands heart against her too (which she knowes will be cruellest to her of all) and withall begun to consume her eldest sister, and that she would this night, or to morrow morning go to the Judge, begge once more for Justice.

Before the judge, Margaret, the bewitched daughter, testifies that Swinow has begun to "harden her Father in Lawes [stepfather's] heart, to make her mothers life more sorrowful." She is worried that her "mothers afflictions, by the hardning of folks hearts against her will be insufferable." In her last fit, Margaret Muschamp proclaims "they sought my mothers life, but could not get it."[142]

The text ends with the indictment of Swinow, but Moore never tells us whether she persuades her husband to believe her and her children. Insisting that the story is one of bringing a witch to justice, she concludes where the formal prosecution begins. Other evidence suggests that although Mary Moore managed to get an indictment, she never succeeded in getting Dorothy Swinow apprehended, tried, or convicted.[143] This was, in part, because Swinow was a colonel's wife and thus less socially vulnerable than most suspected witches. Mary Moore's other story, the story of the hardening of her husband's heart, remains unresolved, although Moore's text insists that it is caused by the witch and will, like the possession of the children, end when the witch is brought to justice. Unique among the pamphlet accounts of witchcraft in identifying its writer as a woman, this text reveals the difficulties in creating one family out of two by means of marriage. In the case of the Muschamps and Moores, as told by Mary Moore, in making this familial friction visible, accusations of witchcraft both displaced blame for it onto an outsider and exacerbated it.

Finally, Edmond Bower's *Dr. Lamb Revived, or, Witchcraft Condemn'd in Anne Bodenham a Servant of His* (1653) explicitly addresses and

---

142. *Wonderfull News from the North,* sigs. B2, C3v, C4, C4v, D2.
143. Notestein, *History of Witchcraft,* pp. 209–10, 363.

dismisses the possibility that accusations of witchcraft might be used to cover up murderous conflict within stepfamilies. Insisting throughout that Anne Bodenham is a guilty witch, Bower defends the young women who accuse her and censures their stepmother for implying that they are the agents of a murder plot rather than the victims of witchcraft. According to Bower's rather confusing narrative, the story begins when Mrs. Goddard suspects her stepdaughters of trying to poison her and employs Anne Bodenham, a cunning-woman, to help her counter the attempts on her life. From Bodenham, the stepmother seeks magical, nonviolent ways "to make the young Gentlewomen exemplary . . . [and] to bring them upon their knees." In an elaborate plot, Mrs. Goddard's maid is sent to buy arsenic, supposedly to be burnt as a preventative. The stepdaughters, "hearing of these transactions about poyson, and that it should be laid to their charge, that they had a designe, and provided to poyson their Mother; being much moved at it, and to vindicate themselves, that no such aspersion might lie on them," start to act as detectives.[144] Inquiring in town about recent purchases of poison, they learn that the maid has made such a purchase; the maid then flees town, apparently at her mistress' (the stepmother's) urging. It is at this point that the stepdaughters accuse the cunning-woman, who is suddenly transformed thereby from an ally in alleviating stepfamily tension to its source; from an advisor of prophylactic counterplots to the head schemer.

Although Bower narrates the very complicated suspicions of the stepmother and her stepdaughters, the plots and counterplots, he insists that he is interested only in the maid and the witch as criminal perpetrators. Despite the fact that he does not wish to cast aspersions on any of the other parties, he dismisses Mrs. Goddard's suspicions and questions her wisdom in consulting a known witch. Bower acknowledges that rumors have circulated claiming that the "true" story is not the one he tells, but one of murderous stepdaughters: "There was for

144. Bower, *Dr. Lamb Revived*, sigs. B4v, C. On Bodenham, see also Mack, *Visionary Women*, pp. 75–77. On Bodenham's notorious mentor, Dr. Lambe, see the *Dictionary of National Biography*, and *A Briefe Description of the Notorious Life of John Lambe* (Amsterdam, 1628). Lambe was associated with the infamous duke of Buckingham. When a London crowd attacked him in 1628, they referred to him as "the duke's devil." Lambe's career seems to have inspired a 1630s play, *Dr. Lambe and the Witches*, no longer extant. Many years later, Bower still uses Bodenham's association with Lambe to discredit her and increase his pamphlet's sensational value and marketability.

some short time some conceivings or thinkings that the young Gentle-women, Mris. *Sarah* and Mris. *Anne Goddard,* should plot and attempt to poyson their Mother in Law [stepmother]"; but, he insists, they have vindicated themselves, not least by being the ones to start the investigation. Since they worked to "finde out the ground-work of the plot" and uncover the witch, "they are so far from lying under any imputation, that it is to be acknowledged by all that they were the instruments of its discovery, and therefore Mris. *Goddard* or others have no ground to co[n]jecture any such thing against them."[145] Bower acknowledges other "conceivings or thinkings" about the case, but he refutes them. Especially in that last clause, Bower seems eager not only to tell yet another story of witchcraft and its discovery and punishment but to convince Mrs. Goddard that "the plot" is not the reputed one to poison her, but Anne Bodenham's plot against both mother and stepdaughters. In this case, unlike the two previous cases, the witch was convicted and executed. Attributing domestic conflict to the witch, *Doctor Lamb Revived* decisively eliminates the scapegoat through execution. But Bower's text leaves one wondering: How did the Goddards get along after Anne Bodenham was dead?

Of all the protagonists in accounts of domestic crime that I have examined in this book—petty traitors, petty tyrants, infanticidal parents, and witches—witches are the least familiar, in various senses of that word. Wives still kill their husbands, husbands their wives, and parents their children; although we no longer categorize people as masters and servants, employees still kill their employers. Most legal systems define all these kinds of murder as criminal, even if they do not distinguish petty treason and infanticide from other forms of homicide or grant them particular significance. Western cultures do not, however, define witchcraft as a crime, nor does the dominant culture take occult power very seriously. We think of the witch, therefore, as an inhabitant of stories, not of our own communities and households, a threat to our persons and property.

The witch is also less "familiar" than the other protagonists in that she was not usually a member of the households in which her crimes took effect. Nonetheless, witchcraft was often understood as a domestic

---

145. Bower, *Dr. Lamb Revived,* sig. C2v.

crime in early modern England. Witches were construed as dangerous in their familiarity with their victims as well as in their demonic otherness. Like other popular representations, those of witchcraft shaped and articulated anxieties about interdependency and intimacy; in particular, these accounts suggest the ways that anxieties about personal vulnerability and familial conflict could be managed by blaming a witch and her ally, the devil. As Michael MacDonald argues, the devil could become the personification of "unacceptable feelings and actions."[146] On the one hand, witches threatened the household from the outside—knocking on the door to make demands, prying, stealing, and cursing; even their gifts were unwelcome and hazardous. On the other hand, witches enabled families and households to disclaim responsibility for internal conflicts, displacing it onto the troublesome neighbor just outside the door.

As the cases of friction in the Wright, Moore, and Goddard households reveal, the decline in belief in witches left families with only themselves to blame. From the skeptical perspective, the threat in these cases lay in Katherine Wright's abusive stepfather, in the inability of the Moores and Muschamps to resolve the conflicts among previous and present allegiances, in Mrs. Goddard's stepdaughters' plots to poison her or her attempts to implicate them. The witch's disappearance as a potential scapegoat intensified the scrutiny of the family. Although the witch ceased to crowd courtrooms and scaffolds and to haunt the popular imagination, the outsider within, the dangerous familiar, remained at home.

146. MacDonald, *Mystical Bedlam*, p. 202.

EPILOGUE

Eighteenth-century novels are haunted by the ghosts of criminal women from an earlier era and their gruesome fates. In Daniel Defoe's *Moll Flanders* (1722), Moll faces the possibility of being burned at the stake for counterfeiting (a form of petty treason): "The very Thoughts of being burnt at a Stake, struck terror into my very Soul, chill'd my Blood, and gave me the Vapours to such a degree as I could not think of it without trembling."[1] In Henry Fielding's *Amelia* (1751), the narrator places Miss Matthews's "wretched Story" of attempting to kill her seducer in a tradition of other transgressive women ranging from biblical and classical precedents like Dalila and Medea to Katherine Hayes, who was burned at the stake in 1726 for bludgeoning her husband to death.[2] In Elizabeth Inchbald's *Nature and Art* (1796), a woman falsely suspected of having an illegitimate child is closely questioned: "Beguiled by solicitations, and terrified by threats, like women formerly accused

1. Daniel Defoe, *Moll Flanders,* ed. Edward Kelly (New York: W. W. Norton, 1973), p. 199.
2. Henry Fielding, *Amelia,* ed. Martin C. Battestin (Middletown, Conn.: Wesleyan University Press, 1983), pp. 44–47.

of witchcraft, and other wretches put to the torture,—she thought her present sufferings worse than any that could possibly succeed; and felt inclined to confess a falsehood."[3] Yet, by the time these novels were written, the petty traitors and witches who haunt the heroines—grim reminders of a history of criminal women *and* of how harshly they might be punished—were, increasingly, ghosts from a receding past, as much as inhabitants of a contemporary social scene.

By the eighteenth century, women's murders of their husbands and servants' murders of their masters were only rarely adjudged as petty treason; Frank McLynn finds that by the end of the century, "public opinion had forced a *de facto* abandonment of petty treason."[4] Witchcraft statutes were repealed in 1736. Although the harsh Jacobean infanticide statute of 1624 remained on the books until 1803, by the 1720s courts were interpreting it more leniently, and by the 1760s most women were tried under homicide laws rather than the 1624 statute. The petty traitors, infanticidal mothers, and witches that have been the central protagonists of this book were less frequently the protagonists of scaffold spectacles. They also ceased to figure as prominently in popular, ephemeral texts. Although legal and social changes cooperated to spare these particular transgressors and popular culture marginalized them, the novel, with its interest in the domestic lives of nonaristocratic, English characters, continued the focus on domestic conflict, often representing women and servants as the sources of that conflict, as dangerous familiars.[5]

3. Elizabeth Inchbald, *Nature and Art,* vol. 27 of *The British Novelists,* ed. Mrs. Barbauld (London, 1810), p. 300. The novel also presents readers with the kind of text on which I have focused, "a printed sheet of paper" or a broadside containing "the last dying words, speech, and confession" of the criminalized heroine, Agnes Primrose.

4. Frank McLynn, *Crime and Punishment in Eighteenth-Century England* (Oxford: Oxford University Press, 1991), p. 124. McLynn argues that in the eighteenth century women's murders "arose within a family or intimate context" (p. 117), as they had in the earlier period. McLynn discusses petty treason, including the case of Katherine Hayes mentioned in *Amelia,* on pp. 121–24; he discusses infanticide on pp. 110–15. See also chaps. 6 and 7, passim.

5. Of the many studies of the novel's origins, I have been most influenced by: Nancy Armstrong, *Desire and Domestic Fiction: A Political History of the Novel* (Oxford: Oxford University Press, 1987); Laura Brown, *English Dramatic Form, 1660–1760: An Essay in Generic History* (New Haven: Yale University Press, 1981); Lennard J. Davis, *Factual Fictions: The Origins of the English Novel* (New York: Columbia University Press, 1983); Lincoln B. Faller, *Turned to Account: The Forms and Functions of Criminal Biography in Late Seventeenth- and Early Eighteenth-Century England* (Cambridge: Cambridge Uni-

While novels feature women and/or servants as protagonists and organize their plots around domestic conflict, they use various strategies to displace or repress the violence so central to earlier accounts of domestic crime. The novels I discuss still represent women's agency negatively, but they do not necessarily render women's consciousness and access to language as transgressive and violent. They achieve this by dividing the heroine in two. In Defoe's *Roxana* (1724), for instance, the servant Amy kills Roxana's troublesome daughter, not with Roxana's explicit consent but in accordance with Roxana's frustration and desire to escape the daughter and her demands. Although Roxana is shocked that Amy murders her daughter, she admits that "had [the daughter] died by any ordinary Distemper, I shou'd have shed but very few Tears for her." Roxana further claims that she cannot revenge her daughter because "to have fall'n upon *Amy*, had been to have murther'd myself." [6] In her close identification with Roxana, Amy enacts Roxana's desire to kill her child; Roxana desires, but does not enact, domestic violence.

George Lillo's *The London Merchant* (1731), a hugely popular domestic tragedy, positions the hero, George Barnwell, between two women: Millwood, the villainous whore, persuades him to betray his master and kill his uncle, and Maria, the virtuous prospective wife, comforts and supports him and helps him toward repentance. [7] Millwood combines sexuality, violence, and agency; Maria combines marriageability, virtue, and passivity. In *Amelia,* the heroine, the ideal wife, rarely acts and never tells her own story; her narrative is subsumed by her husband's. She is positioned between two fallen women who act as agents and narrators. In debtor's prison, one, Miss Matthews, tells Amelia's husband, Captain Booth, the story of her seduction and her

versity Press, 1987); Frances Ferguson, "Rape and the Rise of the Novel," *Representations* 20 (1987): 88–112; J. Paul Hunter, *Before Novels: The Cultural Contexts of Eighteenth-Century English Fiction* (New York: W. W. Norton, 1990); Michael McKeon, *The Origins of the English Novel, 1600–1740* (Baltimore: Johns Hopkins University Press, 1987); John Richetti, *Popular Fiction before Richardson: Narrative Patterns, 1700–1739* (Oxford: Clarendon Press, 1969); Paul Salzman, *English Prose Fiction, 1558–1700: A Critical History* (Oxford: Clarendon Press, 1985); and Jane Spencer, *The Rise of the Woman Novelist from Aphra Behn to Jane Austen* (Oxford: Basil Blackwell, 1986).

6. Daniel Defoe, *Roxana, The Fortunate Mistress,* ed. David Blewett (Harmondsworth: Penguin, 1982), p. 350.

7. On *The London Merchant,* see Brown, *English Dramatic Form,* pp. 147 and 157–65; and Ralph Cohen, "History and Genre," *New Literary History* 17.2 (1986): 203–18.

attempt to kill her seducer; she then has sex with him. The other, Mrs. Bennet, saves Amelia from possible ruin at the hands of a treacherous nobleman by telling Amelia the story of her own ruin. At Amelia's request, Mrs. Bennet also attends a masquerade disguised as Amelia; the fallen woman is able to venture into public as the virtuous homebody would rather not.

Both of these female characters act as sexual surrogates for Amelia; they have adventures, largely sexual, so that she may be spared them. They are allowed to tell their stories at great length; these stories constitute substantial portions of the novel (Books I and VII). Similarly, Moll and Roxana narrate their own stories and confidently insist that they have no obligation to recount other people's stories: "As this is to be my own Story, not my Husbands, I return to that Part which relates to myself"; "There was another Daughter I had ... But I return to my own Story."[8] In contrast, Amelia's story is her husband's story; it is a sign of her virtue that she does not have a separate narrative. Here, as in earlier accounts of domestic crime, it is in transgression that women are constituted as subjects; it is in transgression that they are placed at the center of a story as agents and tellers.

The phenomenon of splitting female characters into the virtuous, silent, and aristocratic lady and the voluble, spirited serving woman has been noticed in Shakespearean drama (Desdemona and Emilia in *Othello*; Hermione and Paulina in *The Winter's Tale*). But, as we have seen, accounts of nonaristocratic, and especially criminal women, struggle to combine contradictory traits within a single figure who is not simply demonized. The accounts conjoin, for instance, the wife and the murderess, or the sympathetic victim of abuse, poverty, and isolation and the frightening perpetrator of domestic violence. In a figure such as Roxana, Defoe continues to suggest distressingly unclear distinctions between wife and whore, mother and murderer. Generally, however, works such as *Roxana* or *The London Merchant* sidestep these contradictions, and their implications for gender constructions, class hierarchies, and social order, by splitting violence off from the wife and mother figure and displacing it onto a more easily demonized figure (the servant, the whore, the fallen woman). Nevertheless, they continue

---

8. *Moll Flanders*, p. 266, see also p. 235; *Roxana*, p. 249.

to associate female agency with sexual license, transgression, and violence.

These novels also displace the violence that underlies their plots through the use of dreams and prophecies. In *Roxana,* for example, Roxana's "vapourish Fancy" represents her lover to her as a murder victim: "I thought I perceiv'd his Head all Bloody; and then his Cloaths look'd Bloody too; and immediately it all went off, and he look'd as he really did"; that day he is beset by highwaymen and murdered. Later, when Roxana suspects her daughter has been murdered, she cannot escape the apparition of the daughter as victim: "She haunted my Imagination, if she did not haunt the House; . . . Sometimes I thought I saw her with her Throat cut; sometimes with her Head cut, and her Brains knock'd-out; other-times hang'd up upon a Beam; another time drown'd in the Great Pond at *Camberwell.*"⁹ Neither of these murders is represented in the novel, except in Roxana's violent imaginings. In *Amelia,* Sergeant Atkinson dreams that Colonel James is raping Amelia Booth and, in his sleep, he throttles his wife, mistaking her for the murderous rapist. When he sprinkles his unconscious wife with cherry brandy rather than water, he thinks their bed is awash in blood, "for a more ghastly and horrible Sight than the Bed presented, could not be conceived." The scene becomes a farcical fantasy of wife murder: "I have stabbed her. I have stabbed her. . . . I have killed my poor Wife."¹⁰ In both *Roxana* and *Amelia,* then, visions or dreams of spousal murder and infanticide express the characters' violent desires to get rid of their intimates in a displaced form. The dreams and visions also enable the novels to exploit the titillating appeal of domestic violence without representing that violence as real.

Defoe's novels also explore the possibilities for nonviolent separations between family members. They present a wider array of social options than earlier texts and they do not present the law as determining those options. Moll and Roxana both "lose" numerous spouses and children without either killing them or formally acting to separate themselves (through divorce, legal separation, or adoption). At certain points in the novels, the narrators seem to forget about various spouses and children and the reader has trouble keeping track of them. These aban-

9. *Roxana,* pp. 87, 374.
10. *Amelia,* p. 378.

donments and divestments, however, are represented as allied to violence. Both Moll and Roxana explicitly connect having a child "taken off," that is, taken off one's hands, with murder. As Moll piously asserts, "I wish all those Women who consent to the disposing of their Children out of the way, *as it is call'd* for Decency sake, would consider that 'tis only a contriv'd Method for Murther . . . a Neglect in order to their being Lost; so that 'tis even an intentional Murther, whether the Child lives or dies." Roxana similarly condemns "those She-Butchers, who take Children off of [parents'] Hands, as 'tis called; that is to say, starve 'em, and, in a Word, murther 'em."[11] Although both Moll and Roxana condemn the abandonment of children as infanticidal, each relies upon it.

Compared to earlier representations of domestic crime, these eighteenth-century works offer more sustained critiques of the legal system and its judgments and punishments; these critiques are inflected by gender and class assumptions. While Defoe's novels, focusing on female transgressors, uphold the moral, social, and legal orders that criminalize such women, Fielding's *Amelia* and Lillo's *The London Merchant,* focusing on male offenders, cast doubt on the law and the penal process as corrupt, excessive, and unjust. Combining Defoe's focus on the female transgressor with Fielding's and Lillo's scrutiny of the legal system, Inchbald's *Nature and Art* attributes the system's failures to gender and class inequities. In this novel, the spoiled, privileged William impregnates Agnes Primrose, the humbly born, barely literate heroine, who attempts to murder, and then abandons, their illegitimate child. "Around its little throat was a cord entwined by a slipping noose, and drawn half way—as if the trembling hand of the murderer had revolted from its dreadful office, and he or she had left the infant to pine away in nakedness and hunger, rather than *see* it die."[12] Agnes later claims and raises the child, but her shame and lack of skills make employment difficult; ultimately, she resorts to prostitution, theft, and complicity "in negotiating bills forged on a country banker."[13] For the latter, she is tried before her seducer, now a judge, who does not recognize her

---

11. *Moll Flanders,* pp. 135–36; *Roxana,* p. 116. Moll also contemplates killing a child she robs: "The Devil put me upon killing the Child in the dark Alley, that it might not Cry" (p. 151).

12. Inchbald, *Nature and Art,* p. 290.

13. Ibid., p. 346.

and condemns her to death. The heroine is a bastard-bearer, a prostitute, a thief, a woman who attempts to kill and abandons her child, and a forger who is guilty of the crime for which she is executed; yet the novel censures both the man who personally betrays her and a social and legal system that empowers him to judge and punish Agnes but offers her so few resources or options. The men with power in the novel—William, Senior, a dean before whom Agnes must confess herself the mother of a bastard and take responsibility for her attempt to kill it, and William, Junior, the seducer and judge—are both presented as morally bankrupt. In this novel, the judge's position is one of class and gender privilege, rather than of moral authority.

Some seventeenth-century texts record voices that condemn legal corruption and question particular legal judgments. In *The Witch of Edmonton*, for instance, Mother Sawyer catalogs the many kinds of "witches" on whom "the law casts not an eye."[14] Such voices are often dissonant ones, competing with other perspectives, or, most often, clearly subordinated to a dominant, didactic perspective that supports legal judgments and penalties. In *Amelia* and *Nature and Art*, however, both the novels' structures and the narrators' perspectives find fault with the legal system. In such works, we can see declining confidence in the legal system and its ability to regulate moral conduct; these works no longer assume that a verdict is the last word on an offender's guilt.

Portraying execution as excessive, unjust, and even vulgar, such works also dissociate personal repentance and the public process of disciplining convicts rather than assuming the two processes to be parallel and mutually reinforcing. In *The London Merchant*, for instance, Maria laments that Barnwell's execution will be beneath his virtue and dignity, forcing him "to give a holiday to suburb slaves, and, passing, entertain the savage herd who, elbowing each other for a sight, pursue and press upon him like his fate."[15] The scaffold on

---

14. The last phrase is Sir Arthur's. See *The Witch of Edmonton* in *Three Jacobean Witchcraft Plays*, ed. Peter Corbin and Douglas Sedge (Manchester: Manchester University Press, 1986), 4.1.119–20. I discuss women who challenge the legal process that condemns them and cast blame on men who escape judgment, in " 'Gentlemen, I have one thing more to say': Women on Scaffolds in England, 1563–1680," *Modern Philology*, forthcoming.

15. George Lillo, *The London Merchant*, ed. William H. McBurney (Lincoln: University of Nebraska Press, 1965), 5.10.64–66.

which divine and earthly justice, repentance and punishment, con-joined in earlier texts has become the site only of a "dreadful spectacle" for "a gaping crowd" and an obstacle between the transgressor and divine judgment.

"By the advice of some friends," Lillo did not present on stage a final scene at the place of execution, with gallows, ladders, and a crowd of spectators in view.[16] (He did, however, include this scene in the fifth edition of the play.) Lillo's friends were right. The focus on conscience and internalized self-punishment have made the scaffold scene redundant. Although *The London Merchant* was an extremely popular play, it reveals contempt for the crowd and distaste at the idea that execution is a public, popular entertainment that generates in turn other entertainments (ballads, pamphlets, newspaper accounts, plays such as Lillo's) and cult followings for certain offenders.

That novels such as *Roxana, Moll Flanders,* and *Nature and Art* seem almost obsessively concerned with eliminating children should suggest the limits of genealogical models for the novel's generic de-velopment. If the novel is the offspring of earlier, ephemeral forms such as the pamphlet and ballad, then its relationship to those pro-genitors is likely to be a vexed, uneasy one. J. Paul Hunter argues that the novel coexisted with the forms that preceded and fostered it, rather than supplanting them.[17] Yet, if these diverse kinds of texts coexisted, competed, and coupled in the seventeenth and eighteenth centuries, literary history has subsequently transformed that story of rivalrous, inbreeding siblings into a violent family saga that *inverts* the parent-child dynamic we find in a novel such as *Roxana.* For in this literary history, it is the predecessors who are indecorously, in-conveniently numerous, as well as illegitimate. The offspring, the novel, survived in part through its ruthless voracity, its willingness to consume its parents, the reversal of Roxana's joking claim that "we had eaten up almost every thing, and little remain'd, unless, like one of the pitiful Women of *Jerusalem,* I should eat up my very Children

16. Ibid., p. 82.
17. Hunter, *Before Novels,* p. 28.

themselves." As Roxana's daughter haunts her "like an Evil Spirit," demanding to be owned—"she is my Mother! and will not own me"—the disorderly, bastard siblings and disreputable parents of the seventeenth and eighteenth century's flourishing, favored, legitimate texts clamor to be acknowledged.[18]

18. *Roxana,* pp. 51, 358, 352.

INDEX